Conten~

Maps

List of Illustrations

List of Tables

J. C. Armytage

Emigrants on the quay at Maryport, 1840s

6

Preface and acknowledgements

For centuries a major export from the Cumbrian region had been its people. *From Hellgill to Bridge End* included a chapter on migration within England from and into nine parishes in the Upper Eden Valley with some reference to the wider region. It was clear that internal migration was only part of the story.[1] Overseas birthplaces of children in Cumbria suggested returned emigration. Random enquiries revealed that almost every family knew of at least one relative that had emigrated in the nineteenth century. My husband's aunt and her husband went to Illinois and thrived. My more distant relatives died in the *Lusitania* tragedy while returning home in 1915. But, were they coming as visitors or returning to stay? The answer will never be known. This book extends the previous Upper Eden Valley study to the whole of Cumberland and Westmorland and examines overseas emigration to any destination before the First World War.

Occasionally similar or even substantially different details came from more than one source about individual emigrants. Almost all relatives gave permission to quote from the information they sent me but as some relatives requested privacy and others wished the experience of their emigrant forebears to remain anonymous the notes use the term 'family information' except where the text refers directly to, or quotes from letters, unpublished family memoirs or from published material. The numerical totals and calculations include every emigrant whose details fit the particular aspect under consideration even though, in accordance with relatives' wishes, details are not otherwise identified. I have endeavoured to treat the information so freely and generously given with respect and to reflect accurately what I have learnt from so many people. It has been an interesting and rewarding experience to read about so many Cumberland and Westmorland emigrants who travelled across the world.

My most grateful thanks are due to many people, principally to the relatives who sent letters, extracts from diaries, many pages of handwritten information and family memoirs. My thanks also to Professor N. Goose for his comments on an earlier draft, to Jeremy Godwin for sending extracts from early twentieth century local newspapers, to Don Manning in the Cambridge University Library for producing the illustrations from original engravings owned by me and from photographs and to Philip Judge who produced the excellent maps. Peter Bysouth and Sheila Betts have rescued me from frustration and advanced my limited computer skills during the writing of the text.

The Trustees of the Curwen Archives Trust in Cumbria have once again given generous support. Rod Hodgson and the members of the Hudson Historical

Society in Canada supplied information and photographs. The National Mississippi River Museum and Aquarium, Captain William D. Bowell Sr. River Library, supplied and has given permission for the reproduction of the photograph of George Richardson's factory in Dubuque. As always, John has supported me in this project and his optimism when things were not going well has been a great strength and comfort.

But, above all, my thanks go to the families of the emigrants; some in the UK, others in many countries – not necessarily where the emigrants settled. Without their help this book could not have been written.

N.B. The investigation covers only Cumberland and Westmorland. Where the terms Cumbria or Cumbrians are used in the text they refer only to these counties and not to the parts of Lancashire and Yorkshire that were included in the new county in 1974.

Abbreviations

TCWAAS	Transactions of the Cumberland and Westmorland Antiquarian and Archaeological Society.
CFHS	Cumbria Family History Society.
VCH	Victoria County History.
SC	Select Committee.
RC	Royal Commission.
BPP	British Parliamentary Papers.
EIO	Emigrant's Information Office.

[1] M.E. Shepherd, *From Hellgill to Bridge End: aspects of economic and social change in the Upper Eden Valley, 1840-95*. (Hatfield, 2003)

Conversions
1 mile = 1.6km   1 metre = 39 inches
1 yard = 3 feet   1 foot = 12 inches

£.s.d.
£1 = 20 shillings or 240 pence (wrtten as d.)
1 guinea = £1.1 shilling. 1 shilling = 12 pence
Present day money
£1= 100 pence (written as p.)

Chapter 1: Introduction
Migration and Emigration

If migration within Britain were to be described as 'stirring the pot' then was emigration a safety valve that prevented the 'pot boiling over' or was it simply leakage? Malthusian concerns about unbridled population growth leading to insufficient resources and eventual catastrophe together with the realisation that population totals were unknown led to the decadal censuses from 1801. Between 1751 and 1801 the population of England had increased by one third, by more than 100 per cent from 1801-51 with a further 82 per cent rise from 1851-1901, and although partly fuelled by in-migration from Scotland and Ireland, the increase would have been even greater without emigration.[1] Those who believed in the danger of over-population were in favour of emigration but others believed the country could not afford to lose enterprising and capable people. The Select Committee on Emigration (1826) suggested sending emigrants to Australia and Canada but their recommendations were defeated in parliament. The United Kingdom sent convicts to America in the eighteenth century and to Australia from 1788.[2] Throughout the nineteenth century schemes to assist emigrants were adopted in Britain and countries in the Empire while suitable and carefully selected emigrants were sent by Poor Law Guardians and philanthropic organisations or societies to the newly developing countries.

The majority of emigrants are 'invisible.'[3] Even totals may be unreliable and few sources or official figures break these down into regions or counties. Because statistics were published in various permutations under different criteria, a long series comparison is almost impossible. Only in the 1850s were the national origins (for example the English who even then may have included the Welsh) of those leaving the country stated separately. Official statistics did not include passengers on small ships and perhaps half of all who left 'before the early 1850s were not counted.'[4] It was not until 1863 that all cabin passengers and passengers sailing on mail packets were included. Shipping lists, where they survive, are difficult to use, often unreliable and almost invariably state only the country of origin.[5] Similarly, census enumerations in the destination country stated only the country not the place of birth or residence before emigrating. Because a large proportion of those who sailed from Liverpool were Irish, passenger numbers from that port cannot help in calculating the number of English passengers and emigrant numbers are therefore even more obscure. Emigrants were not separated from passengers in official statistics during the greater part of the period, consequently, 'the published data are unsatisfactory [regarding] the causes and

9

characteristics of British emigration.[6] Even in 1904 a government report stated that 'Board of Trade Returns [did] not yet afford the means of accurately determining the number of ... emigrants or immigrants.'[7] It has been estimated that from 1851-1914 more than 5,000,000 English men, women and children emigrated, 'nearly one third' of whom went after 1900.[8]

Given the huge numbers involved, the complexity of the published data and the difficulty of analysing these, any investigation into nineteenth century emigration is challenging and to seek information about origins, destinations and individual emigrants is difficult. Important published works, for example by Erickson, Baines and others, refer to the need for a smaller scale approach to the subject.[9] 'The most informed and perceptive work may come out of studies of emigration from particular counties and regions.'[10] 'Few studies ... show the areas of Britain from which the emigrants came'[11] and 'we [do not] know in detail much about the different emigration experiences of those going to New Zealand, Australia and North America.'[12] The results of this study of emigration from Cumberland and Westmorland before 1914 (but concentrating on the hundred years from 1815) to any destination should contribute to filling the need.

The sample and sources

Once the project was defined, the task of finding the names of emigrants, their origins and destinations began. Clearly, once an emigrant had left he (or she) did not appear in British records and, as previously stated, the origin of an emigrant was only rarely stated in documents after leaving. For the project to be viable it was necessary to create a sample that would include the names and details of a sufficient number of emigrants, whose origins were distributed over the whole region and who went to a number of different destinations at dates that spread throughout the century from 1815 to 1914. Personal contact and writing to publications such as local newspapers and Family History journals in England resulted in a flood of letters and emails from all over the world. Many days were spent in the British Library at Colindale and in the University of Cambridge Library. Visits to the Cumbria Record Offices in Carlisle and Kendal together with much appreciated co-operation and help from the staff in these and in the Whitehaven office resulted in numerous copies of letters and other documents which added much valuable information. I wrote to all regional newspapers in New Zealand requesting help from readers. New Zealand was chosen as a focus for enquiry because of its small population and the likelihood of contacting some who were sufficiently knowledgeable of, and interested in, their family roots. I was not disappointed. Hundreds of names, places of origin and destinations became known. Many correspondents from England and abroad, sent valuable information. Some sent extracts from, or copies of family memoirs.

Less obvious sources revealed more names. Nineteenth and early twentieth century Electoral Registers contained names of men who lived abroad but still owned property and were therefore eligible to vote in Cumbria. The census enumerations from 1841 but especially from 1851 gave information about returned emigrants from the birthplaces of children and confirmed that the date of leaving was either after an earlier census or within the decade before the next. Letters, reports and birth, marriage or death announcements in newspapers added more names. John Coates of Helbeck Hall, Brough held a farm sale in 1880 because he was 'leaving the country' but no destination was given.[13] Advertisements were an important source of information. Contemporary and later publications, journals and family memoirs gave details not only of a particular emigrant but often the names of other Cumbrians were mentioned in these and in letters which increased the total number in the sample. Wesleyan and Methodist Circuit and chapel records revealed unexpected information. For example, the local Wesleyan and Brough Primitive Methodist Circuit records tell of members having emigrated. In 1850 Z. Young was removed from the Primitive Methodist books because he had gone to America. Thomas Dobinson, a Wesleyan, was stated to have gone to America in the same year. George Yare went to Ireland in 1855. In 1860s and 1870s the records show that several other members of North Westmorland chapels had emigrated including the Slee family from Murton who went to Australia.[14]

The result was that the sample contains the names and at least some information about approximately 4,000 emigrants. All details were entered into an Excel spreadsheet and placed in separate fields covering the year of birth and age at emigrating (where known), place of residence before leaving, occupation before leaving, emigration port, name of ship (if known), initial destination, subsequent place of settlement, occupation in new country, name of the relative who supplied the information or other sources and finally, a field with added brief comments. For many named emigrants at least some of the fields are empty. The total number has changed during the research and writing period as more names and details became known. Even recently, shortly before publication, emigrants are still being discovered, therefore the phrase '*c*.4,000' has been used in the text for consistency and as a simple approximation. But, all calculations and analyses have been made on the basis of the exact total for the particular topic under consideration.

For some emigrants little is known. For example, only a vague destination – North America or 'Australia or New Zealand', was given. Perhaps contact had been lost or never established after leaving. One correspondent wrote that her great uncle (no name given) emigrated in the 1880s having lived in Workington but no destination was known. Clearly, this was of little help in detailed analysis

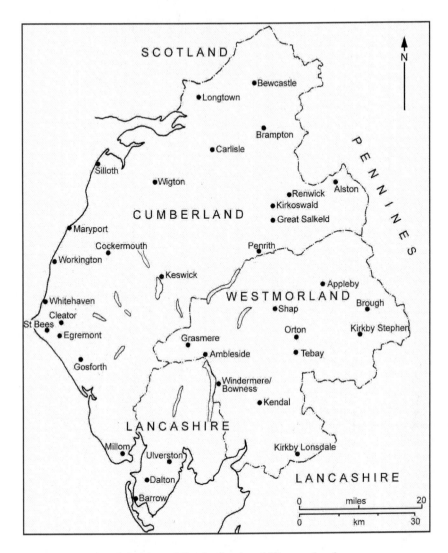

1.1 Map of Cumberland and Westmorland.

but, like all others with similar lack of detail, this emigrant was added to the numerical total of those who had left West Cumberland.

Here, the aim is to investigate emigration from Cumberland and Westmorland and to offer an overview of the region, the emigrants, the journey and of their experience in the new country. As elsewhere in Britain, emigration from Cumbria, 'had been virtually continuous in peacetime since the early eighteenth century' although we have few examples from those early years.[15] So much remains unknown and unknowable but the sample contains examples that are sufficiently varied over time, origin and destination to provide a useful illustration of emigration from the two counties. No investigation could give a comprehensive account. Studying emigration has been described as 'trying to do an unfamiliar jigsaw puzzle in the dark.'[16] It is hoped that this study will throw a glimmer of light on the jigsaw and at least some of the pieces will be in place.

The Cumbrian region

The Cumbrian region occupies the north-western corner of England. It extends from the Scottish border to the boundary with Lancashire, south of the Kent estuary. The region is bounded by the Irish Sea to the west and the Pennines lie to the east. In 1974 the counties of Cumberland and Westmorland, Lancashire North of the Sands and small western sections of the West Riding of Yorkshire were amalgamated to form the new county of Cumbria. Since then the county and region have been virtually synonymous. (Map 1.1)

In simple terms, the physical features of the region comprise the dome-shaped mountainous central Lake District from which a radial series of valleys, rivers and lakes lead to the surrounding lowlands. The Solway Plain lies to the north, a belt of coastal lowlands to the west and south, and the Eden valley in the east beyond which the Pennines roughly form the eastern edge of the Cumbrian region. The Tyne Gap in the north, Stainmore and the lower land connecting south Westmorland to the Yorkshire Dales are the principal routes to the east. A high limestone ridge in the Shap area and including the Shap Fells and Ash Fell, connect the central mountains with the Pennines. This ridge forms the watershed between the River Eden which drains to the north and the Kent and Lune rivers that drain to the south. The more southerly Howgill Fells lie between the Sedbergh district and the Tebay Gorge. (Map 1.2)

Rainfall levels vary widely. The central mountains receive more than 100 inches of rain per year (2,500 mm.) Kendal has about half that amount, 55 inches (1,375 mm.) and Ambleside's total is about 70 inches. (1,750 mm.) The coastal lowlands, the Carlisle area and the Eden valley receive from 30-40 inches. (750-1,000 mm.) Clearly, areas of high rainfall have fewer hours of sunshine than, for example, the coastal lowlands and towns such as Carlisle and Grange over Sands.

The lowlands surrounding the central mountains and the Eden valley are the main arable farming areas. Higher land, for example in the Bewcastle or the Caldbeck districts and the slopes leading to the mountainous core are transitional and support pastoral farming with some crops where a favourable aspect and quality of land allows. But these areas are mainly grassland with some hay (or

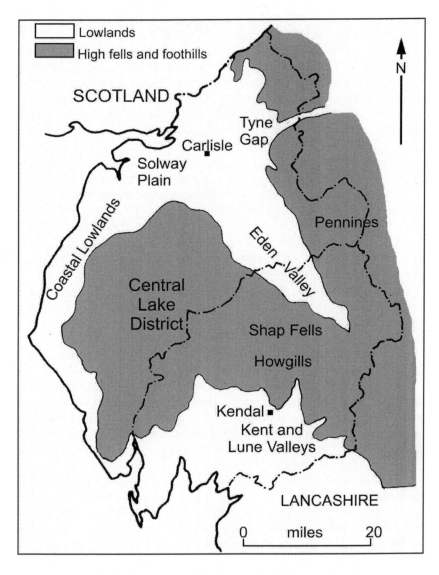

Lowlands

High fells and foothills

N

SCOTLAND

Tyne Gap

Carlisle

Solway Plain

Coastal Lowlands

Pennines

Eden Valley

Central Lake District

Shap Fells

Howgills

Kendal

Kent and Lune Valleys

LANCASHIRE

0   miles   20

1.2 Physical map of Cumberland and Westmorland.

silage today) produced for fodder. The high hills provide grazing for livestock, especially sheep. The main towns lie in the lowlands, for example, Carlisle, Penrith, Kendal, Cockermouth, Whitehaven and Workington. Smaller market towns and villages are found throughout the region with scattered hamlets and dispersed farms in the higher areas.[17]

Population, migration and emigration

During the century after 1815 while internal migration took men and women from, and brought others to, the two counties, thousands emigrated. In-migration as well as natural increase was responsible for population growth in some parts of the region and growth at county level continued until 1891. In Cumberland the increase continued until 1901 but in Westmorland the decline had already started. (Table 1.1) During the half century from 1851-1901 the population in England and Wales had increased by more than 80 per cent. In Cumberland the increase had been by 36.5 per cent and in Westmorland by only 19 per cent.

Table 1.1   County Population 1851-1911

County	1851	1881	1891	1901	1911
Cumberland	195,492	250,687	266,549	266,933	265,746
% Change		+28.2%	+6.3%	+0.1%	-0.4%
Westmorland	58,387	64,191	66,215	64,409	63,575
% Change		+9.9%	+3.15%	-2.7%	-1.3%

Source BPP Census reports

From 1901-1911, the population of England and Wales had increased by 10.9 per cent but Cumberland lost 0.4 per cent of its population and Westmorland had lost almost four per cent in the twenty years since 1891. As with earlier in-migration which was mainly to Carlisle and in the west, the fall in Cumberland was not because of evenly spread migration and emigration from the county but was exacerbated by the 'floods of young men' from West Cumberland who went to the South African mines. The 1911 census, the year in which 'the absolute level of emigration from England reached its peak,' reveals a fall in the population total in both counties and throughout the country emigrants [had been] more numerous than immigrants ... since 1851.' Where population in counties had declined it was 'entirely due to migration and emigration' and not to any change in the birth/death rate balance.[18] (Table 1.1)

It is clear that the exodus from the two counties was substantial. Actual figures are impossible to calculate and almost none were published but the 1841 Census Report did include the result of a survey from January 1st to June 4th 1841. Out of 9,501 emigrants from English counties who emigrated during those five months, 357 were from Cumberland (3.76 per cent) and 61 from Westmorland (0.64 per cent).[19] If replicated in the second seven months of the year, then 500 would have emigrated from Cumberland, a hypothetical total of 857 in the year and 85 from

Westmorland. In 1913, 271,300 emigrated from England. The proportion that came from Cumberland and Westmorland is unknown but as the sample indicates, emigration from the two counties was continuing apace. Baines calculated that Cumberland lost 3.5 per cent of its male and 2.0 per cent of its female population per decade from 1861-1900 (4.3 per cent male and 2.4 per cent female from Westmorland) and the rate of emigration accelerated after 1900.[20]

During the nineteenth century Cumberland's population had increased largely because of need for workers in the developing industries in the west and in Carlisle. A close examination of the population figures reveals that while there were substantial increases in the industrialising communities, in others, especially rural parishes in both Cumberland and Westmorland, low-level in-migration helped to maintain equilibrium but some communities did experience population decline. Table 1.2 shows that in 1901, 20 per cent of Cumberland residents and 29 per cent in Westmorland were incomers yet in Westmorland, where Kendal was a focus for commerce and manufacturing, the population had increased by fewer than 100 from 1881 to 1901 and even 30 years later there had been little increase, which suggests a significant outflow. Many Cumbrians moved to other parts of England including nearby Furness but from 1815-1914 thousands chose emigration.

Simultaneously, emigrants were leaving Cumberland and Westmorland and migrants moved in, for example, the hundreds of Scottish, Irish and others who went to west Cumberland. Why did so many emigrate when the region was apparently so attractive for in-migrants? What were the forces that pushed migrants out or pulled them towards new horizons? As will become clear from the discussion of the Cumbrian economy later, the push factor had an important role in persuading emigrants to leave the Pennine lead mining communities or, as employment in iron ore mining became less secure, from West Cumberland.

Table 1.2 Cumberland & Westmorland birthplace and emigration details 1901

County	1: Birthplace	2: Residence	Total 1&2	Total Co.Pop.	% incomers
Cumberland	*Cumberland*	*elsewhere*	*c61,000**		
Cumberland	*elsewhere*	*Cumberland*	*53,833*	*266,549*	*20.2 %*
Westmorland	*W'tmorland*	*elsewhere*	*c.36,226**		
Westmorland	*elsewhere*	*W'morland*	*18,756*	*64,409*	*29 %*

In 1881 Westmorland's population was 64,124 and 65,408 in 1931
*Source BPP Census Reports   *in England*

Peak years for emigration did not necessarily coincide with specific economic difficulties although they may have encouraged thoughts of the possibility of leaving. Reasons for emigration are complex. It is not simply a question of whether conditions at home pushed and the destination pulled. If that were so why did so many not emigrate? Push factors such as poverty, unemployment, uncertainty and a wish to escape from family, local conditions, and the class system affected far more people than those who emigrated. But for prospective emigrants, the siren call of opportunity was the catalyst. Emigrants believed that they and their children could achieve more in possibly freer conditions abroad even if the reality proved to be years of hard work and no instant path to wealth. Although circumstances helped to 'push' some prospective emigrants, it is unlikely that so many would have risked facing the future far from home without being aware of a simultaneous 'pull' factor. The prospect of making a fortune on the goldfields, of working for higher wages, having the opportunity to acquire land, a sense of achieving greater freedom and the strong belief that they could succeed in a life that must be better overseas were crucial elements in the decision to leave. Migration within Britain, or simply staying at home were the alternatives.

Emigrant letters

As costs fell and journey times shortened, more and more emigrants – or their children, were able to visit their home country, but for the majority, emigration meant separation forever. Communication depended on letters and even a few ill-spelt lines brought pleasure and comfort to relatives. In the early years letters would be received infrequently – perhaps only once a year and postage rates were expensive. For example, in the 1830s, the cost of sending of a letter from, or to, a destination overseas included several layers of charges. But gradually, the price fell. By 1854 letters to New South Wales, for example, cost 6d per half ounce, 4d by 1889 and 2 ½d in 1891. The penny post, as in the United Kingdom, was extended to (and from) Australia in 1911. Newspaper postage had been only 1d from the 1830s; consequently thousands of newspapers were sent to, and received from, relatives overseas. There are many references in the sample to letters of thanks for newspapers received and of having sent newspapers home. A newspaper would convey local news (from overseas or from Cumbria) leaving the writer of a letter free to mention only family news which may account for the lack of wider information in the majority of the sample letters. In the early 1860s, 110,000 newspapers per month were sent to Australia.[21]

In recent decades a number of scholars have offered a critique on the value of letters as a source.[22] As in all written sources, the risk of bias may present a problem especially in letters published in tracts, journals or newspapers where the intention may have been to promote or to be critical of emigration or particular destinations. Most correspondents whose letters were published in the sample editions of the local press simply describe their new life. Occasionally pessimistic or optimistic opinions are expressed which may, of course, have influenced prospective emigrants. Private letters written to family and friends at home, although not free from the danger of bias (few would wish to write of difficulties and may have omitted facts that might cause anxiety), are considered to be a more fruitful and trustworthy source of information. Some of these were published, for example, those from Francis Jollie to William Blamire.[23]

Letters were often short and to save paper and postal costs some were 'cross-written;' a real challenge to read. But, to receive a letter, to see the handwriting and to read the contents was to be as close as possible to the emigrant or the family at home and to gain a glimpse of the other's life gave joy and comfort. A single surviving letter tells us only of life on a single day or short period of time. Other letters would have been different. When a series of letters has survived, perhaps even into the second and third generations, we can follow the fortunes of the emigrant and the family at home over a longer period. Letters from the Wood family who had emigrated from the Penrith area to New South Wales in 1818 were sent to Miss Scott in Penrith over a period of 30 years. Similarly, letters to Joseph Salkeld in Hilton, north Westmorland from his family in North America, extend from *c.*1830 to the 1890s.[24]

Family matters such as births, marriages, illness and death, the progress of sons and daughters are frequent topics and some letters give advice to prospective emigrants which may be positive or cautionary during times of poor employment prospects. Some letters refer to political and national events. Others include news of a family tragedy, for example, the deaths of Joseph Dover in Canada or Anthony Clarke in southern Africa.[25] The Pattinson family letters record the life of their son in India before his death.[26] Some letters give full accounts of the emigrant's experience after leaving home including the voyage, the subsequent journey and their new home. Others contain tantalisingly few details.

Most writers seem satisfied with progress and assure relatives that they had made the right decision. The absence of comments that emigration could have been a mistake is not surprising. The really discontented would make efforts to return home and others would hesitate before admitting to having made the wrong decision. Frequently we are reminded that home was not far from their thoughts and we read of the pleasure brought by receiving a letter. The sense of separation, nostalgia and implicit homesickness is evident in the wish to see Dufton Pike and the Pennines again or in the request for homemade preserves or a root of rhubarb to be sent from home. Writers often refer by name to other emigrants in the neighbourhood who would be known to the recipient – evidence of chain migration and confirming that clusters from the same district had settled in or near the same destination.[27] Letters deposited in the archives or supplied by relatives are almost entirely those sent to Cumbria but it is often possible to gain some insight into the contents of outward letters from comments and answers to questions. Thanks are expressed for gifts, newspapers and other items received and the writers tell of gifts, newspapers and almanacks sent to Cumbria. Only one letter in the sample seems to hint that financial help from home could be helpful and even that is not clear. But money was sent to emigrants. In almost every one of a series of letters from Queensland, Samuel and Margaret White thank their brother and sister in Cumberland for money received.[28] The White letters and those from the Wood family in New South Wales are rare in the sample being written by women.[29] Apart from isolated examples, such as the loss of crops through drought or floods and in one case, financial loss after the failure of a bank, the only financial matters referred to in letters are costs and prices of goods and farm produce or livestock. Occasionally the letters contain offers to send money home to help another family member to emigrate or acknowledge receipt of, or discuss how to transfer money inherited from deceased relatives.

Some emigrants disappeared and never made contact – either being incapable of writing a letter or simply lacking the will to do so. Of course, illiterate or less than fluently literate emigrants are invisible but, as the Cumbrian letters illustrate, emigrants across a broad spectrum of occupations possessed the skill to communicate with their relatives even if there were differences in technical competency. The widespread literacy of emigrants been noted by several commentators.[30] For example, in Ontario (Upper Canada) 'British protestant immigrants' had higher levels of literacy 'than the societies they had left' and they came from regions in Britain with 'relatively high' literacy levels. In Australia, where the literacy level of immigrants was 'very high,' the literacy of immigrants 'correspond[ed] almost exactly' with the rank order of the county of origin and 'letters written by British working people ... gave voice to proletarian colonial Australia.'[31] Literacy levels in Cumberland and Westmorland were among the highest in England throughout the nineteenth century even though there were differences within the region. Schooling for boys and girls had long been part of Cumbrian life – even if attendance was not always regular but literacy was not as widespread amongst the miners in West Cumberland in the first half of the nineteenth century where children as young as nine years were employed underground as in farming communities in Westmorland, for example.[32] The London Lead Company provided schools for the children of their employees in Cumberland and north Westmorland. Local newspapers had been published from the early nineteenth century and Reading Rooms became widely established.[33] Consequently, the majority of Cumbrian emigrants would have been able to exchange letters with their families even if spelling and grammar were poor. The series of letters from Stephen Madgen of Nenthead include one written shortly after his arrival in Australia that he suggests was written for him.[34] Certainly, subsequent letters are in a less fluent hand but he was able to convey what he wished to say.

How representative are these emigrant examples? Even letters and family details do not build a comprehensive picture. Almost all those about whom we have information were at least modestly successful. It is not known if others were in poverty and difficulty. Letters have survived only by chance. Some would have been lost en route and many, although received, have not survived. Some families were 'squirrels' by nature and their letters have been preserved. But unless a family member was sufficiently interested in 'old papers,' letters and photographs and mementoes will have been destroyed. Family bibles often recorded dates of major life events. Letters supplied by relatives and from the archives are only a small and perhaps unrepresentative selection of those written but they help to bring individual emigrant writers to life.

Information extracted from all the sources reflects only this particular sample and, given other examples the picture may have been different. But the sample extends over a period of 150 years and the emigrants who settled in different environments – in towns, cities, rural and mining communities, in far distant parts of the world came from all parts of the two counties.

The national economy

A brief survey of the general trends and conditions in England during the 'long' nineteenth century necessarily smoothes over short term problems, periods of stability and economic growth and political or national events.[35] Alongside unemployment and distress because of change or during periods of commercial and economic depression there were new opportunities but not necessarily near home. Production of coal, iron and steel, manufacturing and commerce expanded to meet the demands of increased internal and overseas trade.

Before the Industrial Revolution most parts of Britain had a wide variety of crafts and industries. Only minerals such as coal, tin or lead were confined to particular areas. Increasingly industrial regions became more specialised. The woollen industry became focused in the West Riding; cotton in Lancashire and in the Glasgow region. Half of the cotton output was exported in the 1820s; three quarters in the 1890s and between one quarter and one third of all woollen and worsted goods were exported throughout the nineteenth century. The growing empire provided a market for British exports consequently at least some of the customers either directly or indirectly were emigrants.

As the scale of manufacturing changed and new technology was introduced, handloom weavers, frame knitters and workers in other local or family based industrial activities could be reduced to penury and destitution. Many had clung to what they knew long after it had become unsustainable. By 1831 handloom weavers could earn only one quarter of the 23 shillings they had earned in 1805.[36] In agriculture too there were many changes. After profitable years up to 1815 when shortage of workers had almost doubled labourers' wages and every possible acre was cultivated, the post-war years were difficult. Thousands of men returned from the army. Unemployment increased with inevitable poverty and distress. Farmers employed fewer workers and for the next 20 years tithe obligations, customary dues, low prices and increased costs led to increasingly narrow margins and reduced working capital but livestock farmers could still make a profit.[37] In the 1830s a North Riding farmer stated 'there was not a township and hardly a family … [that have not] … some … gone to America.'[38] Farming families emigrated throughout the century, even during the 'golden years' in mid-century and certainly before and after those years. For a small owner occupier or tenant farmer already living frugally and using only family labour, costs could not be reduced further. Periodic outbreaks of blight and animal disease, poor harvests caused by drought or rain, fluctuating prices, increased rents, inheritance obligations, large families to be supported on small farms and the risk of losing a tenancy on death were ever present threats. By realising their assets emigrant farmers could take capital with them.[39] Emigrants to Canada in 1842 included English farmers 'who have brought out good means' with them.[40] The alternative was to continue in farming or, if in real difficulty, to become an agricultural labourer or to move to a town and follow an entirely different occupation.

And there were other challenges. Overseas producers in Europe notably in Russia and Prussia and later in North America and beyond found a ready market in Britain. From about 1870 the flood of imported grain caused a collapse in prices and depression in the agricultural sector. By 1910, 80 per cent of wheat used in Britain was imported.[41] Vast quantities of grain, dairy products, eggs, animals and meat (including canned and frozen meat by the 1880s) were imported from many parts of the world. In the context of emigration it is important to recognise that many of these overseas producers had family origins in Britain and some had their roots in Cumbria.

There were also periods of depression and difficulty in the wider national economy. In 1843, for example, it was reported that 'the state of the lower classes … [in] … the UK has continued to be exceedingly depressed … the consequences will doubtless be a continued universal disposition to emigrate.'[42] But it was also stated in the mid-1840s that 'railway building and harvest work' meant that few English working men emigrated and in 1852, the official view was that 'at the present moment there is comparatively little desire among the English labouring classes to emigrate … proof of [their] well-being.' The sample indicates that Cumbrians some of whom who were, but others were not of the labouring classes, continued to emigrate – in fact, more left in the 1850s than in the previous decade.[43] The introduction to an 1858 directory states that more than 23,000 natives of Westmoreland (*sic*) were distributed throughout England 'exclusive of those [who had gone to] Australia and America' and in the Cumberland section, 'a large number of Cumberland folk are to be found ... throughout England and the empire at large.'[44] The sample includes more than 60 emigrants who went to New Zealand in the 1850s when the Canterbury and Otago settlements were attracting immigrants and a total of approximately 360 left in that decade compared with approximately 180 in the 1840s. In the 1850s very few could be described as members of the labouring classes although some went to the gold fields. The majority were from farming families.

The Cumbrian economy[45]

In the eighteenth century crafts and industries were widespread in the Cumbrian region and overseas trade was a long established feature of the West Cumberland economy where the ports had strong connections with lands across the sea. The Lowther family, who developed the town and port of Whitehaven and its coal industry, owned land in the West Indies. Coal was exported to Virginia in the eighteenth century. They and others had trading connections with the Caribbean region, America, the Baltic and more distant lands. For some years Whitehaven was one of the foremost ports in England. Tobacco had been imported from the 1680s and Whitehaven ships carried slaves from Africa to America but not on a scale comparable with Bristol or Liverpool.[46] The Curwens developed Workington. The Senhouses who established Maryport had an estate in Barbados. These families and others increased their wealth from their trading operations and shrewd entrepreneurial investments. Transatlantic trade in coal, rum, sugar, timber and cotton continued to thrive. European, South American and Far Eastern links were also important.

In the nineteenth century ship building and its ancillary trades and fishing remained part of the local economy but as the size of ships increased, Cumberland shipbuilders moved to Liverpool and fishing fleets became focused elsewhere.[47] Here, as in Furness, the exploitation of rich haematite ores, coal mining and iron production increased the industrial capacity and wealth of West Cumberland. Communities grew and harbours were extended. Overseas trade continued. European and American grain was imported and milled at Whitehaven, Maryport and later at Silloth. Ship building, fishing, salt production and local crafts remained as minor players in the local economy. Farming continued to dominate rural areas and Cumbrian farmers weathered the storm of the late century depression by responding to the general improvement in the standard of living and increased national demand for meat and dairy produce. In Cumberland the acreage of pasture had increased by 23 per cent 1871-80 and by 17 per cent in Westmorland; a county where grassland had always been important. In 1881 Mr Coleman reported that in Cumberland 'agricultural depression does not exist' and similar sentiments were expressed by Mr Wilson Fox in 1895.[48] In 1911, 22.5 per cent of Westmorland's working population was engaged in agriculture.[49] But the story is not one of smooth progress.[50]

The former widespread textile industry gradually declined and became concentrated in centres such as Carlisle or Kendal. There were signs of economic difficulties and discontent in, for example, the corn riot in Kendal in 1775, several food riots during the Napoleonic wars and a potato riot in 1812.[51] In 1787 more than 420 textile workers were listed in the '*Westmorland Census*' the returns for which have survived in only a handful of townships with a further 176 weavers, wool and other workers in the partial return for Kendal.[52] In 1788 payment to domestic spinners in Westmorland was reduced and there had been 'tumultuous meetings' of weavers in 1786. In 1795 'female linen spinners in Cumberland [had to] labour hard at [the] wheel, 10 or 11 hours in the day to earn 4d.' In 1799 Kendal weavers gathered at a 'turnout and riot.'[53]

In 1801 Carlisle's manufactures 'were not extensive' but four or five new cotton mills had recently opened. Small-scale 'check' was manufactured in most market towns.[54] Certainly the textile industry was widespread in 1811 but in Maryport, the cotton manufactory had closed in 1810 'caus[ing] unemployment and distress.'[55] The 1826 Select Committee Report on Emigration stated that there was 'distress bordering on actual famine [in areas including] Lancashire, parts of Cheshire, the West Riding of Yorkshire and Cumberland.' The committee recommended that the government should send 1,200 families comprising approximately 6-7,000 adults and children to the North American Colonies who would, 'by their success excite a strong feeling in favour of emigration' and help to 'people our colonies' while also being beneficial 'to the Mother country.'[56] The 1829 directory has more than 100 references to textile manufacture throughout the two counties.[57] There are more than 20 references to textile manufacture in Kendal and at least 25 manufacturers, bleachers or dyers were in or near Carlisle.[58] The expanding cotton industry in Carlisle had attracted a large number of Irish and Scottish in-migrants. Cotton manufacture had ceased in Penrith and Longtown, and in 1828 £900 had been spent on the relief of paupers in Cockermouth.[59] Major fires at a Carlisle cotton mill and at the Egremont flax mill resulted in at least temporary unemployment. The depression in the cotton industry in the Carlisle area was the worst for 20 years. Mechanised factories meant under- and unemployment for hand workers and almost 5,500 families (18-20,000 adults and children) dependent on handloom weaving had seen their livelihood undermined by new mills with power looms exacerbated by general economic problems and over-production. Food prices were high due to poor harvests and many families were in poverty, their diet comprising only 'potatoes, buttermilk and herrings.' More general unemployment meant there was no alternative work. Carlisle people petitioned for assistance towards emigrating. 'They would be happy to go to Canada ... [or] the USA.'[60]

In 1840 Carlisle's textile industry was again in trouble. The handloom weavers had continued in their doomed effort to compete with mechanisation. Twelve hundred weavers were unemployed and 'a quarter of [the] population [was] ... bordering on absolute starvation.'[61] There would be 'a continued universal disposition to emigrate.'[62] The cotton trade had been 'much affected by the American embarrassments' and lack of work in during the past 18 months had resulted in widespread poverty there.[63] Twenty years later the American Civil War had two effects. Few emigrants went to the United States and crucially for the British textile industry, raw cotton imports from America virtually ceased. Once again there was unemployment and 'a great many [were] in distress.' In the winter of 1862-3 Carlisle's Board of Guardians paid more than £7,000 to help *c.*6,000 needy people and Carlisle textile workers were among those who had emigrated under a local scheme; a total of 218 by 1865.[64] After the war, imports of cotton resumed and by 1868 weavers were being recruited in Cumbria by mills at Burnley in Lancashire.[65]

By the 1880s most small manufactories in rural Cumberland and Westmorland had disappeared.[66] In Kendal woollen cloth manufacture remained important and shoes, carpets, tobacco, paper and other products were processed or manufactured. Carlisle's cotton industry continued to have periods of difficulty from the 1860s to the early 1880s. The bankruptcy of Dixon's business in 1872 caused thousands to lose their jobs but other industries in Carlisle including Carr's Biscuits and Cowan and Sheldon's engineering works made progress. Once the cotton crisis was over, Carlisle's textile industry recovered. By the 1880s rural Cumberland and Westmorland had almost no industry of any kind. 'Country mills and small industries [had] passed away' and the 'old industries ... [were] fast becoming extinct' by 1900.[67] Even local crafts had shrunk leaving a village with, at best, only a blacksmith and carpenter.

The mining industry had a similarly problematical history. *Circa* 1800, a recession in the coal trade had caused high levels of poverty in West Cumberland and intermittent economic problems in the local economy occurred throughout the century. In 1811, the Seaton Iron Works employed several hundred men but in 1828-9 'was not working to much advantage at present [and] ... the prosperity of the village [had] decline[d].'[68] Fewer exports to Ireland meant a 27 per cent reduction in the number of trading ships at Workington.[69] Destitute men had built a road at Hensingham before 1829 and in West Cumberland, coal and iron ore mines had periodic difficulties. Other communities and industries suffered periods of unemployment and distress. The population of Cleator fell by 40 per cent from 1821-31. The reopening of a flax mill and the burgeoning iron ore industry over the next 50 years meant the population was 11,400 by 1881. Much of this increase was due to in-migration. However, later difficulties in West Cumberland fuelled the rush to emigrate. In 1868 only 10 of the 21 blast furnaces were in operation in West Cumberland.[70] In 1891, a serious depression in the iron and steel industry caused *c*.5,000 men and boys to be unemployed in Workington.[71] Economic problems and the numbers emigrating were regularly reported in the local press during the late nineteenth century. Cleator's population had fallen to *c*.10,000 in 1901. In 1901 very heavy financial losses meant the closure of Kirk Brothers' iron works.[72] In 1905, only 20 out of 36 blast furnaces were working in West Cumberland, the coal trade was 'shrinking' and a collapse in the pig iron trade reduced the number of furnaces in blast to 12 by 1913.[73] Workers at the Lonsdale Iron Works had to accept a 25 per cent reduction in wages in 1907 to avoid closing the works.[74] There was serious unemployment in Frizington in 1909 after the Margaret Mine closed.[75]

The story of iron ore mining throughout the century in West Cumberland was one of mines opening, being worked out and closing. In Flimby only two mines were working in 1828-9. At St Bees production fell year by year until by 1900 no output figures were given. Millom, in the extreme south west of Cumberland, close to Furness, was a more successful iron ore community. Local mines produced about 500,000 tons per year. Millom, in the extreme south west of Cumberland, close to the border with Furness, was a more successful iron ore community. It grew from a village of 350 to a town of *c*.10,400 by 1901, when the mines and ironworks employed about 1,900 men but there were periods of difficulty. In 1895 500 men had been laid off because of poor trade and a dispute meant that more than 1,000 men had no work. By 1911 Millom's population had fallen to 8,301. Unfortunately the sample contains only nine men and women whose residence before leaving was Millom but it is probable that many of the 2,000 who were no longer in Millom would have emigrated as did iron ore miners from the Cleator Moor district. Lack of information rather than actuality is the key fact here.[76] During that same decade Workington lost 1,044, Maryport lost 373, Aspatria lost 454. Both Cumberland and Westmorland lost population from 1901-1911 and for Westmorland this followed a decline from 1891.[77]

Coal mining remained important throughout the century. When the coal industry was expanding during the 1820s, workers were needed but even the offer of free houses did not persuade those intent on emigrating to take up the offer. Then, and later, coal and iron ore mining and iron and steel manufacturing brought migrant workers and their families to West Cumberland (and Furness) from all parts of the United Kingdom. In 1842 it was reported that Lord Lonsdale's mines offered better wages and conditions than others and, as more horses were used underground, fewer child workers were needed.[78] Coal production more than doubled from 1854-1901 by which time more than 8,600 workers were employed.[79] But, even in the good years, out-migration and emigration were under way. Baines states that the 1880s decade saw the greatest emigration of young adult males from Cumberland up to 1900 but evidence from local sources shows that the wave of emigration to South Africa from West Cumberland continued to gather in intensity from the 1880s up to the outbreak of war.[80] Work in gold and diamond mines attracted many hundreds of men even when local industries were not under stress.

In east Cumberland the mining and processing of lead gave 'employment to most of [the] inhabitants' of Alston Moor in 1829 when 1,100 workers worked in the 38 lead mines. But only five years later there was deep distress there. The population of 6,858 in 1831 had fallen by more than one quarter and 400-500 houses were empty. Seven per cent of those remaining were paupers. Some of the displaced workers had emigrated to Canada or South America. Others had moved to coal mining areas in England.[81] This evidence of a substantial outflow from one particular district (repeated in the 1870s and 1880s after the final collapse of the British lead industry) is a clear example of the 'push' factor at work.

This account of the Cumbrian economy gives credence, but perhaps undue emphasis to the 'push' side of the migration debate. Throughout the century after 1815 West Cumberland also exerted a powerful 'pull' effect. Thousands of in-migrants moved into the area and the highlighted periods of difficulty were interspersed by good years of stability and growth. Nevertheless, there was a considerable degree of endemic poverty and the need for charitable activity to feed families during economic depressions or periods of unemployment. For example, the local press reported that soup kitchens were operating in Whitehaven and Workington in 1879 and 1885 and in Egremont in the early 1900s.[82] Penrith and Appleby suffered from unemployment and distress in the 1880s. In January 1886, poverty in Appleby was caused by low wages and a scarcity of work and a soup kitchen fed 140 in Penrith.[83] Five thousand were unemployed in Workington in 1891 when the West Cumberland iron and steel industry was in the grip of a severe depression.[84] Emigration continued apace throughout the period even in the good years.

By 1900, Carlisle had a varied economic base, was an important railway city and was the focal point and market centre for a large area of Cumberland, north Westmorland and the border regions of Scotland. Industries included engineering, metal box manufacture, textiles, biscuit making and other enterprises. Products made in Carlisle were exported to countries across the world. By the early twentieth century the major points of concern in the regional economy were largely confined to West Cumberland although the outward flow from all parts of the two counties continued even in 1913 when employment in West

Cumberland was said to be 'plentiful.'[85]

Although there were positive as well as negative aspects to Cumbria's economy during the nineteenth century, uncertainty and fears for the future may have influenced even those not directly affected. It could be argued that the scale of the outflow meant that jobs were available for those who had stayed. Cumberland and Westmorland men and women were not parochial in their outlook and although communities experienced an outflow, others moved in and actual decline occurred in relatively few parishes. Not all rural migrants left England. Some moved to Cumbrian towns and both rural and urban Cumbrians moved to other parts of England but, as the evidence shows, many emigrated.

Chapter 1 has highlighted some of the economic problems that may have persuaded Cumbrians to seek work elsewhere. Men and women migrated to all parts of England but a more distant goal – a new and potentially a far better environment overseas was an attractive alternative. Many who emigrated in the decades after 1815 went because of the economic depression and uncertainty about the future. Farmers left not only because of immediate problems but went 'while the going was good' as they faced narrowing margins and gloomy prospects for the future. Such views were not confined to the years after 1815. Periodic revolutions, wars or unrest in Europe, for example in 1830 and 1848, the Crimean war, the Franco-Prussian war of 1870-1, and anxiety about order and stability in England in the later nineteenth century – together with social problems and cyclical periods of 'boom and bust' in the economy fed fears that revolution might be imported into Britain or, at the very least that 'the nation [was] slipping backwards.' Many thought that to continue life as it had been and as they wished it to be required moving to another country.[86] Some in the sample stated that they had left because of over-bearing clergy and lord of the manor attitudes, tithes (until after 1836), dues and taxes. In 1830 Joseph Dover, from north Westmorland wrote from Pittsburgh, 'The love of liberty has so worked upon my mind that I can never think of living again under the yoke of tyranny and oppression any more'[87] Some sought a less class-bound society. Two years later Thomas Hodgson wrote that the rich in Pittsburgh 'were more common than in Westmorland but of all the men I have met with ever since I left Westmorland I never have found a man more inhuman and more degraded in principle than old Mr Heelas. (*sic*) I would like to know how poor Dufton comes on between the wolf and the lion.' [88] In particular, it can certainly be recognised that Alston Moor miners in the 1830s and 1870s and iron ore miners in the last quarter of the century were 'pushed' by circumstances. Others had less pressing reasons. For many Cumbrians the only reason to emigrate was that they wished to follow others and seek a new life and greater opportunities abroad.

Chapter 2:
Origins : who emigrated?

Was dissatisfaction with life at home, lack of prospects or unemployment the only reason for leaving? Not all with similar life experiences decided to leave. Men who did not inherit the family farm whether as a younger son or because they failed to secure the tenancy after the death of parents had different reactions. Some left the land and found work within Britain. After the death of his parents William Elliott of Castle Sowerby, Cumberland, was not able to take on the tenancy of the farm. He left his village, moved no more than 25 miles to Penrith, became a coachman and gardener, married, had a large family and remained there for the rest of his life. Others in a similar position acted differently. Henry Castley of Rosgill, Westmorland went to Canada. Samuel and George Furness of Kings Meaburn went to Australia. Did emigrants have special qualities of enterprise and courage? What persuaded emigrants to leave relatives and friends and everything that was familiar?

It could be argued that the loss of skilled and enterprising men and women had a detrimental effect on their community, but not all ambitious and capable men and women left and the exodus may have helped to stabilise the local economy and thus have had a positive result. Also, by transferring these qualities to emerging nations overseas the emigrants contributed to the new land's potential. Ideal emigrants would be 'young men and women in the prime of life … trained in habits of industry, sobriety and frugality … [and] in possession of a fund of general information which may be useful to them in the new and unforeseen circumstance.'[1] Cumbria was a farming region therefore many emigrants from the two counties had experience on the land. Men with specialised skills such as engineers and miners found work in projects all over the world. Skilled craftsmen were needed to establish communities in new colonies and in existing towns and cities. Farmers, farm workers and female domestic servants were always in demand.

High literacy rates in the two counties meant that Cumbrian men and women were well equipped to make progress at home and abroad.[2] Calculating from the data in the Registrar General's Report for 1851, 84 per cent of men and 66 per cent of women signed marriage registers with their names in Cumberland, 83 per cent and 69 per cent respectively in Westmorland but only 52 per cent of both men and women did so in Hertfordshire.[3] Figures published after the elections of 1880 and 1906 show that of those who voted in the general election, only 0.4 per cent (1880), 0.3 per cent (1906) were illiterate in Westmorland, 0.35 per cent

(1880) and 0.6 per cent (1906) in Cumberland.[4] John Lanigan was not a Cumbrian but his comments seem to fit what must have been 'normal' in the Cumbrian region. He was educated at an elementary school during some of the years between 1875 and 1914 and stated that he 'did not know any children of [his] age who could not read or write, do arithmetic and know something of history and geography.'[5]

Cumberland and Westmorland farm workers were paid far more than their counterparts in southern England. In 1861 half the deposited funds in Penrith Savings Bank were those of farm labourers and servants; male and female.[6] In 1867-70 the average wage in Hertfordshire was 13s 6d but 18s 6d in Cumbria – a differential that applied before and after those years.[7] Later in the century the Vicar of Greystoke commented that 'young farm labourers, both male and female, have plenty of money' and, as many farmers had previously been farm workers, 'they were very provident with money.'[8] The ambition to 'do well' was, for many, part of the Cumbrian psyche and this outward looking population had a long tradition of education, migration and social mobility. English emigrants to Australia have been described as 'well-informed, self reliant and literate' – a description that could be applied to Cumbrians wherever their destination.[9]

Emigration from Cumberland and Westmorland was not new. Edmund Nicholson of Bootle in south west Cumberland was in Portsmouth, Rhode Island in 1650 and more than 40 were in North America or the West Indies before 1800. During the American War of Independence George Hope from Whitehaven was working in a Virginian shipyard building gunboats for the navy and a correspondent wrote of the fight against the rebels in the Philadelphia and New York region during that war.[10] Some early emigrants, for example, Quaker families, left to escape from religious intolerance; others went to plantations or became administrators but some went simply to start a new life. In May and June 1775 two ships left Whitehaven for New York. The *Favourite* carried 101 passengers. The *Lovely Nelly* called at various ports in southern Scotland and the Solway Firth before taking 145 passengers to Nova Scotia. A third un-named ship carried 137 passengers. These are known; there may have been others. Not all passengers would be Cumbrians. Cumberland ports also served north Yorkshire and southern Scotland.[11]

Emigrant numbers fell during the American War of Independence and later wars in Europe and Canada but after 1815 the flow increased. In 1825 the *Cumberland Pacquet* carried an advertisement offering excellent accommodation in brigs bound for the West Indies and 'a fine fast sailing ship,' the 250 ton *Aurora* was to sail direct to Quebec from Whitehaven. The following year the *Arsthorpe* 'a roomy and comfortable brig' would take 20-30 passengers to Quebec from Whitehaven, the 300 ton *Kelsick Wood* would sail from Maryport to Montreal

J. C. Armytage

Maryport harbour, 1840s.

and the 500 ton *Winscales* from Workington to Quebec. In 1836 *The Lady Gordon*, a 600 ton 'fast sailing ship ... unusually roomy betwixt decks' was to sail direct to Quebec from Maryport.[12]

In the 1831 shipping lists analysed by Charlotte Erickson, 19 per cent of emigrants to the United States were recorded as farmers; few were farm labourers.[13] She states that the majority of emigrants had made 'rational and conscious choices' rather than being driven out by circumstances. Poorer emigrants tended to go to Canada.[14] Rural emigration from Cumbria was well underway in the 1830s and the emigrants included farmers.[15]

Table 2.1 shows published statistics for Cumberland ports to British North America over a 27 year period. Emigrant numbers to other destinations and from ports such as Liverpool, Glasgow or London, are unknown. More than 7,800, the majority of whom went to Quebec or Montreal, were recorded as leaving Cumberland ports during these years. In May 1830, for example, 151 emigrants, 'principally from Westmorland,' left Maryport for Quebec and 'went in search of that contentment and prosperity in a foreign land which from various causes they had failed to secure at home.'[16] Other ships may have sailed for other destinations therefore these are minimum totals and are only a fraction of those who emigrated from England.

During stressful economic years, concerns about the future and knowing that

Table 2.1 Emigration from Cumberland to British North America 1825-1852

Port of Departure	1825	1826	1827	1828	1829	1830	1831	1832	1833	1834	1835
Carlisle	-	-	-	-	-	-	-	16	-	-	-
Whitehaven	64	3	95	51	268	522	1086	1664	413	72	-
Maryport	-	-	-	-	-	-	421	884	315	538	182
Workington	-	-	-	-	-	-	399	246	-	29	-
	1836	1837	1840	1843	1846	1847	1850	1851	1852	Total	
Carlisle							24	26	81	147	
Whitehaven	110	-	49	56	-	-	-	-	2*	4455	
Maryport	15	39	-	8	30	11	12	10	63	2538	
Workington	-	-	-	-	-	-	8	-	-	682	
Total										7822	

* To the West Indies   Source: BPP 1833 XXVI p.280, 1837 XLII p.21,1837-38 XL pp.55-6, 1837-8 XLVII p.168, 1847 XXXIII p.171, 1851 XXII, p.368, 1851 XL p.329, 1852-3 XL, App.1.

others who had left were 'doing well' added to the desire to escape. In the late nineteenth century, for example, although some years were better, 1879 was a particularly bad year. Farmers suffered from terrible weather resulting in a poor and exceptionally late harvest. Hundreds were unemployed in Cleator Moor, wages were reduced on the railway, the coal and iron trade in West Cumberland suffered badly, weavers in Carlisle and thread workers in Cockermouth had wages cut by 10 per cent, Kendal's woollen workers had a 'further reduction in wages,' West Cumberland iron mines were working only nine days per fortnight, joiners' wages were reduced by at least 15 per cent and miners in Maryport went on strike after wages were cut by 37 per cent.[17] Recurrent waves of economic depression had occurred throughout the century. But, in spite of problems the coal and iron ore mining industries in West Cumberland did develop with a consequent need for workers. Hundreds of migrants from Scotland, Ireland, Cornwall, and other distant counties moved in. Although a large proportion of the workers were Cumbrians a scan of the census for several mining and industrial communities in the second half of the century shows that few in these industries were from eastern Cumberland or from Westmorland. Members of in-migrant families from other regions were also among the emigrants. West Cumberland's isolation became an increasing factor in an evermore competitive world and local industries especially iron ore mining suffered. From the early 1880s up to 1914 emigration from West Cumberland was 'rife.'[18] In the early twentieth century the West Cumberland industrial communities had high levels of unemployment and much poverty. 'Families [in Egremont were] ... carrying children [and] begging for food ... not having any money at all.' ... Soup kitchens opened, 'people were starving. ... [Anyone] who could afford it' made plans to emigrate.[19] It is clear that for those who could leave, emigration seemed a life-line. Even people who were not directly affected were at least given a gentle nudge into thinking that life could probably be better overseas. But, in the rest of the region, before the mid-century for some, and for the majority later, emigrants went not because of personal or local economic difficulties but because of perceived opportunities abroad coloured by a degree of pessimism about their future in England.

Some emigrated hoping that a better climate might restore their health. For Thomas and Margaret Ostle of Whitehaven the result was good. Margaret's health improved in Western Australia but Henry Graham of Carlisle who took his printing press to Dunedin, New Zealand in 1849 died within two years and Joseph Kilvington of Brough, already in poor health when he left, died in Australia in 1891.[20] Although some children were sent abroad from the region, a decision by the Cockermouth Guardians to send six boys to Canada was reversed in 1905. However, 20-30 young Workington girls had voluntarily responded to an advertisement offering work in Canada.[21]

Many young men and women went alone but families feature strongly in the sample throughout the century and up to 1914. Some emigrant families, especially those who went to North America, travelled in stages with the wife and children following months or even a year or more later. In contrast, those going to the Antipodes tended to leave together. But, Joseph McLintock, a steelworker from Workington went alone to New Zealand in 1908 and found work as a gardener. His wife and child followed a year later.[22] Clearly the comparative costs, length of the journey and communication problems influenced the decision.

The emigrants

The 1841 census recorded individual names and some details for the first time but the enumerations are more comprehensive from 1851. However, if named emigrants in the sample are checked in the previous census, not all can be identified. In some cases the date of leaving is unknown and the often sketchy details of life before emigration as supplied by relatives may be inaccurate. Unless precise age, residence and birthplace details are known, especially in a region where names are common, there are uncertainties. For example several in the census had the name Lancelot Thwaytes and, was John Bramwell a lead miner from Alston or a stone mason from West Cumberland? Two Christopher Siddles in Dufton had similar birth dates – one was a lead miner, the other an agricultural labourer. Some relatives knew only that the emigrant left before 1914 or 'probably in the 1880s.' The enumerations did help to identify some emigrants

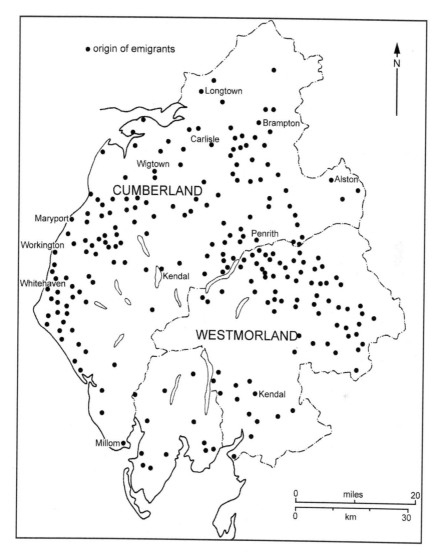

2.1 Map of the known places of origin from which emigrants emigrated.

whose names had appeared in other sources. They could then be placed in a family or work context but there are many for whom we know only the name, perhaps the community from which they emigrated and the country to which they went.

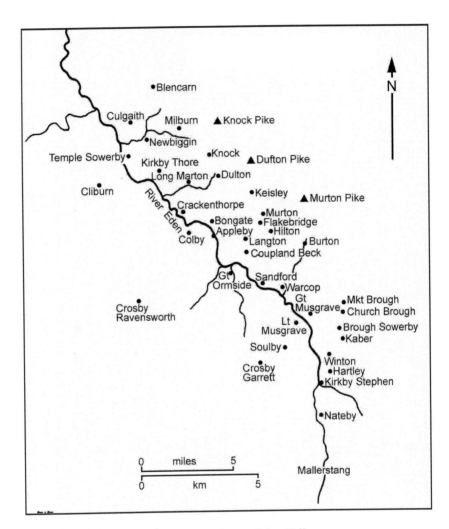

2.2 Map of the Upper Eden Valley.

Some young emigrants appeared in a previous census as scholars and their father's occupation has been noted for use in the wider discussion. Many in the sample were sons or farmers or miners. Others had a different background. The three Studholme brothers who emigrated in 1851 were sons of a Carlisle land agent and surveyor. Philip Colin Threlkeld was the son of the Rector of Milburn. Charles Parker was a law student in 1901. He emigrated in 1904. John Moser was at school in Shrewsbury in 1901 and emigrated as a young solicitor in 1912.

Walter Wilson was an electrical apprentice in 1901.

Emigrants who could not be located anywhere in Britain in the enumerations prior to the departure date stated by relatives may have emigrated at an earlier date. Some who appeared regularly in the enumerations but are missing in one may have emigrated and returned. For example, one Carlisle mill worker was in the 1861 census, 'missing' in 1871, but was living in a nearby village in 1881, married with two young children. Some emigrants returned and then re-emigrated. Giles Walker and his family were in Gosforth in 1871 but not 1861. They had been to Maldon on the Victoria goldfield in Australia. The family re-emigrated to Australia in 1872.

In the sample, as in the rural north more generally, the majority of emigrants in the first half of the nineteenth century were farmers, farm workers and rural craftsmen some of whom sailed directly from Cumberland ports. Farming families who had sailed from Maryport to Montreal in 1848 were said to be intending to settle on the land. The Cumberland families who went to the Vaudreuil area of Lower Canada in the 1820s and 30s included craftsmen and several farmers.[23] They were 'comparatively poor' with 'meagre financial resources' but 'the land provided them with basic riches and the promise of the future.'[24] This 'promise' encapsulates what so many Cumbrian men and women believed and they were willing to travel across the world to find it.

Domestic service was, and remained, almost the only occupation of single female emigrants but, especially in the first half of the nineteenth century the majority of females went as part of a family. Other male occupations were increasingly represented and included millers of grain or saw-millers, lead, coal and iron ore miners, iron and steel workers, railway platelayers, engineers, a wide variety of skilled craftsmen and tradesmen, solicitors, school teachers and ministers of religion. Mining became much more prominent in the sample after the 1870s. Although 'building trade workers, miners and unskilled labourers' were said to be 'over-represented in comparison with the labour force in Britain' among emigrants to the United States in the 1880s, very few in the sample fall into the unskilled category to any destination, at any date.[25] National figures indicate that in the 1880s only one third of emigrants were from rural areas, which suggests that the agricultural depression was not having a major effect on rural employment. However, this must be set against the greatly increased level of overall emigration and the proportion of the working population that lived in rural areas. In Cumbria, rural emigrants continued to leave but many more in the sample left the mining and industrial districts. This again reflects the national picture. The majority of male emigrants to New Zealand from 1854-76 had a rural background.[26] The sample includes a number of families from rural districts who emigrated during these years.

Such results are not surprising in a mainly rural region dominated by agriculture with industries confined to only a few areas. But it is reassuring that as the sample contains a similar broad spread of occupations and emphases that fit the regional economy and reflects the findings of others, this investigation will have relevance and prove useful when compared with other studies.

Origins

Emigrants in the sample were from all parts of the two counties. (Map 2.1) For some we know only that their origin was Cumberland *or* Westmorland and even this distinction cannot always be made with certainty. The numbers that left neighbouring or the same communities and the clusters we find in overseas destinations suggests that they had information and that emigration was discussed among kin, friends and neighbours. It can be demonstrated from several examples that even if emigrants did not leave at the same time, others decided to follow. Apart from larger towns, particular clusters of origin can be seen; for example from the villages of Knock, Milburn, Long Marton, Dufton, Hilton and Murton in north Westmorland. (Map 2.2) More than 100 had emigrated from the Bewcastle district of north Cumberland before 1853 and hundreds went from several mining communities in West Cumberland at the end of the century. Other examples could be cited. Unfortunately lack of detailed information prevented analysis of the entire sample and, of course, an unknown number also left but as Tables 2.3 and 2.4 indicate, there were marked differences in emigration patterns among those for whom sufficient information is available. The figures given and discussed below are calculated only from those whose exact origin is known The date of leaving is known for only approximately 46 per cent of the sample which in itself represents only a fraction of the real and unknown total. (Table 2.2) Consequently, the analysis reflects the true position in only in the most general terms.

Table 2.3 shows the number of emigrants for whom exact details are known from seven towns in the two counties. (Map 1.1) Table 2.4 is concerned with emigrants from rural areas in East Cumberland (mainly the Eden Valley and communities east of Carlisle and Penrith), North Westmorland (mainly the Eden, Lowther and Lyvennet Valleys), the rural area and small communities in and around Cleator and Egremont in West Cumberland and, finally, emigrants from the central Lake District. (Map 1.2)

Differences in origin and destination are demonstrated in these Tables. The attraction of Canada for emigrants from the East Cumberland rural area, North Westmorland villages and Penrith is clear. Many of these had farming or craft skills. Emigrants to South Africa from Arlecdon, Moor Row, Cleator, Cleator Moor and Frizington stand out and although the sample contains fewer from

Table 2.2   Date of Leaving in various categories

	Percentage			
A Century only	14.2%			
'Before or pre-'	24.2%			
'After'	3.4%			
Decade only	5.7%			
No date	6.0%			
Exact date	46.5%			
	100%			
B Century only				
Date	18th c. or earlier	19th c.	20th c.	Total
	2.3%	10.2%	1.7%	14.2%

Source: *Collected information*

Table 2.3   Selected towns. Origins and destinations from the sample

Country	Alston	Appleby	Carlisle	Kendal	Keswick	Penrith	Whitehaven
Australia	18	4	33	16	1	21	5
Canada	20	7	51	30	20	79	30
N. Zealand	3	16	27	6	15	36	24
S. Africa	-	1	7	1	15	10	12
USA	-	9	38	8	17	25	42

Source: *Collected information*

Table 2.4   Selected rural areas. Origins and destinations from the sample

Country	E.Cumb.Vs	N.Westm.Vs	Cleator area	Egremont	Central Lakes
Australia	55	35	9	9	9
Canada	123	128	5	5	35
N. Zealand	23	43	33	31	64
S. Africa	7	4	125	34	4
USA	31	129	37	21	`14

Source: *Collected information*   Vs.=Villages

Egremont the actual number may have been similar. Iron ore mining was a core industry in this area and by the late nineteenth century economic stresses in iron ore production due to the working out of mines and competition from imported ores caused the risk of, or actual, unemployment. Men employed in the West Cumberland mining industry transferred their skills to the gold and diamond mines in South Africa. The Cleator cluster of villages had attracted very large number of immigrants during the years of industrial expansion. Many were now moving on.

Out of more than 2,200 whose exact origins are known, and dividing these into three periods, before 1850 the vast majority from the east of the region (excluding Carlisle) were from rural communities; only four per cent were not rural. In contrast 73 per cent of those with West Cumberland addresses were from towns such as Whitehaven or Workington but some of these had previously moved from nearby villages. Emigrants from the central Lake District came mainly from Keswick, Grasmere or Ambleside. About half of the south Westmorland emigrants were from Kendal.

From 1850-80 approximately 90 per cent from the east of the region had a rural background but there was a change in West Cumberland. Now 64 per cent had a rural address, but by then some small communities were involved in iron ore mining. Emigration had been, and remained, continuous from the west of the region to a number of destinations. After c.1880 'the desire to go to South Africa [grew] apace.'[27] Most were iron ore and coal miners who travelled to the gold and diamond mines. Local newspapers repeatedly reported that groups of young men had emigrated. As the sample includes only named emigrants, the 22 unnamed men from Cleator Moor and Arlecdon, and the 'several Hodbarrow miners' who went to South Africa in 1895, are only two of several examples of emigrants who have not been counted. Hundreds of coalminers and men even at the more successful iron ore mines and iron works in the Millom area in West Cumberland were laid off in 1895.[28] West Cumberland emigrants and others – some with their families – were being 'pushed' towards opportunities and were also 'pulled' by a more certain future in South African mines. They were very different from the speculative gold seekers who had emigrated during the successive waves of gold fever to California, Australia, New Zealand or the Klondike. Many men in the sample went first to the goldfields and then settled, often after moving on to the next 'rush.'

Three quarters of the emigrants from West Cumberland after 1880 were from rural or from newly industrialised communities. The rest were from long-established towns. Two thirds of the emigrants from east Cumberland were rural but, in a region where only the western fringe and Carlisle and Kendal had any significant industry, these percentages are not surprising.

The census has filled in more details. While the majority of the emigrants had a family background in Cumbria it is clear that, for many, migration was part of their family history. Many of the West Cumberland emigrants had at least one parent with an Irish, Welsh, Scottish, Cornish or another distant English birthplace even if the emigrant him- (her) self was Cumbrian. For example,

Thomas Tuite, Robert McCaffery, William Murphy, Michael Keogh and Patrick Branney were from Irish families. James Herold and William Ivey were Cornish. David J. Rees was from a Welsh family and John Quayle and J.C. Looney's families came from the Isle of Man. Other West Cumberland emigrants had been born in rural communities, some locally or in the western Lake District but few were from the east of the region and the Eden Valley.

Some emigrants in the sample had already left Cumbria. William Jackson was in Colne, Lancashire, with his family before emigrating to Australia in 1904. Three sons of a Windermere family living in Lancashire went to New Zealand's North Island and became farmers near Dargaville. Charles R. Carter was born in Kendal but had worked in London as an emigration agent before going to New Zealand. William Slee was a joiner and had lived in New Shildon in County Durham but was with his family in Kirkby Stephen before emigrating to Canada in 1880. His wife and son followed four months later. Other Cumbrians emigrated after moving to towns or cities such as Manchester, Liverpool, Edinburgh and Leeds.

Rural depopulation, whether by migration or emigration was a concern voiced in Penrith and the Eden Valley in 1906.[29] The outflow continued. But the balance had shifted. Before about 1850 a large proportion of the sample emigrated as a family group whereas in the later years there were more lone males and females. This reflects national trends but families were still leaving Cumbria. The Tinnings from Penruddock, two related Kearton families from West Cumberland with north Westmorland connections, the Lightfoots from Carlisle and the extended Armistead family from Killington who emigrated with a total of 28 children are only four examples of the many emigrant families who left Cumbria in the early twentieth century.

Age structure of emigrants

Only about one third of the sample can be analysed by age. Table 2.5 shows that while the majority (both male and female) were young, other age groups were represented. If the ages of the 'flood of young men' leaving for South Africa, were known but assuming that the newspaper descriptions were correct, then the emphasis on youth would have increased significantly.

Forty per cent in Table 2.5 were aged under 21, almost half were aged 21-40 and approximately 11 per cent were over 40.[30] Daniel Skelton, Jane High and John Preston were among several aged over 70. At least four emigrants were born on the voyage and were given a name to mark the event. Ushant Fyfe Donald was born of Cape Ushant. Clara Piako Fallowfield, Annie Tyburnia Sanderson and Jane Dashwood Irving were each named after the ship on which they were born. Death claimed some of our emigrants. At least eight adults and

Table 2.5   Emigrants with known ages, pre-1850 to 1914.*

(A) Under 14	14-20	21-30	31-40	41-50	Over 50
21.1%	19.0%	37.1%	12.1%	7.4%	3.3%
(B) Age	Pre 1850	1851-1880	1881-1914		
Under 14	27.7%	28.2%	!4.5%		
14-20	16.9%	16.8%	21.6%		
21-30	31.8%	33.0%	39.6%		
31-40	14.4%	12.6%	12.5%		
41-50	7.7%	5.7%	8.3%		
Over 50	1.5%	3.7%	3.5%		
	100.0%	100.0%	100.0%		

Source: *Collected information   *Approximately one third of the c.4000 in the sample*

several children failed to reach their destination. Table 2.5 (B) shows how the age structure changed. Overall these analyses support the general finding that emigrants were more likely to be young men and women and that the proportion of families with children fell by the late nineteenth century.[31] But, while the percentage of children under 14 had decreased, the numerical total after 1880 was 45 per cent higher than before 1850. Although the proportion of families with children had fallen, they still formed a significant segment in the sample and in a wider context may be concealed within a greatly increased total. Similarly, the number of those aged over 50 had increased with at least eight being in their 60s when they left after 1880.

Chapter 3:
Destinations

Information, inducements and decisions

How was the decision to emigrate taken? Did publicity persuade undecided people to leave or was information by personal contact or from letters from previous emigrants more influential? Did the decision to emigrate precede the choice of destination? Was it influenced by the prospect of assisted or free passages which would therefore affect the choice of destination? It is clear that information was widely available in the two counties.

In the first half of the century many emigrants financed the venture from their savings, the realisation of assets or inheritance. Some were wealthy. Others had only sufficient for bare necessities until they found work. John Austin of Orton went to Melbourne in 1883 as an unassisted emigrant as did Joseph Stoup and his sister's family in 1901. Some borrowed from family members. In letters established emigrants offer to pay, or actually paid the fare of a brother, for example, if he were prepared to go. It is not clear if the Irving brothers from Kirkoswald borrowed money at the time of leaving or later, but it was to be repaid with interest on the death of their father.[32] Assisted and free passages which enabled many to emigrate were in operation to some destinations throughout the period and, together with other inducements such as free onward travel, became more widely available. The terms and availability varied according to the need for workers and economic circumstances in the new countries. The Walker family from Keswick had free passages to New Zealand in 1842 and the Johnston family and two female relatives from Cummersdale went to Adelaide as assisted emigrants in 1851.[33] Many others in the sample went as assisted emigrants to Australia, New Zealand and Canada before 1914. In 1913 for example, assisted passages to Canada for 'skilled agriculturalists' were advertised at a cost of £4 with employment guaranteed.[34]

Throughout the nineteenth century, although circumstances at home undoubtedly persuaded some Cumbrians to emigrate, it is clear that a powerful influence was the attraction of life overseas especially when these 'new' countries were experiencing economic growth. As elsewhere, many felt the urge to leave but, unless there had been a sense that they could adapt to life in the new country and be at least modestly successful, emigration would not have reached the level that it did – on an ever increasing trajectory, albeit with flat years, during the nineteenth century and up to 1914.

As the nineteenth century progressed sources of information multiplied.

41

Advertising from the 1820s onwards extolled the advantages of overseas destinations, the promise of land and work for skilled men. News from emigrants encouraged enterprising men and women to have the confidence to seek a new and better life.

British North America and the United States were obvious choices in the early years and West Cumberland already had well established links across the Atlantic. In 1825 and probably earlier, sailings from Cumberland ports to North America were advertised and letters tell of life in America from the early 1830s.[1] North Westmorland emigrants who arrived in Pittsburgh c.1830 were met by relatives. Cumbrians were in the West Indies and in the American colonies in the eighteenth century – two examples date from the seventeenth century. Some in the sample were sent to Australia as convicts; others went as free settlers from 1818 onwards and Cumbrians were well represented among the early emigrants to New Zealand.

After 1815 the government had paid for British soldiers to settle in Canada and a series of experimental schemes operated from 1818-27. A Land Settlement Scheme for emigrants to New Brunswick was one of these. At least six Cumbrians in the sample, some with their families were in New Brunswick during these years and one had been there in 1800. Independent emigration to New South Wales and Van Diemen's Land was already under way before the 1826 Select Committee's proposal to send 'the surplus labouring population' and certain groups of emigrants with 'small capital' to Australia was defeated in parliament.[2] The Wood family from near Penrith went to Sydney in 1818 and the Downwards and Allanbys were in Van Diemen's Land before 1825. In 1828 the fare to Australia was about £30.

'There is no doubt that emigrants from the lower reaches of British society made their way to Australia in every decade of the [nineteenth] century' and, although assistance was given such emigrants still needed funds – often provided by relatives.[3] Even before the Poor Law reforms of 1834 there was limited government intervention to support voluntary emigration and some parishes helped the 'deserving' poor to emigrate. From 1816-21 the cost of relieving poverty in Cumbrian communities had tended to increase annually; by more than 100 per cent in Cockermouth and Brampton, 75 per cent in Dalston, by smaller percentages in several with a fall in annual costs only in Longtown and Clifton. In 1836 the *Cumberland Pacquet* carried reports of the Petworth Emigration Committee's work by which at least 1,200 had been sent to Canada.[4] In the same year a total of 2,666 individuals of whom almost half were children were sent overseas from Norfolk.[5] But although there were no schemes of assistance in Cumbria like these, the *Carlisle Journal* reported that a party of cotton spinners and weavers emigrated from Carlisle to the United States in 1832 as a result of weekly subscriptions into an emigration fund.[6] The Maryport overseers of the poor sent William Clarke and his family to Upper Canada with 50 others in 1832. They sailed on a brig at no cost and were given a grant of £30.[7] As in later years emigrants who were chosen to benefit from assisted or free passages were not destitute nor were they 'indigent misfits.' They were 'the deserving poor' – working men and women who wished to emigrate but could not afford to do so.[8] In the Poor Law Report of 1847, no emigrants were sent by Cumberland Guardians and, although Kirkby Stephen, Westmorland was mentioned at a probable cost of £40, no names or destination were given.[9] The Nonconformist Association helped to organise William and Ann Sanderson's emigration to New Zealand in the 1860s and financial help may have been part of this. They took advantage of a New Zealand government scheme that gave land to emigrants who could pay their fare.[10]

The government appointed an Agent General and established an Emigration Department in 1836-7. The work of encouraging emigration began. The *Colonisation Circular* was published from 1843 and from the 1850s Canada promoted its benefits as a destination. Land deals were advertised by organisations and individuals, for example, the Huron Tract near Lake Huron in the first half of the century and in 1903 the Barr Colony scheme that resulted in the founding of Lloydminster, Saskatchewan. Cumbrian emigrants went to both destinations. Other schemes during the century included those of the New Brunswick and the Nova Scotia Land Company in British North America, the New Zealand Company and in the Otago and Canterbury regions in New Zealand. The vast prairie lands in Canada were peopled after promotion by governments and railway companies. The United States advertised opportunities for emigrants to settle in the prairies, Texas and other states but offered no financial assistance beyond advantageous onward fares. But, it must not be forgotten that the land in destination countries was not 'empty.' Indigenous peoples had been, or were displaced. The area around Goderich in the Huron Tract for example, 'used to be the camping ground for the Chippewa Indians' and, although some continued to live nearby in the winter, they had become a 'poor ... dissipated group.'[11] Many died from European diseases and for those who survived, their traditional form of life was no longer possible. The Maori Wars in New Zealand and repeated examples of conflict with Native Americans in Canada and the United States and with aborigines in Australia are testimony to this even though arrangements were made in some instances that allowed for a peaceful 'takeover.'

Agents, governments, companies and emigration societies advertised in the press and publicity material throughout the century sometimes focusing on particular destinations and pausing during economic downturns. In 1837 the

Colonial Office gave loans to selected families and to young single females, several ship owners reduced their fares and more agents were employed at British ports. For those going to Australia, loans were converted into a gift of £30 for families and £12 for young single females.[12] In 1850, there was 'great competition amongst owners and agents' in Liverpool.[13] Although the fare to Australia had fallen to £18 by 1856, it was still a substantial sum and far more than the cost of going to North America. During the years 1831-60, 56 per cent of all emigrants (in specified occupations) from Britain to Australia were at least partially funded by the colonial government, but, taking the century as a whole, more than half of all immigrants to Australia paid their own fare.[14]

In the mid-1830s South Australia embarked on a major advertising campaign and from 1836-40 more than 11,000 prospective emigrants and their families applied for assisted passages. After the mid-1840s, assisted or free passages were offered to fulfil the state's labour needs as required. New Zealand also offered assistance through colonising organisations and later, the government. For example, in the 1860s free land was offered in Auckland province to immigrants who could pay their fare.[15] During the New Zealand Company's existence emigrants were under the agent's care until embarkation, the commission being paid only after the arrival in New Zealand. A fine was imposed on agents if the emigrant did not leave. Emigrants had to be of good character, healthy, vaccinated, with marriage certificate where relevant and be aged 30 or under. No single female could travel alone.[16]

The total numbers that emigrated from the two counties from January 1st 1841 to June 30th 1841 were given in Chapter 1. Of those the government sent 96 emigrants from Cumberland and 41 from Westmorland to New South Wales as 'bounty' emigrants. But these numbers are small compared to the 352 from Devon, 461 from Yorkshire and 1,292 from Lancashire.[17] Similarly, from 1846 to 1850 when the government sent 69 from Cumberland and 10 from Westmorland to Australia or South Africa, 6,813 were sent from Cornwall, 1,889 from Devon and 1,997 from Somerset.[18] Nevertheless, from 1846-69, fewer than seven per cent of all emigrants left under British government schemes indicating both the scale of emigration from Britain and the degree of self-financing. Governments in destination countries also supported emigrants and the Empire was increasingly pushed forward especially in the Edwardian years.[19]

South Africa became a favoured destination as its mineral industry developed. The proportions and difference in numbers in Table 3.1 are noteworthy. Australia and New Zealand needed labour and their assistance schemes aimed to attract working men and women with the result that in 1854-1855, while only 27 per cent of emigrants went to those countries, they took 82 per cent of all the agricultural labourers and 62 per cent of domestic servants. Similarly, in the 1860s

Table 3.1 Passengers including emigrants from British Isles 1820-1911

Year	USA	Br. N. Amer	Aus & NZ	S Africa	Total
1820*	*53.3%*	*31.7%*	*11.1%*	*3.9%*	*7,987*
1840	*44.5%*	*35.4%*	*17.4%*	*0.6%*	*91,236*
1861**	*55.0%*	*11.1%*	*31.9%*	*2.3%*	*69,165*
1880	*75.0%*	*9.4%*	*10.9%*	*4.1%*	*221,790*
1911	*46.7%*	*31.4%*	*5.8%*	*10.0%*	*262,177*

Source: **BPP 1821 XVII Passenger numbers from England. ** BPP 1862 XXII Emigrants from England only. More than 14,000 went to the goldfields.*
1840, 1889, 1911. Britannia's Children, pp. 121, 179, 210-12

when only 18 per cent of British emigrants went to Australasia, again, 82 per cent of all the agricultural labourers and 74 per cent of domestic servants went there.[20] As Table 3.1 illustrates, the United States was the major destination throughout the century and although fewer went in individual years, usually because of economic circumstances, and emigration to Canada, Australia and New Zealand was consistently at a lower level, the trend was for emigration to increase. The peak year for emigration to the United States and to the Antipodes was 1880. In spite of active promotion of Canada as a destination, especially in the first decade of the twentieth century when thousands went the peak year had been 1840. But, in 1836 an emigration report from Canada stated that more emigrants may have been persuaded to choose New York as a destination because of letters from 'settlers in the Upper Province ... complaining of the privations and hardships to which they were exposed ... and the detention they met with at the quarantine station.'[21] By 1900 the booming gold and diamond mining industry in South Africa attracted ever increasing numbers of men.

Table 3.2 shows those in the sample who went to selected countries before 1914. Any whose destination was 'North America,' 'Australia *or* New Zealand' or for whom we have no information have been omitted. In addition, approximately 150 Cumbrians in the sample were in India, China, Europe and other countries throughout the world. (Map 3.1) The data in Table 3.2 do not reflect the primacy of the United States as shown in Table 3.1 but this may be due to lack of information. Furthermore, if all the anonymous emigrants who were reported in the press as attending Cumberland and Westmorland Society events in Canada were added, then its importance as a destination would have been further enhanced. 'Canada had undoubtedly offered a very good opening for agricultural labourers and others willing to work hard. Such men can save ... [and] take up land with a good prospect of bettering themselves for life.'[22] Australia and New Zealand feature strongly in the sample but, as a particular effort was made to contact relatives in New Zealand and the sources revealed

Table 3.2   Destination of emigrants in the sample

excluding those without names, other destinations and no precise destination

Country	Total from the sample	Percentage of the total*
United States	670	21.6%
Canada (Br.N.Am.)	1067	34.5%
Australia	399+114*	12.9%
New Zealand	573	18.5%
South Africa	293	9.5%
West Indies	49	1.6%
South America	43	1.4%
TOTAL	3208 (including the 114)	100.0%

Source: Collected information
*The 399 are known emigrants. The 114 were either in Australia or sentenced to transportation by C&W courts. They are excluded in percentages but discussed in a later chapter

the names of many emigrants to Australia, there may be undue bias towards these countries. Emigration to the United States was undoubtedly very attractive to Cumbrians and, from the sample, this was especially true in the first half of the period whereas the majority of emigrants to South Africa went after 1880.

Sources of Information

Numerous publications, advertisements and accounts in newspapers brought emigration before the public. Local newspapers carried regular, often weekly advertisements placed by agents and national and colonial governments about shipping, onward travel, destinations, bounty offers, free or assisted passages, fares for self-financing emigrants, land grants and employment and other inducements. From the 1830s pamphlets and guides had been produced and commercial publishers did not ignore a growing market. Books, lectures, publicity in libraries and Reading Rooms carried information. From 1831 the Colonial Office, and after 1886 the Emigration Information Office, church and other voluntary organisations, locally organised emigration societies, philanthropists, local clergy and, later, the Trade Unions were active in publishing or distributing information. Emigration journals, guide books and other publications multiplied as the century progressed. *Sidney's Emigrant's Journal*, the *Emigrant Settler's Guide*, the *Emigrant and Colonial Gazette* and handbooks published by the British and other governments gave information about a number of destinations and accounts of life overseas.

In 1855 the *Daily Telegraph and Courier* carried advertisements for the *Cape of Good Hope Almanac* and a map of railways in America and Canada could be obtained from the *Railroad Journal* offices via the Colonial Newspaper Agency

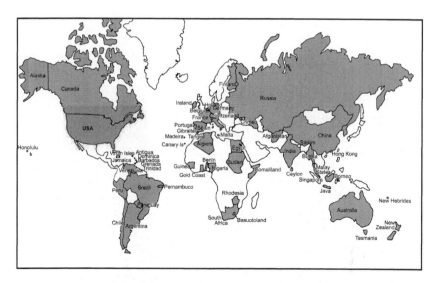

3.1 World map showing destinations of Cumbrians before 1914.

which also advertised newspapers 'from every British Colony and settlement.'[23] Journals such as the *Illustrated London News* carried articles, news items and pictures. Newspapers in destination countries were advertised in emigration literature as 'available by post' and some, for example, *The Colonist, The Australian and New Zealand Gazette* and the *Australian Circular* were published in London.[24] Emigrant letters from the 1830s onwards comment on newspapers sent to and received from Cumbria. Among the regular readers of the *Cumberland and Westmorland Herald* in 1912 were a 'Westmorland lad' in Rhodesia and the Laidlaw family from Bassenthwaite in Kamloops, British Columbia.[25]

The Emigration Information Office (EIO) produced a massive amount of information. For example, in 1887 the office received 10,221 letters, 5,975 visitors and dispatched more than 35,000 replies and circulars per quarter. Posters were sent to every post office, to clubs and institutions. Some were displayed in railway stations. Circulars were sent to clubs, Co-operative Societies, trade and charitable societies, libraries, Boards of Guardians and directly to applicants. Handbooks for each of 10 countries were published and sixpenny pamphlets sold well. Teachers requested these and other publications to aid their work in schools. The *Canadian Handbook,* for example, comprised 96 pages with maps.[26] In 1898 information was displayed in libraries in Carlisle, Frizington, Kendal, Millom, Penrith, Whitehaven and Workington.[27] In 1901, 22.5 per cent of enquiries to the EIO had been from skilled mechanics; in 1907 the percentage was 31 per cent and requests for information about Australia and New Zealand almost doubled.[28] By 1908, posters were in 1,100 libraries and institutions; 435,500 free circulars and 213,000 copies of monthly supplements were distributed.[29] Whereas in 1886-7 8,217 enquiries were received and 12,688 replies sent, in 1907 enquiries had risen to 18,874 and replies to 67,903.[30]

Clearly there was enormous interest in emigration from individuals but also from national charitable institutions and philanthropic societies as a means of helping the unemployed under the terms of the Unemployment Act (1905). More than 40 societies were listed in a Royal Commission report in 1912.[31] The Salvation Army advertised opportunities for women in Canada in the Cumberland press in 1914.[32]

Although most publications originated in London, their distribution was widespread and in a largely literate society such as Cumberland and Westmorland information about emigration would be widely circulated. As well as encouragement, prospective emigrants were warned to beware of 'unscrupulous persons' or syndicates who made 'extravagant promises.[33] Letters describing life overseas, articles, information and advertisements were published in local newspapers. Land in Texas was advertised in a Carlisle newspaper in 1853.[34] Colonial governments sent agents and former emigrants to promote recruitment drives. In 1872, 1874 and 1875 Thomas Graham lectured in Shap, Hackthorpe, Plumpton, Pooley Bridge, Murton and Appleby promoting emigration to Canada, emphasising the 'advantages, capabilities and resources' of that country.[35] Similar lectures and 'magic lantern shows' about Canada and New Zealand were reported in other years. James Adams, the official agent for emigration to New Zealand and a member of the Otago Executive Council, spoke in Kirkby Stephen in 1875. Mr Capstick, a north Westmorland emigrant who 'had done very well' sent letters to the meeting telling of his experiences.[36]

The Canadian government vigorously promoted Canada in advertisements, publications and from the mid-1890s employed agents and collaborated with brokers and shipping companies in Britain to find emigrants who would take land in the west. In 1895 Saskatchewan, 'a beautiful region' was described as having 'clumps of spruce' providing building timber, abundant fish and game, excellent farming land and was, 'to a considerable extent unoccupied.' Alberta was especially suitable for dairy farming.[37] In a speech in London in 1901 the Canadian High Commissioner emphasised the need to interest prospective emigrants by providing good information but also by encouraging settlers to keep in touch with friends and family at home with the hope that others would be encouraged to join them.[38] Manitoba, with its 'rich deep soil' held 'unbounded opportunities' and was a 'vacant land awaiting the arrival of settlers.'[39] The original inhabitants were not mentioned. Canadian railway companies were also recruiting emigrants for their lands as the new cross-continental railway and its branches opened up the far western provinces. In 1907 thousands of copies of a promotional booklet with details of wages or various trades in the different provinces had been sent to 'members of the British working class' by the Canadian Provincial governments.[40]

Reports of lectures, lantern slide shows and visits promoting emigration to Canada, Australia, New Zealand and Rhodesia continued to appear in the local press and, presumably, Cumbria was not the only region targeted by the agents and representatives.[41] In 1907 for example, a Canadian farmer was due to meet prospective emigrants in Mr Hodgson's shop in Penrith and Mr Baker, a Canadian delegate, was to be at Mr Whitehead's shop in Appleby. Canadian Pacific Railway advertisements sought workers and offered 160 acre land grants in the western provinces. Mr Lee from Great Salkeld wrote of life in Manitoba and encouraged others to follow him. Newspapers also published letters from Cumbrian emigrants to Australia.[42] In February and March 1909, two meetings in Penrith encouraged prospective farmers in the audience to emigrate. Mr Bardgett spoke of opportunities in Rhodesia. Mr Carey from Belle Plains, Saskatchewan and George Aylesworth from Ontario promoted Canada. Meetings were also held in Stainton, Greystoke, Clifton, Great Salkeld and Appleby.[43] Mr Brunskill, a Cumbrian emigrant, was sent to England by the Dominion Department of Immigration as a recruitment agent in 1910 and 'spent a very busy' few months giving lectures with slides.[44] In 1914 Mr Holmes, a Canadian government emigration agent who had spent 25 years in Manitoba gave lectures in Brough, Maulds Meaburn, Temple Sowerby and Asby in north Westmorland, and as he seemed to be based in Carlisle, probably in other parts of the region as well.[45]

Published information was helpful but could exaggerate the opportunities in, and advantages of, destinations. Advice from friends or relatives was more reliable and persuasive. A letter conveying a sense of well being would reassure the family at home and, perhaps, encourage others to go. John Gibson's letters from Australia are realistic, even pessimistic at times. In the late 1830s he told his friend Walter Murray in Cumberland – 'Take warning … and stay at home.' There was no work for tradesmen and 'all government work is stopped.' Australia was 'worse than England, there is now in this colony thousands of people walking about … their families are starving … and hundreds more [are landing] every week.'[46] And this was before the 1841 depression when there was considerable distress in and around Melbourne. However, as letters took six months to reach home, any warning or encouragement would be out of date long before being read in Cumbria. Robert Gibson asked 'old John' to 'come over and help me build a wood house' in New Diggings, Wisconsin in 1851.[47] In a letter from

Melbourne in 1853, one Keswick emigrant reported that diggers going to the goldfields needed a gun, knife or sword and a year later Stephen Madgen of Alston thought Melbourne was 'not so good as it has been represented and I believe it never has been' but still recommended William Stout to emigrate.[48] Henry Forrest wrote from Canada asking his brother to join him and added 'bring me a wife.'[49]

Exhibitions such as those in London (1851, 1886 and 1908), in Liverpool and Edinburgh (1886) and Glasgow (1888) focused attention on the world and contributed to an increased awareness of 'our overseas possessions.' Charles Dickens and Anthony Trollope wrote about their visits to North America and Trollope also visited Australasia.[50] In 1858 James Caird wrote enthusiastically about the opportunities for farmers in Iowa and Illinois but was less complimentary about Canada.[51] In 1862 Trollope complained that Quebec, (population 42,000 in 1851) 'had little to recommend it apart from the beauty of its situation.' Ottawa had miles of broad streets but 'the city is not yet built' and Toronto's roads were 'very bad.'[52] Some found to their cost that the claims of the publicists were not justified. The Huron Tract was promoted as a newly opened destination in the 1830s but there was no quick transformation and 'poor emigrants had to work for years.'[53] Thomas Sowerby from Renwick and the Snowden family of Carlisle were early pioneers there. Other Cumbrian families followed.

The work of agents was crucial. Brokers and publishers were pursuing a profitable line of business by the mid-1850s. Agents were paid a fee for every emigrant they recruited but Charles Dickens was unimpressed by those who 'tempt the credulous [and offer] monstrous inducements ... which can never be realised.'[54] In 1858, 77 emigration or shipping agents were listed in the Liverpool directory; 102 in 1893.[55] From the mid-nineteenth century local agents, usually in business in the community, such as J. Braithwaite in Kirkby Stephen, James Steel in Carlisle, George Irwin in Whitehaven, Joseph Barwise in Maryport, William Jobling in Carlisle and Thomas Webster in Kendal advertised in the local press, supplied information and offered inclusive fares including onward travel to many destinations. In 1894 agents included Robert H. Beeby and William Pollard in Cleator Moor, Edward L. Irving in Carlisle, John J. Wilson in Egremont, M. de Rome, John Monkhouse and Edward Haythornthwaite in Kendal.[56] Mr Whitehead in Appleby and J. Braithwaite in Kirkby Stephen continued as agents in the Upper Eden Valley. In 1905 John Rothery was an agent in Whitehaven. Daniel McAllister and William McClean were agents in Cleator Moor in the early twentieth century. In 1906 a total of 11 emigration or shipping agents were listed in Cumberland and three in Kendal.[57] Prospective emigrants from south Cumberland may have contacted agents in Barrow in Furness.

The United States

Occasionally, identifying the correct destination can be difficult or impossible. For example, Mrs H. Gowling from Brough died in Elkhorn, USA in 1891. She and four children had recently joined her husband who 'had been there for some time.'[58] But, which Elkhorn? Did she die in Kentucky, Nebraska or Wisconsin. Or was it Elk Horn in Iowa? Fortunately such uncertainties in the USA and other countries were few in the sample.

Cumbrians had been in Virginia from the seventeenth century and have been identified in Virginia's lead mining region in the eighteenth century. Before the War of Independence in the 1770s when 13 of the 18 American colonies became the United States, British convicts and indentured servants had been part of the labour force. Slaves from Africa were taken to plantations in the southern states and the West Indies. Cumberland men were active in trade, as plantation owners or managers, farmers and in transporting slaves and Bailyn identified 30 emigrants to America from Cumberland and 26 from Westmorland in his 1773-1776 sample.[59]

Fewer emigrated during the wars in America and Europe but later the number increased hugely. Cumberland men fought for the Crown during the War of Independence and on both sides during the Civil War in the 1860s. Daniel Brocklebank had a shipbuilding business in Maine but returned to Whitehaven to avoid the war. Robert Rathnell, a Westmorland man, was in New York in 1778 and told of the rebels 'in the Jerseys and Long Island.' By 1782, he was on a naval ship near Barbados where they 'engaged with the French, telling his relatives at home that 'our fleet [is] far superior.'[60] Thomas Barwise of Whitehaven was in America by 1818.[61] Cumbrians in New York and Pittsburgh in the 1830s wrote to their families telling of life there. Eastern cities grew and westward expansion continued. Agents recruited emigrants from Britain and Europe.[62] Clashes with the native population over land were fiercely fought and the Civil War rent the nation. Joseph Forster paid for a substitute to fight during that war because he could not leave his family and farm.[63] One Cumbrian emigrant living in the southern states wrote that during the war, normal business was impossible. Samuel Hodgson's son was 'in rather poor health after returning from the army in 1866 and John Hodgson's son had 'nearly starved to death ... in prison after ... passing through some of the severest battles of the war unscathed.'[64] James Walker was in the army in 1862. He wrote from Nashville having walked 180 miles with the troops from Alabama. The fighting against the rebels had been 'mainly skirmishes.' He believed the war could last three years. But this is an intriguing letter. It seems that Mrs Walker, James's mother had returned home, possibly because of the war. He advises her that if she were to return to the northern states she would be safe and by doing so she 'would be

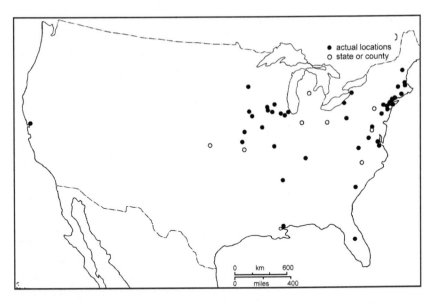

3.2 The United States showing known destinations before 1860.

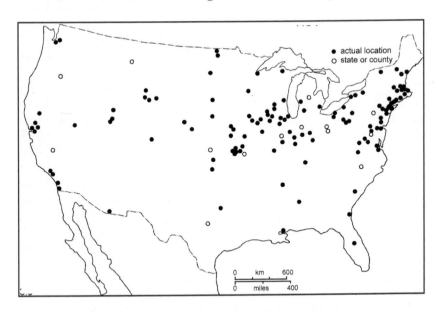

3.3 The United States showing known destinations before 1914.

entitled to my bounty and pension if I get killed and then you could go back.'[65]

Maps 3.2 and 3.3 show the distribution of named Cumbrian emigrants in the United States before 1860, and during the whole period. Inevitably the greatest concentration was in the east in the early years and although the south received fewer, some went to Virginia, Alabama, Louisiana and Texas. The move westwards is very clear as migrants settled on the vast prairie lands but thousands were also needed for the growing industrial and commercial needs of burgeoning towns and cities. Philadelphia was already a large city when William Shaw arrived *c*.1840. Fifteen others in the sample were there between 1841 and 1909. A group of north Westmorland emigrants settled in Birmingham close to Pittsburgh in the 1830s. Thirty years later, Trollope thought Pittsburgh, dominated by its coal, iron and steel industries, to be 'without exception the blackest place I ever saw – soot, grease and dinginess. Thick brown smoke covers the city.'[66]

In 1848, Robert James of Thursby near Carlisle visited the United States. He found good farms in New York State where land cost $20-$50 per acre but labour was scarce, excellent dairy farms in Ohio and cheap farms in Tennessee. Kentucky was 'in a high state of cultivation.' An 'industrious Englishman would do well in East Tennessee' where land cost only $2-$10 per acre. Farmers in Indiana were 'a great deal better off than in England' and a blacksmith reported that life in Ohio was good.[67] In 1855 John Coulthard of Dufton died in St Clair, Missouri; one of several Cumbrians in that state.[68] In 1860 Michigan, Wisconsin and Iowa had 'participated to the full in the surprising development of the North West [and were] becoming the granary of Europe.'[69] From the early 1860s onwards land was offered to settlers in Minnesota, Wisconsin, Montana, the Dakotas and Wyoming where in 1880, the population was only *c*.20,800. Cumbrian emigrants settled in these states and farther west in California. Other emigrants worked in mines or in other occupations throughout the United States.

When north Westmorland emigrants went to Iowa in the early 1850s they were part of a major influx. Iowa had abundant lead, rich agricultural land and 'there will be money to be made for many years in towns' such as Dubuque which was 'the great metropolis of the mineral region.'[70] George Richardson, from Church Brough, did just that. He established a very successful boot and shoe manufacturing business in Dubuque.[71] In 1862 Trollope confirmed predictions and wrote that 'very large sums of money' had been made in the Dubuque and surrounding lead mining region.[72] Towns in Wisconsin, Iowa and Illinois were doing well. The region had good communications by river before railways were built.

J. Irving and J. Pattinson, both from Penrith, were in Stockton, California, a town of 18,000 inhabitants in 1885. Stockton was 80 miles from San Francisco, in the centre of a wheat growing district which was irrigated by thousands of water pumps powered by wind.[73] In 1905, John Braithwaite was among several

Eigenthum d. Verleger

Dubuque, Iowa, in the 1850s.

Cumbrians in Kansas. Others were in Indiana.[74] Christopher Gelder was in North Dakota. John Labourne, an engineer, died in Lead City, South Dakota in 1905.[75] Cities such as Chicago, Minneapolis, Cleveland and Los Angeles also attracted Cumbrian immigrants. Chicago had been an insignificant settlement in 1830 but had grown rapidly. Good communications by rail and water increased its role as a marketing centre for the mid-west and exporter of produce. In 1871 a Penrith man was reported to be safe and had 'lost nothing' in a severe fire in Chicago. Many other Cumbrians were there.[76]

San Francisco had developed from a tiny settlement and mission in 1840 into a thriving port and city, its early expansion being driven by the Californian gold rush from 1849. Cumberland and Westmorland emigrants settled in the San Francisco area during the next 50-60 years. In 1906 local newspapers reported that all (a large number) were safe after the earthquake and official papers highlighted the great need for construction workers to rebuild the city in 1907. In that year there was a major economic crisis and emigrants from other parts of the United States returned home because of unemployment.[77] The sample also includes emigrants in 19 communities in Pennsylvania, 12 in Illinois, 10 in Iowa, eight in Nebraska and six in Ohio.

Canada

The main destinations in Canada of named emigrants are shown in Maps 3.4 and 3.5. Some of the earliest settlers were in New Brunswick, Nova Scotia and the Vaudreuil area of Lower Canada. Upper Canada also attracted early emigrants. George Longley of Newbiggin, Westmorland had emigrated in 1808. He died at Maitland, Ontario 34 years later.[78] Halifax, Nova Scotia was the entry port for many emigrants but few stayed even before the railway was built. Of the 148 known destinations 45 per cent were in Eastern Canada. Most emigrants were in the eastern provinces before c.1870 and, in spite of the 'rush to the west,' Cumbrians continued to settle in Ontario and Quebec throughout the period.

By 1847 Canada West was 'the place to go.' The roughly triangular region between the Great Lakes contained sufficient land 'for generations to come. ... First choose a site for the house then build a shanty, buy a cow and calf, clear the undergrowth, buy supplies and in winter clear and chop trees. Tap sugar maple trees in March.'[79] It sounded easy but the reality was hard. Towns were growing. In the 1840s Thomas Gash of Whitehaven was in Hamilton, a town at the head of Lake Ontario with a population of about 12,000. He was working as a stone cutter. Hamilton was 'thriving, well situated but drunken'. Everything looked 'rough, prosperous and cheap.'[80] Toronto was 'a large wealthy city of 24,000, but was also a 'drunken place.'[81] In the mid-nineteenth century Isaac Thompson, a Cumberland farmer, emigrated to Bertie, Ontario with his family and his servants. Promoters of the Huron Tract scheme advertised for pioneer settlers from the mid-1820s. Their publicity is an example of exaggerated promises. Instead of finding that there would be an easy transition from virgin forest to good farming land, little had been prepared and the initial years were much more difficult than the settlers had expected. Thomas Sowerby of Renwick and Thomas Snowden of Carlisle and his family were there in the 1830s.

The 1859 *Canada and the Western States Handbook* stated that un-cleared land cost £5 per acre. A two storey 16 by 24 ft log house with shingle roof cost £18; a frame barn cost £100 but 'most settlers build their own buildings, helped by neighbours and make their own furniture. ... Almost every article of convenience or luxury must be made at home or dispensed with.' But the prospects were far better than in towns where 'a large number ... find there is nothing to do and return home dissatisfied because they did not ... find out about employment ... before leaving.' Some had been 'decoyed into coming.' Medical men would find 'an uphill struggle' and there were few opportunities for commercial assistants.[82]

In 1871 only approximately 51,000 people (excluding Indians) were in the North West territories, Manitoba and British Columbia. From 1872 the government offered 160 acres with extra benefits for $10. In 1896 the

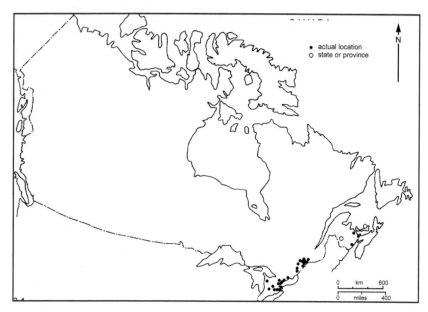

3.4 British North America (Canada) showing known destinations before 1860.

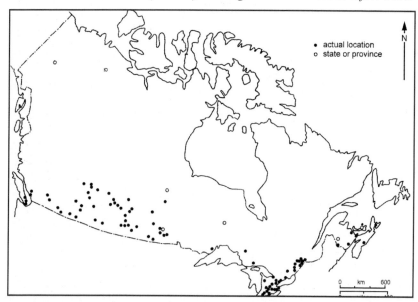

3.5 British North America (Canada) showing known destinations before 1914.

government increased its campaign to attract immigrants to the west which contributed to the huge increase in Canada's population from c.5.4 million in 1901 to 7.2 million in 1911. For example, an advertisement in 1909 stated that 160 acres of government land in Canada was free. Two years rent in England would buy a 'partly improved' farm outright in Canada where there was the prospect of 'contentment, independence early in life, healthy climate, bountiful harvests and good markets, profitable dairying and excellent fruit.' Free maps and full particulars to be obtained from government agents in York or London.[83]

Massive numbers went to western provinces. They were the new pioneers. Some had moved north from the United States, some were from the east but most had crossed the Atlantic. Among these were many hundreds of Cumbrians who flocked to Saskatchewan, Manitoba, Alberta and British Columbia. The sample includes more than 70 named emigrants in Alberta, c.70 in Manitoba and more than 90 in British Columbia. Two letters from Manitoba in 1913, one from a Penrithian, commented on the excellent food for workers – including beef, that all farm implements had seats attached therefore work was easier, that wages were good and a hired man not only ate with the family but, after two years could afford to hire a horse and implements then work as a contractor. Land cost only £4 to £9 per acre.[84] In 1871, Winnipeg had only 241 inhabitants, but illustrating its rapid growth, about the same number attended the Cumberland and Westmorland Society's celebratory dinner there in 1913 when the population had reached 136,035. Winnipeg was the 'gateway to the west' and was a conduit for exporting produce from the western prairies. There was a thriving Cumberland and Westmorland Wrestling Society and in 1909 Frank Dobinson formerly of Warcop won a silver cup for Cumberland and Westmorland style wrestling at the Scottish Sports in Winnipeg.[85]

The sample contains c.50 named destinations in western Canada. Twenty of these were in Saskatchewan where Regina, 'on bleak level prairies' became the capital in 1905. By 1911 its population was c.30,000. More than 100 members from the surrounding area attended a Cumberland and Westmorland Society Dinner in 1911 and when damage from a cyclone was reported in 1912, 'all Penrithians [upwards of 50] were uninjured.'[86] Several families from south Westmorland settled in the Battleford area. Thomas Laidlow of Bassenthwaite, was in Kamloops, B.C. in 1912 and reported that others were in the vicinity. Mr H.M. Jenkins, a solicitor from Keswick and his family added to that number when they went to Kamloops in 1913.[87] Vancouver's Cumberland and Westmorland Society held a dinner in 1913.[88] Emigrants from north Westmorland were in Medicine Hat in Alberta in 1909.[89] This had been ranching territory but much of the land became peopled by homesteaders. More than 100, 'almost all [of whom] were natives of Cumberland or Westmorland' attended the Calgary

Cumberland and Westmorland Society's social evening in 1914.[90] These burgeoning local societies, and Cumberland and Westmorland Wrestling Societies indicate the scale of emigration and the desire of Cumbrians in Western Canada to celebrate and confirm their roots. The formation and membership of such societies and organisations in Canada and in other countries not only confirmed pride in their common heritage and their desire to keep in touch with fellow Cumbrians but also helped to create a sense of community in the new environment.

Over vast tracts of North America, railways 'facilitated' settlement.[91] They were a vital link for communication, for bringing in supplies and taking out produce. 'Railways are the precursors of cultivation ... through primeval forests and over prairies. ... People settle on their edges. ... They created the value of the land.' In forest regions, 'year by year, the forest reced[ed] before the persevering cultivator' – a process that continued for many years.[92] As lines were extended land was allocated to more homesteaders but prairies tended to be dry lands as some settlers found to their cost. Homesteading was recommended, for example by Joseph Turner of Penrith who wrote in 1908 that 'emigrants to cities made a great mistake. ... Go to farming straightaway.'[93] More than 14,600 homesteads had been occupied in the north western region in 1901-2 and Cumbrian emigrants took full advantage of cheap or free land and other promotional benefits. 'Personally conducted parties of emigrants in charge of Canadian officials left Liverpool at regular intervals during the season.'[94] On entry, every emigrant had to have at least £5 in cash, a ticket to his (her) destination and, if found to have no means of support within two years of arrival could be deported.[95]

Although some information painted an unrealistic picture, the best advice came from those with experience of a homesteader's life. For example, that emigrants should think carefully and expect hard exhausting work. Life in Canada was very different from England. Thomas Hetherington who had 480 acres at Lumsden, Saskatchewan in 1906 was encouraging. He wrote that 160 acres cost only $10. Oxen or horses and implements could be bought on credit and 'there are thousands of acres in the west almost like an ordinary lea field in Cumberland [but] the sod is tougher and there are more stones.'[96] In Canada, rich and poor mixed freely and after some years of effort, the emigrant 'could afford to visit England.' The severity of Canadian winters meant that outdoor work was largely confined to the summer months and the winter was a time for 'enjoyment and visiting,' by sleigh during the snowy weather but not for the poor in towns.[97] Emigrants were advised to arrive in spring or early summer and winter unemployment remained a problem. In 1908 'thousands of sturdy English and Scottish mechanics and labourers'

G.H.Andrews

Waterfront Montreal, 1840-50.

were living in shacks in poverty. Food and fuel were being distributed. There was 'intense suffering. ... In summertime ... one would never think there were poor people in Toronto' but in winter 'life in Canada is not all sunshine.' Thousands were unemployed.[98]

Many Cumbrian emigrants went to cities and larger centres and followed a number of occupations. More than 20 in the sample had settled in Montreal where Robert Salkeld of Whitehaven was manager of the Bank of North America in 1901.[99] Septimus Stephenson died at the Centre Star Mine, Rossland, B.C. in 1905. In the same year Charles Lister of Whitehaven died of typhoid at the Copper Cliff Mines, Ontario. Local newspapers reported that coal mines were thriving in Nova Scotia in 1908 which may have encouraged Cumberland emigrants to go there.[100] Gold, copper, lead, and zinc were all mined in the 1850s and very rich iron ore had been found near Lake Huron.[101] Nanaimo, a coal mining town on Vancouver Island where 42 per cent of miners had an English birthplace in 1891, had attracted men from West Cumberland.[102] 'All eight of the Cumberland miners killed in the Nanaimo disaster of 1887 were from villages no more than 15 miles apart.'[103] But not all Cumbrian emigrants in Nanaimo were miners. The Revd. Wilkinson was a Methodist minister there.

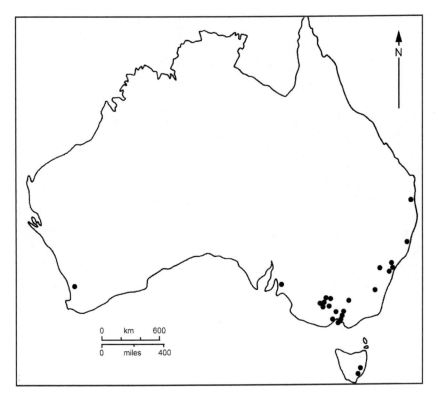

3.6 Australia - Destinations before 1860

Australia.

Maps 3.6 and 3.7 show identified destinations in Australia. Initially settlement was only on the coastal belt in New South Wales but after the Blue Mountains were crossed in 1813 and with further exploration, settlement began on the interior lands where John Wood, a Cumbrian, took land in 1818. Van Diemen's Land became a separate state in 1825 and Victoria in 1851. South Australia was founded in 1836 and Queensland became a separate state from 1859. By c.1830 about 4,000,000 acres were being farmed in New South Wales. Grain and other crops were grown and vast areas were used for grazing sheep and cattle. Others in the sample were early settlers in Van Diemen's Land. Richard Downward and his family from Workington settled in Sorell, formerly Pitt Water about 13 miles from Hobart in 1822. He became a miller and landowner. Thomas Dent, a married farmer from Kirkby Stephen and Mr and Mrs Molloy were among the first emigrants to the Swan River Settlement in

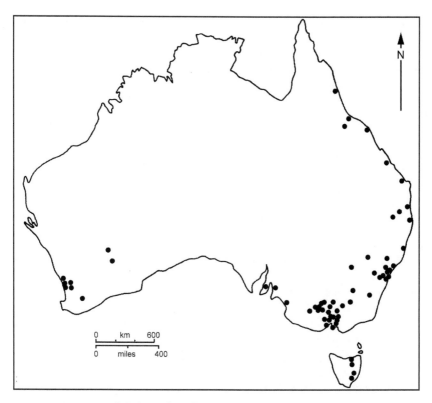

3.7 Australia - Destinations before 1914

Western Australia in 1830.[104] Georgiana Molloy was from near Carlisle.

By the 1820s great progress had been made in New South Wales. Small numbers of free settlers were arriving but the population was dominated by a very large number of convicts, ex-convicts and those holding tickets of leave. Clearly some settlers or administrators had been able to build up significant assets by 1825 when a farm near Sydney was advertised for sale. It comprised a 'genteel residence' with nine rooms, a good cellar, kitchen, coach house, stabling, granaries, a smith's forge and other buildings, 700 acres of wood, meadow with garden, orchards, a brickyard, a good water supply, a stone quarry and lime kilns. All were within a ring fence with access to two creeks. Furniture, 100 horned cattle, 300 sheep, six mares and three horses were to be sold.[105] The reason for sale is unknown.

In 1838, a great shortage of workers in New South Wales was reported. But the problem was not only a lack of labour. Serious economic difficulties in

Australia were developing and in the 1840s immigration was stopped which exacerbated the scarcity of workers. In a letter dated January 15th 1843, Mary Lowe wrote from Sidmouth Valley, 'We still feel very much the want of an industrious peasantry. If thousands were to come from England there is an abundance of employment. ... Want of labour is felt to a great extent in this country.' And in 1845 she wrote, 'Money ... is very scarce and [there is] a great deal of distress. You cannot sell anything.' She blamed Sir George Gipp, the Governor, who on his arrival found the colony 'flourishing and rich and ... he leaves it miserable ... and ruined.'[106] Immigration resumed in 1847 and in 1850 passenger ships to Australia were full. The Watson family from Renwick emigrated at this time.

Of the total number of emigrants who left the two counties in the next five months of 1841 as recorded in the Census Report, 96 from Cumberland and 41 from Westmorland were 'bounty' emigrants. They were financed by the government to travel to New South Wales.[107] By then overland routes to Melbourne and Adelaide had been explored and more distant interior lands were being settled. In 1848 the government sent 16 emigrants from Cumberland to Australia. A total of 114 went from Cumberland and 20 from Westmorland (including children) under the same scheme in the next three years. Again, these numbers are insignificant compared to the hundreds who were sent from Cambridgeshire and more than 6,000 from Cornwall where the local economy was under severe strain.[108]

From 1851 there was a more compelling reason for going to Australia. Thousands went after the discovery of gold first near Bathurst, NSW in 1851, then in Victoria. Gold seekers paid their own fares but increased numbers of assisted emigrants were also able to emigrate. For several years New South Wales offered bounties to emigrants with particular skills. The 'gold effect' and the greatly increased emigrant numbers are indicated by comparing the figures for the years 1848 and 1852. In 1848, when immigration had only recently resumed after the economic crisis, 1,252 unassisted and 5,952 assisted emigrants went to Australia. Four years later, in 1852, the totals were 37,255 and 20,313 respectively.[109] At least 20 in the sample were at diggings in Victoria c.1853 and other Cumbrian emigrants seem to have been gold seekers before settling into another occupation. In 1859 'the agricultural population was vastly outnumbered by gold miners' leaving a shortage of labour in all sectors of the economy.[110] In 1871 more than 12,000 were at diggings in Queensland.

In 1853, a Cumberland emigrant described Sydney as 'a large, stirring town with a great many excellent buildings.' There was 'a very fine park and botanic garden, one of the finest harbours in the world,' churches, a museum, societies and 'every possible need was catered for.'[111] John Gibson had described Melbourne as being 'about the size of Carlisle' in 1837 when its population was

GOVERNMENT EMIGRATION
TO
NEW SOUTH WALES.
REDUCED RATES.

FARMERS, MECHANICS, MINERS, DOMESTIC SERVANTS, FARM and other LABOURERS, &c., are provided by the Agent-General for New South Wales with passages from Plymouth to Sydney, and thence by rail or steamer to other parts of the Colony, as under:—

Married or single, not exceeding 50 years of age, Passage, *including bedding and mess outfit* £2

Children from 3 to 12 years of age, Passage, *including bedding and mess outfit* £1

Children under 3 years of age, Free.

The Bedding and Mess Outfit become the property of the Emigrant.

Forms of Application with full particulars may be obtained from the "Emigration Department," New South Wales Government, 3, Westminster Chambers, Victoria Street, London, S.W.

Government supported emigration to New South Wales, c.1880

under 6,000 but 'lack of basic amenities [was] irritating and even dangerous.'[112] In 1851 the state of Victoria was created. Almost simultaneously gold was discovered and Melbourne became a 'great sea of canvas.' The hinterland exploded into growth. In 1853 James Forster of Irthington thought Melbourne was 'a commodious well built city, rising in wealth and importance.' It had grown 'from savage wilderness' to 'one of the chief cities of the Empire' by 1877.[113]

In the 1870s agents offered free or assisted passages to emigrants with specific skills, such as trained artisans and farm workers but only if required. In 1872, for example, no assistance was given to those bound for Victoria and only for female domestic servants and farm workers to Queensland. Assistance was also offered by Queensland to shepherds, railway mechanics, and workers in building trades provided they paid the balance of their fare within 12 months. They would then be eligible for a land grant.[114] Assisted passages were available for emigrants to South Australia or New South Wales. Artisans, agricultural and other labourers, miners, gardeners and single or widowed female domestic servants not exceeding the age of 40 could emigrate to South Australia at a cost of £4 and 'persons approved by emigration agents' and emigrants who paid all the costs of their passage 'were entitled to land warrants up to £20 per passenger over 12 years and £10 aged 0-12 ... for occupying and cultivating Crown Lands' – in effect this was assistance.[115] In 1877 reduced fares were offered to similarly qualified workers sailing from Plymouth to New South Wales. Adults paid £2, children 3-12 paid £1 and younger children were free.[116] Cumberland emigrants were in Adelaide, in the Yorke Peninsula and other communities in South Australia from c.1860.

In 1871-2 Anthony Trollope was in Western Australia where transportation had only recently ended and c.10,000 of the State's 25,000 population were convicted men and women. Fremantle was 'a hot, white, ugly town with a very large prison, a lunatic asylum and a hospital for worn-out convicts.' Perth was 'a pretty town' of 6,000 inhabitants but Trollope was assailed by 'musquitoes.'(sic)[117] In 1895 gold was found at Coolgardie, Western Australia and attracted huge numbers of migrants and immigrants. At that time, good land in New South Wales could be bought for £1 per acre, paid for in instalments. In 1908 coconut farming in Queensland was recommended in the local press and wheelwrights, carpenters, engineers and especially blacksmiths would be considered for assisted passages.[118] Other crops in Queensland mentioned in emigrant letters were sugar, pineapples and cotton.[119] Cumbrians were in Ipswich, Brisbane and at a number of diggings in Queensland.

A continuing problem, also encountered in other destinations, was the preponderance of men. In 1847 out of a total of approximately 195,000 European inhabitants in New South Wales, only 39.5 per cent were female and there was a proposal to send more single young women but the imbalance continued for many years in spite of efforts to reduce the difference.[120] Sixty years later, in 1907 the local press stated that 'special efforts' should be made to persuade women to emigrate to Australia, New Zealand and British Columbia in Canada to correct the imbalance in the sexes.[121] In 1910, free passages and the promise of high wages were offered to female domestic servants and to farm workers bound for Queensland but 'domestic servants must be prepared to undertake the general work of a household [including] cooking. ... Laundrywork was [usually] done at home. ... Parlour maids were not much in demand.'[122]

As in other destination countries, clusters of friends and relatives can be identified. Wagga Wagga was a community situated in good farming country more than 300 miles from Sydney with a population of 2,500 in 1875. Christopher, John D. and Thomas Norman went to Wagga Wagga c.1870. Andrew Holliday and his two sisters went there in 1883. Their brother Jabez followed in 1885 and a cousin, another Andrew Holliday with two sisters settled there in 1902. Mr M. Potter from Great Salkeld was farming in Wagga Wagga from about 1903. Wheat and wine were the main products with stock rearing being an important activity.

The convict population included some Cumbrians. Free emigrants in the sample went in increasing numbers from 1818. Apart from those who took land the emigrants followed a wide range of occupations including crafts and trades, business of all kinds and the professions. Some went to coal mines in the Newcastle area, to the Victoria goldfield, to gold mines at Charters Towers in Queensland or Maryborough in Victoria to Broken Hill in New South Wales or to Western Australia and other mineral extracting areas such as the Yorke Peninsula. Many in the sample who initially searched for gold settled in Australia. Others moved to New Zealand or went home.

New Zealand.

The New Zealand Company sent emigrants to the North Island where they founded New Plymouth and Port Nicholson (Wellington) and to Nelson on the South Island. Later problems and war with the Maoris particularly affected the North Island. The history of the Company, its relationship with the British government and with the indigenous peoples is complex and it ceased operation in 1850.[123] In essence, in 1840, the Company was given leave to 'purchase, sell, settle on and cultivate lands in New Zealand, to convey emigrants thither provided that the emigration was supervised by the government.'[124] Emigrants were offered free passages in the early 1840s. In spite of the great distance, this was an attractive offer and the sample includes several who were selected and sailed on the first ships. A total of 98 Cumbrians applied for free passages during the years of the Company's existence. Only 14 applicants were from Westmorland whereas Cockermouth alone accounted for 27, Carlisle 26 and Whitehaven 19. Some of these were family or neighbourhood groups who wished to emigrate together.[125] Occupations included quarry worker, shepherd, carpenter, cartwright, blacksmith, a carpet manufacturer, a clock and watch maker, several agricultural workers and a dressmaker. However, of 32 families and single applicants listed in the Company documents consulted, only 11 had embarkation numbers including the dressmaker who was to travel 'under the protection of a relative' which may indicate that only about one third actually went. Forty three per cent of applicants from Cumberland and 16 per cent from Westmorland were accepted from 1839-50 compared with 40 per cent of the approximately 6,000 applicants from England. Although many fewer applied to emigrate to New Zealand than went to North America during these years there was considerable interest in the new destination.[126]

The Nelson project was given careful thought and promoted as having 'a good climate ... with good harbour and anchorages, near to Wellington and New Plymouth with good easily cleared land.' It would be necessary to 'build a comfortable house, lay out a garden and cultivate subsistence land for a year or

3.8 New Zealand - Destinations before 1860

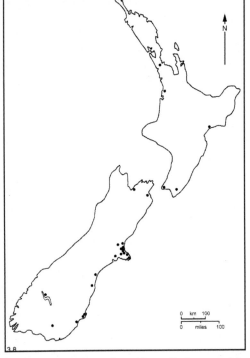

two' and to make roads. Two hundred acres of town, suburban and country land cost £300. It was hoped that 'congregations of various denominations would spring up' with schools and leisure activities such as music, drama and dancing but not at balls – seen to be the 'worst kind of social pleasure.'[127]

A large number of settlers were sent with the hope that the colony would have a dynamic and trouble free start. Surveyors, civil engineers and others went earlier to prepare the site. Ships were to leave only five weeks after advertisements appeared in the local press, necessitating a quick decision, and thereafter ships sailed at monthly intervals to Nelson, New Plymouth and Wellington. Land could be purchased before leaving. Applications were invited for free passages. The New Zealand Company also advertised for workers, farmers and small capitalists, not entitled to free travel to emigrate. They paid 50 guineas per couple (1st class) or £20 per adult in other cabins.[128] Cumbrians were among the first arrivals.

But investors bought only about 10 per cent of the land and few of those were among the emigrants. Even several years later not all the land was taken. Lack of bridges and roads here and in the other new settlements hindered expansion of cultivable land. Food had to be imported and there were difficult times for all the early settlers in New Zealand. Emigrants were advised to take money, strong and serviceable clothing, all ironwork necessary for a house, farming implements, cart wheels, a blacksmith's forge and tools but not furniture.[129] By 1848, Nelson was reported to have made 'considerable progress and the population had reached 3,800.

Some contemporary correspondents described claims about New Zealand as over-optimistic and stated 'the reality.' For example, 'the islands are uncultivated

*3.9 New Zealand -
Destinations before 1914*

wastes either of mountains covered by dense forest, of plains and lowlands covered with high fern shrubs or of swamps and marshes covered with rush or flax without any open spots of grassland for pasturage or verdant downs and hills for sheep.'[130] This was 'an isolated colony, three months from home with no social or cultural activities. ... Colonists need money, strength and a contented spirit ... [amid] the trials of pioneering life.'[131] Instead of the Company spending money on printing 'puffing journals' and cultivating parliamentary influence, building roads would have helped 'a great population of small farmers' to occupy land.[132]

In 1841 Wellington was described as being 'adjacent to the finest portions of the country' with 'natural advantages.' Already the town had 'many handsome and substantially built houses.' 'Influential settlers' were there but allocated land could be up to 100 miles from the town; 'inaccessible and worthless without roads.' 'The mountains were higher, the morasses deeper and the forests denser than in England.' The Wanganui district was 'impenetrable' by land with 'unfordable rivers.' Here, as in Nelson, there were food shortages and settlers including Cumbrians had to rely on native 'sweet potatoes and Chilean flour.'[133]

The South Island proved particularly attractive to emigrants from the two counties. The Canterbury Association offered assisted passages from 1850 and favourable terms for buying or leasing land. Otago was intended to be largely Scottish but several Cumbrians made their homes there. In 1848 more than 2,000 sections of land were available for lease or purchase. Each section was, as in other New Zealand colonies, divided into three, a small town holding, a few suburban acres with the major portion of land being 'rural.' Here, the allotment was one quarter of an acre in the town, 10 acres nearby and 50 acres of rural land at a cost of £120 10s.[134]

Dunedin's site was not ideal. 'Hills and gullies ascend[ed] to the heights from the shore.'[135] Mountains, swamps, flax and fern meant hard work and expense before farming beyond the town could begin. Although both Canterbury and Otago were suitable for pastoral farming, prices quoted for wool sales in the early days were 'imaginative'.[136] Gold on the west coast brought thousands to the South Island in the 1860s. Lyttelton, Christchurch and Dunedin developed and numerous smaller settlements grew in their hinterland. The Taieri Plain offered opportunities for arable farming with sheep on pastoral land. The Powley and Robinson families from Kirkby Stephen became farmers in the Dunedin district together with other members of their families.

The sample contains no reference to Cumbrians being initial settlers in New Plymouth but several were in the nearby Taranaki region later. Throughout New Zealand land was cleared, farms established and vast pastoral areas supported thousands of sheep. Two Studholme brothers from Carlisle raised livestock on the Waimate Run. Men and women from all parts of the two counties settled throughout the island as Maps 3.8 and 3.9 indicate. Many were farmers. Some were miners and a wide range of other occupations were represented. Villages and towns grew organically to serve the settlers but others, for example, Feilding in the North Island were created. Cumbrian emigrants were nearby.[137]

More than 40 men and women from Cumberland and Westmorland in the Canterbury region are named in Volume 3 of the *Cyclopaedia of New Zealand*. Many others are in the Otago and other volumes.[138] With a few exceptions, only those who were alive at the turn of the century are included. Early emigrants would have died before publication. More than 30 from West Cumberland are known to have been in the coal mining area near Greymouth on the west coast of the South Island. The sample includes 520 identified by name in all parts of New Zealand but the majority were in the South Island. Other unnamed emigrants (or lacking clear identification) who were mentioned in correspondence and newspapers have not been counted.

South Africa.

Not all Cumbrian emigrants to South Africa were miners. Some farmed or became fruit growers, others settled in towns as teachers or in other occupations but, as Map 3.10 shows, the majority were clustered in the gold and diamond mining area. The 284 named men and women in the sample who went to South Africa are only a minimum number. William Collins from West Cumberland was in South Africa before 1830 working as a teacher. Later he became a farmer. His last farm (in the 1870s) was called St Bees.[139] Newspaper reports tell of emigrants who went in 'large parties,' in groups, the un-named friends who accompanied

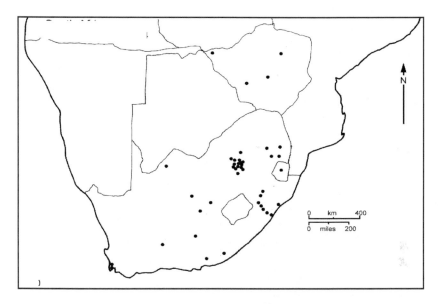

3.10 Southern Africa - Destinations before 1914

them and many other unknown Cumbrian men and women were also there. In the 1890s James Airey had a farm and sold dairy products and garden produce in nearby Krugersdorp which had become a mining centre.[140] In the early twentieth century a Waberthwaite man gave a lecture in Whitehaven on his experience as a dairy farmer. Mr E. Martin went to join Baden Powell's police force in 1901.[141] Henry Richardson of Penrith was Treasurer and Town Clerk of Springs, Transvaal where Thomas Snaith of Kirkby Stephen was a bank manager.[142] But, from about 1880, most Cumbrian emigrants went to the gold, copper or diamond mines. Diamonds were found at Harrismith and Kimberley in the 1860s. The population at Kimberley had reached more than 13,500 by 1885. Anthony Trollope thought Kimberley was 'foul with dust and flies, reeks with brandy and ... not a tree near it.'[143] Many gold mines had opened. Johannesburg and settlements in the area grew rapidly. In 1905 the *Maryport News* reported that parties of emigrants left West Cumberland weekly.[144]

Workers were also needed to construct and operate the expanding railway system in Southern Africa. Before Samuel Hastings of Whitehaven had to return home because of family health problems he had worked on the railway. Mr L. Coates of Orton, Westmorland was employed on the railway at Kimberley.[145] Essie Metcalfe wrote to her Carlisle relatives from the Zambesi Bridge site, a link in the projected Cape to Cairo railway, in 1904 where her brother in law was

Union Castle Line advertisement

an engineer on the project.[146] In 1909 Rhodesia was advertised in the local press as 'splendid cattle country with abundant well-watered pastures.' Grain crops, cotton, tobacco and fruit would thrive, there were 300 days of sunshine per year and 'millions of acres of cheap land' were available.[147] Mining also drew men to Rhodesia where Joseph Kearney of Whitehaven was the manager of a coal mine and where several other Whitehaven men also worked.[148]

The Boer Wars and unemployment due to an economic depression in the years 1905-6 caused immigrants to leave South Africa. As the majority of Cumbrians had not settled there, they could return home. But for many, the mines caused death, injury or chronic ill-health. Local newspapers record fatal accidents and death from illness overseas. For many miners in South Africa and elsewhere, a more insidious but powerful agent of illness in the form of respiratory disease was exposure to mineral dust created by drilling machines in hard rock mines. Miners developed tuberculosis where their work was in damp conditions. But still West Cumberland men went to South Africa in their hundreds. In 1887, diamonds worth £4.2 million and gold worth £250,000 were exported - £4.6 million and £8.25 million respectively in 1896.

The West Indies

Most emigrants to the West Indies had a specific purpose in going there. From the mid-seventeenth century onwards West Cumberland men owned property or plantations growing sugar cane or cotton in Barbados, Tobago, Jamaica, Antigua and other islands. The sample contains the names of 30 men who were in the West Indies during the late eighteenth and early nineteenth centuries including James Crow of Lanercost in Barbados and members of the Plaskett family of Threlkeld and James Graham of Scotby in St Croix. Thomas Dixon of Egremont and Robert Peel's three sons from Armathwaite were in Jamaica in the early 1840s.[150] The majority were sugar planters or their employees; others were sojourners - in the army, in administration or were clergymen. When William Robinson from the Penrith area died in Demerara in 1839 from yellow fever, he was only one of many who succumbed to disease in that region. Elizabeth Ferguson, wife of an army officer wrote that 'the men were dying so fast in Demerara it was thought advisable to move ... I was very thankful to leave ... it is a dismal place.'[151] In 1841 bounties were given to almost 900 agricultural workers, female domestic servants and others for travel to the West Indies to provide much needed labour.[152]

South America and other destinations

Cumbrians in European countries have been excluded from the sample. Those in South America were in several countries for example, Chile, Argentina,

Paraguay, Peru and Brazil at least from the 1840s. In the four years from 1845-1848 (inclusive), more than 2,300 passengers or emigrants went to Central and South America from Britain.[153] Government handbooks and publicity repeatedly warned emigrants of the difficulties they might encounter in Spanish speaking countries compared with 'the advantages offered by our own English colonies.'[154] The language did not deter Thomas and Rosetta Blamire and James Wigstone who moved to Spain as protestant missionaries c.1860 but this was to a European environment. Periodic political upheavals were cited and 'language, laws and conditions of life and employment were totally different from those to which they were accustomed.'[155] Advertisements offered passages to the River Plate region in 1871 where an agricultural colony was to be formed. Many years earlier Joseph Fell had been a pilot on the River Plate.[156]

Mr R. Martindale of Wigton and Gertrude Watson went to Peru. Anne and James Steward were in Montevideo in the 1840s.[157] Chile seems to have been a favoured destination. The Dobson family from Kendal went there in 1895, took land and stayed. It is not known where their land was but in 1897 British subjects were in distress on the island of Chiloe, in southern Chile because of 'ill-advised emigration.'[158] James Hodgson worked as a plasterer in Santiago in 1905 and Mrs Muir from Musgrave was with her husband in Vina del Mar, near Valparaiso in 1906.[159] John Ferguson of Penrith was an engineer in Valparaiso in 1914.[160] In 1890 c.6,000 British emigrants went to Argentina only a year before a revolution.[161] Richard Burnes of Cleator Moor worked at a cold storage depot at La Plata and Thomas Horsfield of Kirkby Stephen, a railway worker went to Buenos Aires in 1912.[162]

Place names

Although so many emigrated from Cumberland and Westmorland, a scan of present day atlases reveals comparatively few places with names that have namesakes in the two counties and of these, not all are necessarily connected with Cumbria. For example, Windermere Lake in British Columbia was not a place where Cumbrians initially settled.[163] Clifton, Hilton, Brampton and even Appleby may not have Cumbrian connections and the name Cumberland may be associated with the Duke not the county. Therefore, there are potential difficulties in making the association. But, many names do have local connections. There is a Cumberland in New Jersey, a Westmorland in Pennsylvania, and at least two other Westmorlands in North America. In the United States there is an Egremont, a Kendall (*sic*), several Carlisles, a Whitehaven, Milburn, Colby, Grasmere, Penrith, four Keswicks, Windermere, an Eden and more than one Carleton but few other names suggest any connection.

In New Zealand, surprisingly few place names can be associated with the two counties but they include Eden Park in Auckland, Inglewood in the Taranaki, Eskdale, Walton, Dacre, Lake Grassmere,(sic) Carleton, Renwick, Staveley, Inglewood Mill at Wetheral Station, Eamont Lodge, near Wanganui, Lonsdale, Milburn, Renwick and Winton. The village of Aglionby near Wellington was named after a director of the New Zealand Company who was a member of the family that had its roots in, and continued associations with Aglionby near Carlisle.[164]

Australia has at least one Inglewood and a Harrington, Grasmere, Lowther, Langdale, Penrith, Alstonville, Hartley, Kendall,(sic) Keswick, Rydal, Thirlmere, Winton, Casterton and Eskdale. The small township of Eden was founded in the 1840s on Twofold Bay, New South Wales, close to the border with Victoria. Names of islands in the Cumberland Isles in the Great Barrier Reef include St Bees, Carlisle, Brampton, Scawfell, Cockermouth and Keswick. Cumberland and Westmorland are counties in Tasmania. Keswick, Winton, Derwent and Ulverstone, now in Cumbria, could be counted. But, even a few years after settlements were named, the association may be unknown to local residents. The daughter of John Wood had emigrated as a small child with the family from near Penrith, Cumberland in 1818. Initially they lived in Sydney but later moved into the hinterland. As an adult, more than twenty years later, she wrote that she did not know why Penrith near Sydney was given that name.[165]

In Canada, more than 20 names could be connected with Cumbria. Nova Scotia has a Cumberland and Westmorland. Staveley, Silverdale, Inglewood, at least two Carlisles, three Carletons, Brampton, Keswick, Keswick Bridge, Lowther Island, Brougham and Bowness are other places with Cumbrian names. Farms too were given names to remind the owners of home, for example, Glendidden, Lowther, Sandford, Newlands, Wythburn, Lang Rigg, Eamont Lodge, Lamplugh, St Bees, Buttermere, Isel, Blencathra, Blencarn, Orton and Ulverston (then Lancashire). John Airey lived at Penrith House, Woburn, Massachusetts and James Dinsdale from north Westmorland lived in Dinsdale, Iowa in 1914 which, although that was his own name not a Cumbrian place name, suggests he was a very early settler there.

Destinations were very different and the impact of the environment upon new arrivals was equally varied. Few stayed in the ports at which they arrived and many moved at least once before setting down their roots; some never did settle but kept moving. Cumbrians were part of the history and settlement of new lands and of established cities and industries. Whether the destination was a huge city like New York, dense forest, a vast sparsely inhabited prairie, or an empty bay in New Zealand their new life was ahead. But, first – the journey.

Chapter 4:
The Journey

West Cumberland had a long history of overseas contacts. In the 1830s and 1840s locally built ships were going to South America, New South Wales, Van Diemen's Land, California, New Orleans, Chile via Cape Horn and China.[1] But the majority of Cumbrians may have travelled only to local market centres, especially in the pre-railway years. Joseph Grave from Cockermouth had never visited Whitehaven, only 15 miles from home before he sailed to Liverpool in 1837.[2] Emigrants from east Cumberland and Westmorland were even less likely to have seen the sea and the reality of travelling across the ocean on a ship was unknown and unimaginable.

The journey to the port

In 1811 coaches and waggon or carrier services connected Carlisle with Whitehaven, London, Liverpool, Newcastle and Glasgow.[3] Emigrants may have sailed from these as well as from Cumberland ports. Coastal ships regularly went to Liverpool from Port Carlisle, Whitehaven and Maryport; a faster and often a more comfortable journey than the 118 miles by road from Carlisle (80 from Kendal). Local coach or carrier services connected with these. If the port of embarkation was London, Cumbrians could sail from Newcastle, reached by road until the railway connected Carlisle with Newcastle in the 1830s. The weekly sailings to London cost £2 2s or £1 10s. This is the route chosen by three Cumberland men who sailed to Newcastle from London in the early twentieth century.[4]

Very few emigrants in the sample left an account of their journey to the port. Before railways, travel was by coach, a carrier's cart or waggon or on foot. The 110 emigrants from Alston Moor must have travelled across Cumberland to Whitehaven by road in 1818 before embarking on the tiny single decked brigantine, *The Jason* to sail to Upper Canada.[5] Emigrants from Swaledale in the 1830s went 'with horses and carts [or] with hill ponies loaded as packhorses. ... Wives and children rode on the carts and men not riding on horses set out to walk.' Their route was via Wensleydale to Lancaster where they joined the road from Westmorland and east Cumberland and on to Preston and Liverpool.[6] The 'great many' families from the 'eastern parts of Cumberland' who sailed from Maryport in 1832 with 'cartloads' of luggage and furniture must have travelled by road across the county to the coast.[7] In the 1830s several thousand emigrants sailed from Cumberland ports to Canada and others went first to Liverpool by

J. C. Armytage

Liverpool, 1841.

steamer. Emigrants also sailed from other ports to different destinations.

In the early years of the nineteenth century Mrs Molloy wrote 'we rose at six, dispatched our men with the packages, trunks etc. and at half past eight [we] walked from Parton following the waggon laden with the remaining boxes and my poor beehive.' At Kendal they had 'a long detention' before travelling to Gosport.[8] Robert S. Hall had visited his uncle at Hornby, south Westmorland in 1853-4. Before returning to North America he had walked to Kendal to 'purchas[e] merchandise' then, on the day of his departure Robert's cousins took him and his luggage on a cart as far as Lancaster where he embarked on a Liverpool bound vessel before boarding the ship that took him across the Atlantic.[9] The railway could have taken Robert to Liverpool but he chose to travel by road and sea. By 1908 when the Spedding family and more than 30 others, mainly miners and their families, emigrated to New Zealand, they travelled to London from Egremont in West Cumberland in two special coaches attached to the train. Arriving at Euston an omnibus took them to Fenchurch Street. The boat train took them to the Royal Albert Docks where they boarded the *S.S Marathon*, a 6,000 ton coal fired ship 'with a clipper bow,' for their voyage to Australia. Their ultimate destination was New Zealand.[10]

From the 1840s, railways transformed travel but it took until 1846 for Cumberland and Westmorland to be connected directly to London. Gradually more lines were built, branch lines extended until rail travel was, together with connecting coach or omnibus services, within reach of most communities. Granville described Euston, the terminus in London for Cumberland and Westmorland travellers, as 'swarming with bustle' in 1840. First class carriages carried luggage on top. Second class carriages were 'closed with glass windows ... sufficiently snug in winter but [were without] the luxury of cushions, stuffing etc.' These carriages were followed by the post office coach, 'the tender, the luggage van and the truck for private carriages.' Granville foresaw the future. 'Cheap and speedy' travel by rail would 'induce the whole nation ... to be on the move. ... Restlessness will be the order of the day.'[11]

Travellers to London or to Liverpool from Cumberland and Westmorland had a choice of transport and routes. Although there was no railway line through Cumbria to the south before 1846, the line to Newcastle from Carlisle had opened in 1838. From Newcastle travellers could go to London by sea or, after the Newcastle to London link was established, by rail. Alternatively, Cumbrians could travel by mail coach calling at Penrith at 7.45 a.m. and at Appleby and Brough before connecting with the 3.47 p.m. train to London at Darlington. This train arrived in London at 5.00 a.m. the next morning. The rail fare was £3 8s first class, £2 6s second class in 1843.[12] Coaches from Carlisle, Penrith, south Westmorland and the Lake District ran to Kendal and Lancaster where they connected with the London trains or, by changing at Preston, passengers could travel to Liverpool. To shorten the road journey, the twice daily 'swift' canal packet boat sailed from Kendal to Lancaster at a cost of cost 3s first class, 2s second class. The boats were warmed in cold weather, breakfast and refreshments were served and a free omnibus transferred passengers to the railway at Lancaster.[13] After the line was extended northwards to Carlisle in 1846 there was direct connection with Liverpool (changing at Preston) and London, a journey of more than 12 hours. Coaches connected with the railway at stations such as Milnthorpe from Ulverston and other centres in the south western district. The coach to Penrith from Keswick, for example, cost 7s inside, 5s outside.[14] Tourists visited the Lake District in ever increasing numbers after rail travel presented a speedy and reliable means of reaching this previously remote region. The coaches and omnibuses that met trains to take visitors into the central Lakes area also transported local people and emigrants on their outward journeys.

Costs differed according to the transport used. The rail fare from Carlisle to Lancaster in 1849 was from 9s 9d to 14s whereas by sea, the voyage from Port Carlisle to Liverpool on the *Royal Victoria, The Queen* or *The Victoria* was 3s to 10s. If the traveller went first to Newcastle, the voyage to London by sea cost

12s to £1.[15] But the decision was not simply one of money. Train travel was quicker and after about 1850 was the preferred link between home and the port. From Maryport, for example, a local train called at several stations to connect with the 10.20 a.m. service from Whitehaven calling at Broughton, Ulverston (1.30 p.m.) Preston (change for Liverpool) and on to London arriving at 11 p.m. Coastal steamers continued operating. An eight hour voyage from Whitehaven to Liverpool cost 8s or 4s on deck with connecting trains from Carlisle at 4s to 10s. There were also weekly steamers from Maryport; twice weekly from Silloth.[16] When Joseph Grave sailed to Liverpool in 1837 he went by coach to Whitehaven and embarked on the steamer, *The Countess of Lonsdale* in the evening. The sea was calm and the ship docked early the next morning after sailing past the Cheshire coast. 'It was a beautiful sight all along the river.'[17]

Once the emigrant had arrived at the station in Liverpool, a coach to the docks cost 2s to 2s 6d. A 'car' was cheaper – 1s 4d to 1s 8d. Men with handcarts, horse-drawn carts or even runners could be hired to take luggage but travellers could be 'at the mercy of swindl[ers].[18] In 1865 the press reported that Liverpool's reputation suffered because of 'the plunder of emigrants and the absence of proper accommodation' before sailing. 'As soon as [they] arrive ... they are beset by a tribe of people ... whose business is ... to "fleece" the emigrant and [take his cash] ... by fair means or foul.' It was often necessary to stay at least overnight in lodging houses, some of which catered solely for emigrants. These could be acceptable or be 'destitute of comfort and convenience' where profiteering was the motive.[19] The 1858 directory contains several pages of lodging houses in Liverpool.[20] Emigrants and others going to the docks had to 'brave the exorbitant demands of those who craved payment' such as cabmen, porters or runners and avoid the attention of pickpockets.[21]

Once the rail network covered the country the journey to more distant embarkation ports including Gravesend, London, Glasgow, Plymouth and Southampton was not a problem apart from time and expense. In 1859 the rail fare from Carlisle to London was 25s third class and 66s first class. For the determined sea traveller for whom time was not important, steamships went from Liverpool to Bristol (12s 6d cabin or 5s deck) and fortnightly from Liverpool to Plymouth, Portsmouth and Southampton en route for London at a cost of £1 (1st class cabin), to only 10s on deck.[22]

After arriving in London from Buckinghamshire in 1844, the Mundy family were taken in 'a large van' to the Deptford depot where they slept with 300 others in 'rough bunks' before boarding their ship to Australia.[23] Twenty years later, Thomas Hetherington and his family sailed to Australia from Plymouth. Their home at Hethersgill was in north east Cumberland, less than 20 miles from Carlisle but they chose to travel across country to Lanchester, County Durham, then by rail via York, Bristol and Exeter to Plymouth. They thought the depot in Plymouth was 'a very rough place ... plenty of meat [was] served [but] in a very rough way' however 'things [were] all very clean.' All their breakable goods had been packed in straw but, finding that straw was not allowed on board, everything had to be repacked using cloth which indicates that the family were taking more than personal luggage and were prepared for setting up their new home in Australia. Only about half a dozen of the emigrant families in the Plymouth depot 'belonged to the North Country.'[24]

Newspapers refer to presentations to emigrants from employers, churches and other organisations and to the groups of friends and relations who gathered at stations to say farewell; occasionally accompanied by the local brass band.

The ships

Advertisements in the press and other references give little or no information about the ship itself. Brigs were ocean-going trading and passenger ships, about 70 to 160 ft long and up to c.500 tons. Such ships left West Cumberland ports for many parts of the world in the first quarter of the nineteenth century and continued in use for many years. In 1819 a passenger service was operating from Whitehaven to New Brunswick – a destination for early Cumbrian emigrants including Richard Hodgson, Joseph Sewell and their families. Thomas Ostle followed in 1822.[25] In 1818, the Alston emigrants sailed in the two-masted brigantine, the *Jason*.[26] Local newspapers reported the arrival from (or departure for) the Baltic and other European ports, Trinidad, Barbados, Rio de Janeiro, Montevideo, New Orleans, Mobile, New Brunswick, Quebec, Hobart, Valparaiso, Sierra Leone and Singapore.[27]

In 1825 advertisements stated that 250 ton brigs sailing to the West Indies offered 'excellent accommodation' and the *Aurora*, 'a fine fast sailing ship' of 250 tons would sail to Quebec from Whitehaven.[28] The 300 ton 'coppered' *Kelsick Wood* was to sail from Maryport to Montreal and the 500 ton *Winscales*, 'purpose built for passengers' went to Quebec from Workington in 1826. In March, the same year a 'copper fastened' brig, the *Arsthorpe*, was to sail from Whitehaven to Quebec with 20-30 passengers. 'Those wishing to emigrate' would have 'roomy and comfortable accommodation.'[29] In 1830 a Maryport agent invited applications for a sailing to Quebec on the *Itinerant*. Five weeks later it was reported that 151 people, mainly from Westmorland had left for Quebec. Some of these may have travelled on the *Itinerant*.[xxx]

The *Charlotte Farrie* took 50 emigrants to Canada from Glasson Dock in 1842. In the same year the *Eveline* sailed from Maryport and the *Grace* from Port Carlisle, taking passengers to Quebec. In September 1842 the 600 ton Cumberland built *Winscales* – 'a splendid vessel,' was to leave Liverpool taking emigrants to Port Phillip and Sydney.[31] Was this the same *Winscales* as in 1825? In 1847 the *Isabella*, *Nestor* and *Hope* took a total of 33 passengers to Quebec from West Cumberland ports and in 1848 11 passengers sailed to Canada in the *Fawcett*.[32] For so many to have left Cumberland in small ships, most of which carried few passengers, many voyages were necessary. The *Meteor*, built in Whitehaven went several times to Australia and Tasmania before 1850.[33]

In the early 1840s steam ships such as the *Royal Victoria* were used on coastal routes from Newcastle to London and from Port Carlisle, Silloth, Maryport and Whitehaven to Liverpool. At 450 tons, the *Royal Victoria* was larger than sailing ships bound for New Zealand and offered 'provisions, beds and bedding' at 'most moderate terms.'[34] In 1842 applications were invited from 'labouring persons duly qualified' for free passages from London to Nelson and Wellington. A number of Cumbrians applied, some of whom were successful.[35] The *Thomas Harrison* which carried emigrants from the two counties to Nelson in 1842 was only 355 tons and the 391 ton *George Fyfe* went to Wellington.

Early steamships were equipped with masts and sails in case of engine failure and to save fuel. They were faster than sailing ships but the need to carry huge quantities of coal and extra crew added weight and took valuable space. Coaling stations were needed on long voyages for example, to Australia, New Zealand or India. Although it became both practicable and profitable to use steam on the Atlantic route by the mid-century as regular advertisements indicate, it is often unclear whether the ships were in fact steam powered and even into the early twentieth century, sail was still used on the Antipodean route by some shipping lines.[36] The first Atlantic steam ships were driven by paddles, travelled at about 10 knots and took 12-14 days compared to the three to five weeks or more that adverse weather conditions could impose on a sailing ship. In 1855 a *c*.400 ton sailing ship took 55 days to reach London from Trinidad by which time food and water were in short supply.[37]

In the 1840s steamships were small and uncomfortable with little space even for cabin passengers. Charles Dickens commented 'Nothing smaller for sleeping was ever made except coffins.'[38] Steerage travel was unpleasant in both steam and sailing ships in the first half of the century and passengers endured overcrowded, ill-ventilated, dark and insanitary conditions even in good weather. In bad weather they were 'battened below.'[39] But the standard of accommodation offered to passengers improved over time. In 1858 the White Star Line advertised that their twice monthly sailings to Australia were in 'the largest and fastest [ships] afloat' with 'elegant saloons' and 'exceedingly lofty' steerage accommodation.[40] Continued developments in ship design and technical progress meant that meant that steerage passengers travelled in much improved conditions on trans-Atlantic and long distance ships even if not approaching the comfort

and luxury enjoyed by first class passengers. In 1908 the Spedding family and their friends seem to have been contented with their accommodation on the *Marathon*. 'Three mothers and five children' shared a large cabin. The men and boys were in separate but probably similar accommodation. Mr Spedding describes the voyage as 'uneventful' although they encountered storms and rough seas with 'terrific waves.' Broken crockery and water were 'swishing about' the floor. After three days in Melbourne they sailed to Sydney where the cargo of 'locomotives and tractor engines' was unloaded, then went to Wellington, New Zealand by a fast steamship, the *Maheno*. Their final destination was Runanga, near Greymouth, reached after a nine week journey from Cumbria.[41]

But some ships offered little comfort even in the late nineteenth century and beyond. George Callcott described the voyage to the United States in 1885. The accommodation was in 'great barn-like room ... partion[ed] like the stalls in a stable with 24 berths [per] stall. ... Of course there was no privacy. Modesty was left behind.' Tables were planks on trestles. Seats were wooden benches. About 90 per cent of the 1,000 passengers on board were in steerage.[42] But this was crossing the Atlantic. Similar conditions were described by steerage passengers on the long voyage to Australia when perhaps 200 people slept in one dark dormitory and, as these ships carried wool or other cargo on the return journey, any partitions to make cabins were temporary and flimsy unless passengers were in First Class accommodation. In 1912 when Edith Spark and her family emigrated to Western Australia from Garrigill they embarked on the steamship *Ajana* at Avonmouth Docks after travelling by rail from Carlisle. As in earlier years and other examples, this ship carried emigrants and other passengers on the outward voyage but cargo such as wool and other bulky goods on the return journey therefore cabins and other partitioned accommodation was of a temporary nature. The cabin Edith shared with her mother and sisters was 'small [and] dark with ... not even a chair to sit on.' Her father and brothers would be in a similar cabin. The dining hall was filled with 'about 200 or so fearfully rough-looking people' and the first meal was dreadful. The bunks were uncomfortable – made of straw or something equally as hard.'[43]

Sixty years earlier, in the early 1850s the *Great Britain* was converted from a steamship with sails into a steam assisted sailing ship. The gold rush in Australia coincided with the *Great Britain's* entry into the Australian run – a service that continued for more than 20 years. The ship carried 600 passengers in three classes and steerage.[44] A cargo of wool, other goods but especially gold was carried on the return journey. James Huddart of Whitehaven sailed to Australia on the *Great*

Opposite: Orient Pacific Line. Late nineteenth century advertisement.

Britain in 1861 – a voyage of 62 days. John Airey from Orton, Westmorland was another who emigrated on the *Great Britain*. Anthony Trollope worked at his writing throughout the voyage to Melbourne on the *Great Britain* in 1871.[45] The *Great Britain* served the Australia route until 1876, a voyage taking only approximately 60 to 80 days which may be compared to the 138 days taken to reach New Zealand by the 1,000 ton *Geelong*, the 'famous fast-sailing full poop passenger ship' in 1862; 'a time of slow starvation and anxiety.' Advertisements stated that the *Geelong* went 'direct to the goldfields' at a cost of 20 guineas or 16 guineas in an open berth with children at half price, including provisions.[46] Even on the trans-Atlantic route, Sarah Jordan of Carlisle went by sailing ship *c.*1890.

By 1850-60 iron hulls had replaced wood, paddles were being replaced by screws and ships had doubled in size to about 1,000 tons. Improvements continued until in the 1880s steel-hulled ships such as the 7,000 ton *Servia*, lit by electricity and lavishly appointed, travelled at *c.*17 knots across the Atlantic. By 1914, when Bill Atkinson from north Westmorland sailed to New York on the *Mauretania,* there had been a transformation of travel conditions and length of voyage. Ships were huge and offered a standard of comfort unimaginable in earlier years. The *Mauretania* carried more than 2,000 passengers, a crew of 800, needed 7,000 tons of coal to fire 192 furnaces and was the fastest ship afloat.[47]

Local newspapers advertised passages to many destinations – often weekly. In 1879, for example, the White Star Line and the National Line ships to New York from Liverpool, took 6½ days in summer, 9½ in winter at a cost of 10-12 guineas (cheaper in steerage). Passengers could book onward tickets to all parts of North America with especially favourable rates to Texas.[48] The Anchor Line had a direct service to New York from Barrow in Furness for a few years from 1879.[49] In 1880 John Braithwaite, the Kirkby Stephen postmaster and agent advertised this three weekly service at a cost of £10 10s - £12 12s. Steerage passengers were charged £6 6s.[50]

Shipping companies offered assisted passages to Canada but only paying passengers were taken to the United States. Through tickets at special rates could be booked to Montreal, Toronto, Chicago and the Western States in America. Union Castle Line ships went to South Africa weekly from 1872 taking about 16-17 days. Holt Line ships were among those serving South America. The New Zealand Line, established in 1873, operated steamships from about 1880 but continued to use sail until 1899. Their ships and others took advantage of the prevailing wind systems and went via Cape Town but returned via Cape Horn thus circumnavigating the world.[51]

Opposite: White Star Line advertisement, c.1890

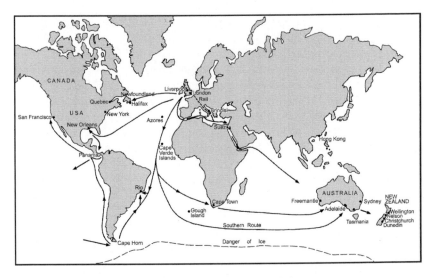

4.1 World map showing destinations and shipping routes.

Map 4.1 shows the main shipping routes. From the mid-century, ships sailed non-stop to Australasia instead of calling at Cape Town. By following an apparently longer curved route more than 500 miles south of the Cape the journey time was shortened but scarcity of food and water could be a problem. Ships were far from any port and apart from the chance sighting of another ship were completely alone. In these southern seas, the temperatures were low, passengers suffered from the cold but, more importantly, icing of the rigging and icebergs could threaten safety. In 1865, a passenger on the *Great Britain* described seeing icebergs that resembled 'a large palace in ruins' or 'a large island' but 'admiration' was mixed with 'awe allied to fear.'[52]

Some travellers shortened the long sea voyage to India or Australia, especially after the Suez Canal connected the Mediterranean with the Red Sea in 1869. The British base at Aden provided a coaling depot. By journeying overland to Italy passengers could join their ship at Brindisi or at Alexandria after crossing the Mediterranean by steamer where they could see Cleopatra's Needle and explore the city and bazaars. From Alexandria an overnight train journey took the traveller to Suez to join their ship. The overland route saved more than a week of travelling time which gave steam a significant competitive boost in spite of higher fares. For example, a passenger could leave London on or before the second Thursday after the ship had left England, cross the Channel by ferry, then travel by rail via Cologne, Munich and Bologna to Brindisi (1,391 miles) in 52 hours, or via Paris and Milan to Venice thence by steamer to Brindisi or to Alexandria.[53] Thomas G.

Deutsch-Australische Dampfschiffs Gesellschaft, Hamburg.

HAMBURG ≗ AUSTRALIA
VIA ANTWERP.

Under Contract with the Belgian Government.

Fourweekly Direct Service between Hamburg and Adelaide, Melbourne and Sydney.

Goods and Passengers taken at Through Rates to other Australian or New Zealand Ports.

Seven Large First-Class Steel Steamers:—
BARMEN, CHEMNITZ, ELBERFELD, ERLANGEN, ESSEN, SOLINGEN, SOMMERFELD.

Carrying only Steerage Passengers, berthed in the poop; fitted with all modern appliances, electric light, bath-rooms; also special arrangements for proper ventilation, &c.
SEPARATE COMPARTMENTS FOR FEMALES AND FAMILIES.

Fare from London to Adelaide, Melbourne, or Sydney,
£13 13s.

PASSENGER AGENTS IN LONDON: SMITH, SUNDIUS & CO., 158, Leadenhall Street.
FREIGHT   ,,   ,,   H. D. BORET, 93, Leadenhall Street.
   ,,   ,,   ANTWERP: EIFFE & Co., 1, Canal St. Pierre.
   ,,   ,,   HAMBURG: KNÖHR & BURCHARD and ROB. M. SLOMAN, JR.
Agents in Australia: G. von der HEYDE, General Agent, Sydney, 81, Pitt Street.
JAMES SERVICE & CO., Melbourne.
GEO. WILLS & CO., Adelaide.

German shipping line including the fare from London to Adelaide, c.1890

Brunskill, a Westmorland man, but apparently living in Liverpool, went to India c.1890. He left Liverpool on Friday February 12th by the 7.10 a.m. train, arrived in London at 12.30 p.m. then to Dover by the 3.25 train from Charing Cross. He crossed the Channel and took the 7.00 p.m. Pullman train (with sleeper carriages) from Calais via Paris to Brindisi where he arrived at 5.00 p.m. on Sunday afternoon after a journey of approximately 58 hours.[54]

In 1885 the Orient Line advertised a fortnightly service via the Suez Canal to Adelaide, Melbourne and Sydney at a cost of 50 guineas first class, 20 guineas third class and a steerage fare of 16 guineas for men only. Steamers to Melbourne took 43-60 days compared with the 95 day voyage under sail but sailing ships were cheaper and continued on the Australian route into the twentieth century. Through tickets could be booked to Tasmania and New Zealand.[55] Even after the Canal had shortened the distance and length of the voyage to the east and to the Antipodes, not all steam ships used that route. When the Spedding family emigrated to New Zealand in 1908 they went via Cape Town, Melbourne and Sydney.[56]

To reach the west of the United States the route lay either by sea round Cape Horn or by crossing the 52 mile wide Isthmus of Panama to Panama City, where malaria, cholera and other tropical diseases were rife. Until 1855 when a railway crossed the isthmus, the journey had been by small boat, mule and on foot through mosquito infested country. There remained a 3,500 miles voyage to San Francisco. Before the trans-continental railway was built, thousands of migrants trekked overland to the west – more than 1,800 miles from the Mississippi/Missouri area across plains, deserts and mountains, living in ox-drawn covered waggons. Later migrants travelled to the west of Canada and the United States by rail and by water. Dubuque, Iowa, was 1,142 miles from New York. A combined rail and steamer ticket from New York cost £13 10s in 1877.[58] Other emigrants including some in the sample sailed to New Orleans. A newspaper advertisement in 1877 suggested that emigrants to Australia could travel across the Atlantic then overland to the west coast of the United States. Ships from San Francisco sailed monthly to Australia or New Zealand via Honolulu and Fiji.[58] Three years later the Dominion Line quoted the cost of fortnightly passages from Liverpool to New Orleans and Texas via Corunna and Havana as £20 or £6 6s steerage.[59] River steamers then took the emigrants north, some went as far as the upper reaches of the Mississippi and its tributaries, for example, to Dubuque but, as the rail network developed, passenger traffic on river boats tended to decline.

It is not surprising that many early emigrants who had crossed the ocean on tiny brigs never wished to board a ship again. But this changed. By the turn of the century the majority of emigrants still travelled as steerage passengers but, even if conditions in some ships were cramped and uncomfortable, there had been a huge improvement compared with the 1830s. Some emigrants returned for the Great Exhibition of 1851 and we read of many others who visited home. In 1859, it is estimated that about one third of the passengers who sailed to Australia on the *Great Britain* were returning after visiting England. Some had collected their families or parents. Some were re-emigrating.[60] Elizabeth and Eli Foster visited England five times from New Zealand after they emigrated in 1906.[61] By the 1880s men and women were regularly crossing the Atlantic to work for a season. The cost had almost halved since c.1850. Visitors and businessmen came to Britain and the British went to North America. Mr Braithwaite of Kirkby Stephen visited the western United States in 1889-90 and Hall Anderson whose grandparents had emigrated from north Westmorland made an annual visit from Canada to Scotland in the 1890s to sell his cattle and visit his Hilton relatives.[62]

Opposite: Pacific Mail Company - American overland route to London from Australia and New Zealand, c.1880.

The voyage

Some accounts of voyages are remarkably full and interesting. Emigrants to Australasia and those sailing to India commented on many days with only the restless ocean to see, sometimes enlivened by flying fish, birds, whales, sharks and porpoises. Thomas Hetherington mentioned seeing albatross and cape pigeons.[63] In the early years ships sailing to Cape Town, to Australia or New Zealand called at the Cape Verde Islands to replenish supplies before the long run south. St Antonio, in the Cape Verde Islands was described as 'very mountainous and where the King of Portugal sent his prisoners.'[64] Sibella Crozier described passing Madeira – 'a rugged mountain rising abruptly out of the ocean.'[65] In extreme circumstances, sailing ships even called at Rio de Janeiro before heading east across the southern Atlantic. (Map 4.1) Sailing ships to the Antipodes called at Cape Town before the southerly route was adopted. In later years, steamships re-coaled there.

From letters and other accounts we learn of dark, overcrowded and often damp accommodation in steerage. Some had uncongenial companions and the diet was unappetising and monotonous. Food in the early years consisted mainly of salt meat, rice, biscuits with lime juice being doled out to prevent scurvy. When ships in the southern seas sighted vessels travelling in the opposite direction, mail could be exchanged and gifts of fruit or other items received. Water was scarce, often rank with a foul taste. Emigrants were advised to take a water filter and occasionally, especially on the Australian routes, shortage of both water and food was a reality. In later years, food as well as accommodation on board had improved. Norman Spedding remembers good meals on his voyage to New Zealand.[66] When Anthony Tyson went to Canada in 1899 the passengers were 'packed like sardines' in a ship that carried many foreign immigrants.[67] Few accounts mention other passengers; usually only when illness, death, psychological problems or their disagreeable or even criminal behaviour seemed worthy of note.

In 1829 Georgiana Molloy and her husband emigrated to the Swan River Settlement in Western Australia. Mrs Molloy's account of the journey tells of the voyage as far as South Africa which lasted almost three months. Throughout the journey she was 'very sick and weak, still ill, very ill indeed, too weak to attend service' with occasional improvements – 'tolerably well, better,' even an encouraging 'much better than for many weeks.' But it did not last and sickness returned. However, she gives a wealth of interesting details such as a description of the Cape Verde Islands where she thought bananas to be 'long green thick pods like beans but much thicker.' She ate a ripe one – 'it taste[d] like a mixture of cucumber, beans, fig and vegetable marrow, they grow in large clusters and I think are insipid.' She mentions ships seen, the condition of her bees, the crossing

A. Willmore

Steamship leaving Twofold Bay, NSW en route for Sydney or Melbourne

of the line ceremony (in every account of a voyage beyond the equator) a fracas on board and the Christmas feast of 'preserved soup, turkey and fowls and claret.' Presumably she was in better health on Christmas Day! At last Table Mountain and Robben Island were sighted and soon they ate 'fresh figs, peaches and grapes.'[68]

In 1908, when the Spedding family went to New Zealand, the ship called at Tenerife which they thought to be 'full of interest.' In Cape Town they ate ham and eggs during a three day stay – a real treat after the journey and a meal especially appreciated by Cumberland people. The women bought ostrich feathers and silk. Ostrich feathers were hugely fashionable in Edwardian England. In 1889 for example, the value of exported feathers from South Africa was *c.* £348,000; gold was £1.4 million, diamond exports were *c.* £4 million. Ten years later, exports of ostrich feathers were worth c.£500,000 and c.£1 million by 1905.[69]

Thomas Hodgson and his family went to the United States from the Hilton area in the mid-1830s. Thomas wrote that the 'sea was very boisterous.' He and his wife were ill for the whole voyage but their children and other north

Westmorland passengers were less affected. They were 'so thronged together [in their accommodation on the ship] that it made it unwholesome and unnatural to the greatest degree.'[70] One graphic description by Mr T. Raine describes his voyage to New York in 1888 as 'rather rough. … I cleaned my stomach out and then I was all right [but, although] it was very amusing to see the passengers hanging about vomiting … it had a sickly effect on you.'[71]

In 1841 William Shaw and his parents from Cargo near Carlisle, went to Philadelphia via New York. William's mother was seasick throughout the rough 43 day voyage. During a storm 'boxes, water bottles, pans and tins [were] flying about from one side of the ship to the other.' In New York they met friends.[72] There are several references in the sample of meeting known contacts in the new country, some by chance, others by arrangement. A few years later, for example, another Carlisle emigrant was met by a friend when he arrived in Boston. William Shortridge and a friend went to South Africa from Egremont in 1891. He wrote that he had 'met Mr Rigg' in Cape Town and Mrs Thomas, Mrs Denly and Jack Bennet in Natal Bay.[73] Others wrote of meeting friends or acquaintances while en route to their final destination far from the port of arrival. Not only do these references demonstrate that emigrants made contact with Cumbrians who had emigrated earlier but also that, by quoting the names, they would be known in their home communities.

The Shaw's experience in a storm was also not unusual. The *Great Britain* ran into storms during voyages to Australia when sails were destroyed, crockery was smashed and sacks of coal were washed overboard.[74] Daniel Shilton described a storm encountered on his voyage to New Zealand in 1877. All sails except one were stowed, passengers were sent below deck, huge waves struck the ship, torrents of water came through the main hatch and, at the height of the storm the ship had several feet of water on deck. Bulwarks were washed away, iron plate was smashed and 'delved in.' Iron railings on the forecastle and the cabin lifeboat (as well as many other things) were destroyed. Some passengers prayed, others wept but eventually 'I rose up in bed … and to my delight saw a star in the sky … we are saved.'[75] Another account of the same voyage mentions icebergs in the southern ocean.

The Revd. Holme wrote of his voyage to England from Valparaiso in 1856. Rounding Cape Horn 'was much the usual story;' storms, very heavy seas, 'all possible discomfort,' a rolling ship which suffered damage to booms, spars, sails and the 'main yard.' The weather was too bad to hold the Easter service but the South Atlantic was worse with more damage to sails and superstructure. The port bulwarks were washed away 'filling the lower deck with water … everything was mighty uncomfortable.'[76] Such conditions were endured by many but the tropics held their own difficulties. Ships could be becalmed. The heat was intense

Barque in London Docks.

below decks. Passengers on the *Great Britain* described the steerage accommodation as a 'great oven.' Even sleeping on deck and sheltering in the shade of the sails by day brought little relief as they sailed through the tropics.[77]

A voyage across the seas does not immediately suggest the presence of animals. But, ships, especially those going to the newer settlements in the Antipodes, carried livestock including a milch cow and animals including poultry to be slaughtered for food on the journey. Farm animals, poultry, dogs, bees, birds and horses were taken to the new colonies. In 1843 George Ferguson had to help after horses had 'broken out of their stabling' during a storm near Newfoundland. The Powleys of Kirkby Stephen went to the Canterbury district of New Zealand in 1852. The 502 ton *Tasmania,* a wooden three masted barque was only 120 ft long and carried 41 cabin and 90 steerage passengers from London.[78] The emigrants took furniture, crockery, tools, seeds, plants, clothes and extra food for the journey. 'The *Tasmania* carried pigs and sheep. ... Livestock, for fresh meat, were kept in cages on the upper deck. ... Chickens ... were particularly tiresome as the noise of their pecking penetrated the deck' Not only pecking would be heard as an account of voyages on the *Great Britain* makes clear.

The *Great Britain* carried so many animals to Australia that it was said to be like sailing in a farmyard. Passengers were awakened by cocks crowing and noisy pigs, sheep, cattle, dogs, hens and ducks. In 1865, for example, the ship carried 126 sheep, 30 pigs, 2 bullocks, a milch cow, 510 fowl, 286 ducks, 65 geese, 32 turkeys and 6 rabbits.[79] Domestic animals such as horses and dogs and many species of wild birds, plants, shrubs, fruit trees and bushes, and young trees were taken to new lands on emigrant ships.

Thomas Hetherington went to New Zealand on the sailing ship *La Hogue* in 1879. This was a wooden ship of *c.*1,300 tons. He wrote 'we have more room ... than in the Depot. We have a very nice place, the store is [near] and our mess table and bunks is (*sic*) next to it. [We] and another [family] ... all mess together. Mary and me sleep together and the children above. We have a mattress, bolster, three blankets and a rug ... [and] we are not as bad as I expected.' 'The deck was 'just like a farmyard with sheep, pigs, ducks and drakes, hens and cocks ... and a very nice greenhouse.' One of the pigs, being taken to Sydney for an 'exhibition' died. Dogs, small birds and other animals were also carried. But, during a storm, water poured through the skylights, the cabins filled with water, one of the boats was smashed, poultry drowned and the greenhouse and some of the livestock were washed overboard.[80]

Single men and women were given accommodation at opposite ends of the ship separated by married couples with their families. Emigrant literature recommended taking books and anything to help fill the long days at sea. Passengers sailing to New Zealand described how they sewed, knitted and one commented that she had crocheted more than 250,000 stitches on the voyage to make a cover for her piano.[81]

The long voyage to the Antipodes went through rough northern waters, the heat of the tropics and the very cold southern ocean where storms, freezing conditions and the danger of icebergs were common. John Gibson experienced snow and saw 'a great many icebergs' on the way to Melbourne in 1837. It was so cold that 'we could scarce keep heat either in bed or moving about.'[82] In 1851 the *Reliance* sailed from Plymouth. This 750 ton, 145ft long ship carried 313 emigrants including John Errington, his family and his sister Margaret. They arrived in Adelaide after about 14 weeks with 302 on board which suggests that 11 had died – or more if there had been births. The ship had sailed farther south than expected, even the rigging froze.[83] Both warm and cool clothing, bedding, adequate food and water supplies were essential during such a long voyage, usually non-stop and far from land.

Storms, dismasting or being swamped by waves were dangerous but there was also the risk of running into the coast, rocks or sandbanks. Skill and a degree of luck were needed. Navigation depended on clear sightings and even then there were concerns about a ship's position until the use of accurate chronometers became standard. Although the longitude problem was effectively solved in the eighteenth century, it was not until after the mid-nineteenth century that ships ceased to rely on lunar observations. And, that depended on clear skies. In 1837, John Gibson wrote 'we had a narrow escape from running into Goffe's Island in the South Atlantic.'[84] Ships approaching Melbourne were often 50 miles from their calculated position. Fog and darkness added to uncertainties. Thick fog obscured the coast when Henry Mundy's ship approached Port Phillip in 1844 and similar conditions are mentioned in other accounts.[85] Charles Dickens' ship ran aground near Halifax, Nova Scotia but was safely re-floated.[86] In 1843, George Ferguson wrote that his ship 'hit hard ground' after the tide fell but they 'got off' with the next tide. This was near the Gulf of St Lawrence.[87] In 1853-4 Robert Hall's voyage to Canada went well, many huge icebergs were sighted near Labrador but the ship ran aground off Newfoundland causing 'no small stir among the passengers.' After failing to reverse off the rocks, passengers were put on shore, coal was thrown overboard, cargo was unloaded including 'railcar springs, wheels and axles, casks of cutlery, nails, bar iron and boiler plate' which tells of some of Britain's exports. Huts were built on land for shelter. After three days the ship was re-floated and resumed its voyage to Quebec where it arrived 18 days after leaving Liverpool.[88] The *Geltwood,* a Harrington ship was wrecked off the South Australian coast in 1876 but, overall more ships were lost on the north Atlantic route, and not only in the early years as the loss of the *Titanic* in 1912 indicates.[89] Fire was always a hazard at sea. A fire on the *Piako* in 1880 was successfully extinguished. During that voyage to New Zealand Thomas Fallowfield's wife gave birth to a daughter named Clara Piako.[90]

Outbreaks of disease too could be disastrous on crowded emigrant ships. Infectious diseases such as measles or smallpox could occur but more usual were the twin problems of diarrhoea and vomiting which caused illness among adults and often resulted in the death of young children. In 1838, George and Sarah Brunskill sailed from Plymouth bound for Australia. In a single day both their young children died as they crossed the Bay of Biscay. In all, 17 children died during that three month voyage to Australia and three were born, one of whom also died.[91] John and Sarah Walker from Aspatria lost their son on the voyage and their daughter died soon after their arrival in Australia.[92] When Joseph and Ann Simpson emigrated to South Australia *c.*1850, their daughter was among seventeen children who died and 'was buried in the deep ... [in] the Bay of Biscay.'[93]

Voyage duration was variable under sail. Several in the sample were among the first emigrants to New Zealand. John Nixon, his wife and two daughters had free passages on the *Lord Auckland*. They left in August 1841 and arrived at Nelson in February 1842; a voyage of five months. The Walker family from Keswick sailed on the *Thomas Harrison* in 1842.

The Vipond family from Garrigill were on the *Wellington* for almost six months in 1881 but the *Howrah,* sailing in 1875 from Gravesend to Wellington took only 92 days. The *Great Britain*'s voyage to Australia in 1861 took 62 days. In 1879 Thomas Hetherington wrote that on some days *La Hogue*, a wooden three masted ship carrying 400 passengers, covered 200 miles, on others the ship could appear to be stationary. *La Hogue* carried a cargo of wool on the return journey.[94] William Shortridge's voyage to South Africa on the *Lismore Castle* in 1891 took about 31 days.[95]

When ships neared their destination, emigrants gained a first view of the land to which they had committed their lives. Four months after the last sight of land Thomas Hetherington saw the New Zealand coast for the first time. There were 'mountains all around, some covered with snow' and he looked forward to 'fresh meat and potatoes.' Hartley Dawson also went to New Zealand. He wrote that there were not many houses at Bluff Harbour and the view was of 'an abundance of peaks capped with snow.'[96] While few mentioned the topography or appearance of their destination, the relief of arriving at last is mentioned by several correspondents. On arrival at Wellington in 1872, one emigrant wrote '[I saw] large mountains ... cows and sheep were grazing ... this was the most beautiful sight I ever saw.'[97]

Whatever the shortcomings and privations on the voyage the time to leave the ship had come. This meant the severing of the final link with home – a known environment. Fellow passengers had become either companions or people from whom they wished to distance themselves but were part of a shared experience. After disembarking they were 'all assembled on the wharf, our luggage around us ... like birds ... [who] did not know where to fly. ... Each stood asking advice of his neighbours.'[98] What lay ahead? The future was unknown.

Chapter 5:
Arrival: First Steps in a New Land

First Impressions
North America

The voyage was over. Emigrants disembarked and dispersed. Everything and everywhere was different from home. Although many of those with professional qualifications and particular skills settled in towns or cities, others chose instead to take land or homesteads and follow a new vocation. Some never moved from their first destination; others changed their occupations and their location at least once. New York was already a large city when John Fowler arrived from London in 1830. He had sailed past 'rich cultivated lands ... handsome villas ... and fortifications.' He saw Castle Garden, many churches and public buildings and 'crowds of shipping in the Bay' but was 'assailed by bugs' in his lodgings in the city and mosquitoes caused 'torment beyond measure.' Shops and stores sold 'goods of every description from every nation.' It was a 'scene of great bustle and business.' New streets such as Broadway were spacious but older streets were 'irregular;' comments repeated in later years by other visitors.[1]

In 1838 J. S. Buckingham, also from London went from New York by sea to Charleston. He sailed past the 'heights of Brooklyn [and] the beautiful villas on Staten Island.' The view as his ship (towed by a steamer) passed through the Narrows was 'among the finest pictures of maritime scenery that can be imagined.'[2] Both these descriptions of New York roughly coincide with the arrival of the Hodgson and Hall families from north Westmorland before they moved on to join friends and relations in Pittsburgh. From Charleston, Mr Buckingham went to New Orleans where levées protected the city from flooding. It was 'one of the most expensive places in the world.' Four hundred ships were in the harbour where bales of cotton awaited loading. Five hundred steam vessels worked on the Mississippi along the 1,200 miles to the Missouri junction and beyond.[3] Several Cumbrians in the sample landed at New Orleans and continued to their destinations on Mississippi steamboats. Not all travellers appreciated the grandeur of the Mississippi. Charles Dickens described the river as 'liquid mud ... [a] foul stream.' The 'marshes swarm[ed] with frogs,' there were a 'few wretched cabins' beside the river, mosquitoes were a problem and 'it was very hot.[4]

William Crook from Bolton le Moor was in New York in 1832 where, about ten years later, Dickens commented that parts were 'pleasing' but in other areas poverty, 'filth and wretchedness' prevailed.[5] In a letter William thanked his sister for a watch chain. Four years later his brother George Crook, also in New York, wrote that the city was very crowded with 'strangers of every colour and clime.' He requested 'a large shipment of preserves – strawberries, gooseberries etc.' which 'would be very acceptable.' Later in the year his letter tells of their crop of grapes – 'a splendid dessert,' and acknowledges receipt of a newspaper and the preserves. Apart from the strawberry which had 'fermented a little,' all were in 'good order.' At such an early date it is remarkable that home-made jam should be sent and had survived the journey. Shrimps had also been sent but they had not kept well! However good life was, emigrants still hankered after familiar things from home.[6]

After quarantine at Staten Island, immigrants went to Castle Garden, the main reception area for New York from *c*.1850 until Ellis Island opened in 1892. Castle Garden removed much of the risk of fraudulent and criminal exploitation of new arrivals which had been rife. The St George, St Andrew or St Patrick Societies had previously helped immigrants avoid 'the tricks of the swindlers.'[7] Approved lodging houses were recommended and onward travel arrangements made. After 1892, immigrants were subjected to careful scrutiny and questioning at Ellis Island. Correct documents and money were needed before being allowed entry. If rejected the immigrant was sent back to Britain. In Canada, Grosse Island, about 30 miles from Quebec, performed a similar function. From 1832 it was the quarantine station and all were subjected to rigorous checks. During the summer season when the St Lawrence was ice-free, ships sailed to Quebec and Montreal. Samuel Strickland, from Suffolk, sailed up the St Lawrence in 1825 and passed through wild country where wolves could be heard howling. Farther on they saw many islands and 'shores dotted with farmhouses and adorned with fine gardens and orchards.' He was filled with 'wonder and delight' at everything he saw and believed Canada to be 'the most beautiful country in the world.'[8] Quebec's harbour was crowded with ships and had good lodging houses for new arrivals but they were recommended not to 'tarry long.' The fort overlooking the city was 'much higher than Edinburgh,' on a 'precipitous cliff,' houses, churches and the cathedral were roofed with tin – a 'splendid look on a bright sunshiny day but roads and footpaths were intolerably bad.'[9]

Samuel Strickland reached Montreal in 45 days from London. He described it then, as others did in the mid-1830s as 'a handsome town' but there were also 'narrow garbage strewn streets with mean houses, no drainage or sewage, ill-clad children, drunks, lodging houses and much unpleasantness.' Diseases, even cholera were constant worries in the summer.[10] Charles Dickens described the St Lawrence near Montreal as beautiful – 'a noble stream' winding its way among the 'thousand green and richly wooded islands.'[11] Captain George Ferguson, a Cumberland man, who was stationed in Montreal in 1844 chose to live 46 miles

G.H.Andrews

River steamer on the St Lawrence, near Montreal, 1840s

away at 'one of the most beautiful and healthy spots in Canada,' connected by a daily steamer service on the St Lawrence with Montreal and Quebec.[12] By 1850 a fleet of 'large and commodious' steamers on the St Lawrence each with a speed equal to that of an R.M.S trans-Atlantic steamship had cut the journey from Buffalo to Montreal to less than four days.[13]

The majority of emigrants in the sample left no record of their first impressions and only a few described their new surroundings. Jack Hudson described the countryside in southern Africa as 'very mountainous, like Wasdale but not so high' with a 'beautiful waterfall' nearby.'[14] George Barrington, from London, arrived at Botany Bay, New South Wales, as a convict in 1791. He thought the coast was reminiscent of that near Portsmouth and commented on the Governor's impressive stone house in Sydney, the officers' brick houses, and log houses all covered with shingles or thatch.[15] John Wood, his wife and children arrived at Sydney on September 13th 1818. They were invited to attend a reception at Government House. 'Of course, we went and were received by the Governor and his lady as first settlers. We were treated with great civility.'[16] In the 1830s John Gibson thought Sydney was 'most elegantly built' beside 'the most splendid and large natural bay.'[17] In 1844 the Mundy family from Buckinghamshire, found Melbourne roads mainly un-surfaced but commented on the fine public buildings, banks and hotels.[18] George and Sarah Brunskill arrived in South Australia in 1839. They landed at 'one of the most sandy places you can imagine swarming with fleas' before walking to Adelaide across 'ground [that] appeared burnt up.' Their luggage was carried on a bullock cart to a hotel where they stayed until the rest of their belongings, including a prefabricated house could be taken to their land which they named Sandford after George's Westmorland birthplace. Sarah remarked that there was no 'twilight as in England.'[19] An English immigrant described the coastal scenery near Brisbane as reminiscent of the 'hills around Cambridge.' Clearly this was not the view of a Cumbrian who could not have described such topography as hilly.[20]

Letters often quoted prices of food and of agricultural produce and gave family news but few describe the landscape, birds, animals, their new home and daily life. Several refer to bedbugs, mosquitoes, fleas, flies, caterpillars, locusts and other troublesome insects. One correspondent mentioned seeing fireflies and hummingbirds in New York, another wrote about the grapevines, fig and orange trees and the vegetables she grew in her Adelaide garden. To relatives at home such comments would have conveyed the difference between a garden in South Australia and Cumberland. But the vegetables would be familiar. Occasionally letters included measurements or sketches of the new home. Mr and Mrs Molloy were near Fremantle, W. Australia in 1834 and later moved to Geographe Bay. A letter includes a sketch plan of their house that was 'capable of being enlarged.[21]

In 1830 when Joseph Dover wrote that 'the poorest family in Pittsburgh lives better than the richest in Milburn' he was sending a reassuring message to his family that all was well and his prospects were good.[22] He wrote of catastrophic floods in 1832, caused when the 'Allegamy and Mongahela (sic) rivers ... that intersect each other immediately below Pittsburgh and form the Ohio river [were] in torrent.'[23] In other correspondence from him and from other north Westmorland emigrants in or near Pittsburgh we learn that newspapers were exchanged and that an almanac had been sent home. Thomas Hodgson described Pittsburgh in 1832 as a place 'of all nations and all colours ... Irish, Welsh, Dutch and Germans is (sic) very numerous.' We learn that to reach the market they had to cross the river, nearly half a mile wide, that one of the bridges was 'down' and the roads were very bad. 'People come many miles to the Pittsburgh market' which was 'crowded ... like Brough Hill [Fair].' Tobacco, whisky and apples were 'all very plentiful.' Whisky at 36 cents per gallon 'is used as common water.'[24] John Hodgson sent a map to Hilton in 1848 to show 'our market town' of 40,000 inhabitants. 'You will observe ... the city lies between two rivers. ... Eight miles up and one mile back from the river you will see my house.' By then he was a miller and 'some of my flour [may] go to England.' He wrote that there was employment and 'good money' for anyone who will work. Some north Westmorland men were in the salt works, others were 'sinking shafts' or were

Prefabricated iron buildings were exported from England

miners or builders. But there are few comments in any letters about the home and immediate surroundings or social life. In 1832 William Crook commented that the nearest church in New York was 'wealthy and respectable' and his 'comfortable bedroom and neat parlour [were] tastefully furnished' with mahogany chairs and a sofa bed. This would give his family reassurance that he was living in a good neighbourhood and helped his family in Cumbria to visualise his surroundings.[25]

More than 50 years later, in 1888, Mr R. Harrison was in New York. He walked on Broadway and Fifth Avenue, visited Brooklyn and drank iced lemonade but not alcohol. 'The place is full of [saloons]. It is a great country for drink and wickedness.' He moved on to Buffalo, NY where he intended to make 'a good pile of money.' There were many different nationalities – 'I have always found them nice fellows.' He wrote of the trams and electric light – not to be found in his Eden Valley village at that time but also 'bed bugs [that were] too plentiful to be pleasant.' He had read newspapers from home and refers to the new Croglin waterworks. Mr Harrison 'would not come back to Ainstable and work for them old farmers for a fortune. I am only sorry I did not get out before I did' but he had not met 'any nice girls since [he] left the old country.'[26]

Pittsburgh and New York were very different from Little York where William Atkinson was at about the same time; but which Little York? At such an early date it was probably in New Jersey not Illinois. In 1831 William thought it was 'a very strange place – the streets run straight through the town.' He worked on the land and while 'ploughing among the stumps beside the woods' he heard sounds which caused him to be afraid as there were 'bears and wolfs' (*sic*) in the forest.[27] In only a few words, William created a picture of a place very different from his Westmorland home, of a small town built on a grid pattern, of a country where wild animals roamed in the forest and although cleared land was being cultivated, massive tree stumps remained.

In contrast to New York or recently cleared land with a nearby small town, Captain Ferguson and his family lived on an estate close to the St Lawrence River in Lower Canada in the 1840s. He had rented an old French house with verandahs, gardens, two ice houses and a 140 acre farm. The family had a staff of six, including a butler and clearly lived well. Captain Ferguson wrote that he would willingly pay the 'passage out but not home again' for a good cook or nurse from home. His description of the estate and its location would help his family to imagine the setting but who in Cumberland could understand the reality of that great river and its surroundings with only the Eden and other small Cumbrian rivers for comparison?

In the 1880s George Calcott wrote from Texas that the very high temperatures were difficult to 'get used to.' His house had only single walls because wood was scarce and timber had to be 'hauled out into the country.'[28] Such a building would afford little protection from the heat.

In 1907 Matthew Lee, a Great Salkeld emigrant to Canada received the *C & W Herald* weekly and wrote that Manitoba was 'just the country for a poor man to start in [and] for mature emigrants to place their children in a better position.' Lake Manitoba had a railway, post office, telephone connections and a good bracing climate. There were opportunities for sport and, it seems, a good social life. It was 'a good place to go.'[30] In 1913, a Westmorland family in the Cariboo district, British Columbia wrote that there were 'more Indians than whites' and, in spite of 'thousands [of in-migrants] arriving every week ... vast tracts were still unoccupied.' At first one lived in the 'primitive conditions of an unopened country' but the first log cabin became a chicken house once a new home was built. British Columbia was beautiful and 'to travel here is never to be forgotten.'[31]

New Zealand

At the other side of the world, Francis Jollie from Brampton was one of several Cumbrians and their families to arrive at the New Zealand Company's new settlement at Nelson in early 1842. From his letters, from newspapers and other publications there is a wealth of information about Nelson's early days. Tracks and house sites had already been marked by surveyors when the first emigrant ships arrived. Building materials and other supplies, bullocks, a milch cow and calf, goats, pigs, dogs, cats and poultry had been brought from England. Some goods were traded for pigs, wood and potatoes from the Maoris. 'Wooden houses, tents, sheds formed of boughs, houses with clay walls and thatched roofs and heaps of goods and chattels … were scattered around.' But cultivable land was scarce. The area was 'covered by low herbage' with timber nearby. Much of this low herbage was in fact, flax, fern, woodland and swamp with some grassland in the Waimea area, all of which needed a great deal of work to convert into good farm land. Until roads were made access to the country district was difficult. Nelson was 'a small clearing strewn with tents, whares (*sic*) and cottages set among forbidding mountains.'[32] But, its climate was good.

Horses, cattle and sheep had arrived but the settlement was 'overrun by rats.' Good terriers, traps and guns were required. Seeds of all kinds, soft fruits such as gooseberries, currants and raspberries, grass and clover seed, potatoes, rhubarb and tree seeds were also needed.[33] By March 1842 when the population was approaching 2,000, an advertisement in the *Nelson Examiner* offered furniture, agricultural implements, cooking stoves and 'all indispensable items for emigrants' to be shipped from London, Birmingham or Sheffield. Even in the early years, it seems that provided that emigrants had capital, everything needed for a comfortable life could be bought and sent from England. Some emigrants had taken prefabricated houses with them. But establishing the new settlements, clearing and fencing land, preparing for cultivation, building bridges, roads and other infrastructure necessities could not be bypassed or eased by having money, especially when few wage labourers were in the colony.

In June 1842 Francis Jollie reported that they 'were progressing … on the whole, very satisfactorily.'[34] By the end of the year, about half of the inhabitants had houses or cabins. The rest lived in tents or huts. Warehouses, a court and a gaol had been built. A temporary church, school and other community buildings were soon erected. 'Town acres' had been allocated and settlers were 'comfortably ensconced upon them.' Building materials were 'excessively dear and scarce' and although coal and limestone were found nearby, initially there was no mortar. Bricks, made on site for chimneys were expensive. The town was situated 'advantageously,' but outlying land was either 'far too hilly' or 'too low and swampy.' Workers and capital were needed. By December 1842, Francis Jollie was no longer a 'dweller in tents.' He had a comfortable mansion, 'the largest in town' which had cost £400 compared with 'modest conventional cottages' at £100 or a wooden cabin at £40. He employed a father and son named Graham from Renwick, Cumberland; 'steady, honest folks,' to clear, drain and cultivate his land. [35]

Some of the Cumbrians known to be in Nelson in 1842 were John Nixon and family from Ireby, Dinah Bowes, Daniel and Eleanor Richardson and family, Thomas and Mary Marsden from Hensingham and John Walker and his family from Keswick. John and Sarah Walker went under the New Zealand Company's auspices – others may also have sailed as part of the scheme. Eight years later, John Walker's brother George and his family from Grasmere arrived followed by their brother Edward in 1862 who had probably having been in Australia first. William and Harriet Gill from Grasmere emigrated to Nelson c.1857. It seems almost certain that communication from earlier emigrants had encouraged others in the Grasmere area to choose New Zealand and some went to Nelson. It also indicates a propensity to emigrate from the central Lakes area. The Spedding family thought Nelson was a very busy port when they called there en route for Greymouth in 1908.

The Canterbury Settlement scheme on New Zealand's South Island dates from 1850. A year later the *Lyttelton Times* reported that the population was 1,100 but new settlers moved quickly from the coast to the plains. Barracks and 'habitations' – anything from 'iron stores to turf cabins or blanket tents [had] sprung up.' Of the first five cows, only two survived. One fell over a cliff and two died after eating poisonous vegetation.' During the first year advertisements included sheep, heifers, bulls, horses and milk cows and other items ranging from seeds and fruit trees to boats, frame and prefabricated houses, garden sheds, wire for fencing, doors, windows, tools, dungarees, gunpowder, chairs, sherry, brandy, whisky, canned herrings, jam, sugar, butter, slates, bricks, and pianos.[36] A serious fire in 1851 destroyed many dwellings in the nearby Riccarton bush and 'raged … to the edge of farms and houses.' All timber was burnt – a great misfortune in an area where wood was so scarce. None was left even to construct fences.[37]

Christchurch lay nine miles inland from Lyttelton and access was a problem. The first few miles were 'steep, narrow [and] inaccessible to carts;' suitable only for pack horses. Everything had to be carried. Once the ridge, 'a hill perpendicular,' had been surmounted the road was good and level. A new route was planned and progress had been made apart from crossing the Raupo Swamp. But there was 'great disappointment' at the state and appearance of Christchurch among new arrivals. The land was swampy with dense scrub and although it was 'in a good situation' it was 'decidedly ugly' with only 'a few woe-begone houses.'[38] Francis Jollie's brother Edward was a surveyor engaged in the early planning of both Lyttelton and Christchurch. He also explored much of the interior and is commemorated in Christchurch Cathedral.[39]

Some accounts written by emigrants strike a cautious or critical tone and balance the generally positive, encouraging and even exaggerated optimism of guides and publicity material. For example, several comments published in *Sidney's Emigrant's Journal* painted a bleak picture of the Canterbury region and other destinations. Fertile ground was 'extremely rare. ... Mountains and swamps occupy three quarters of the country.' Rural land, allotted to settlers in Nelson, Wellington and, to a lesser degree, in other new settlements, could be as much as 100 miles distant and was almost impossible to reach for lack of roads and bridges. 'The climate is damp; wet in winter [and] soils are either rich or barren.' Clearing the land was expensive and prices quoted for wool sales were 'over-optimistic.'[40]

In 1853, new settlers arriving at Lyttelton were greeted by hail, rain and wind with a view of snow covered hills but by then there were 'wide streets, neat houses, shops, stores, hotels, coffee rooms an emigration barracks, police court, a neat sea wall and an excellent and convenient jetty.'[41] However, six years later an immigrant thought that Lyttelton was 'devoid of natural beauty' like 'a cartload of boxes chucked out on a hillside' and 'the walk to Christchurch ... a depressing and uninteresting' place, was 'dusty and unpleasant' through a 'flax swamp.' The 'streets, all running at right angles were more like riverbeds with tussock grass everywhere; ... [and] houses like packing cases [lay] about in fields.' Outside the settlement 'a monotonous plain stretched to the south as far as the eye could see.' It was 'a howling wilderness.'[42] But it was this plain and that wilderness that, after initial years of hard work, provided so many settlers with farmland and a means to independence and success. In 1857, an emigrant who had been farming near Christchurch for five years wrote to the *Carlisle Patriot* that although he was 'plagued by rats and mice' others who were prepared for rough living at first should join him.[43] By 1862, Christchurch had a number of two and three storey houses, a theatre, some large stone buildings, a substantial Town Hall was under construction, the streets were being surfaced and the 'swampy banks of the Avon' had become ... a well-built and thriving city.'[44]

Cumbrians were among the first to arrive in both Canterbury and Otago – as they had been in Nelson. When Edward Bland Atkinson of Bongate, Appleby landed in Otago in 1848, he 'enjoyed a meal of fish and sweet potatoes with the natives.'[45] Cumbrians in Canterbury include Charles and George Leech from Penrith, Thomas, Isaac and Edward Wilson, their families, parents and siblings from Grasmere, Jonathan Brown of Oughterside, Henry Moffat, his nephew Joseph, his niece and either sister or sister in law from Catterlen, Thomas Bell

Prefabricated iron bungalow

Howson from Skelton, Daniel Shilton, John and Mary Salkeld and three brothers from Carlisle, John, Michael and Paul Studholme. Henry B. Graham and his family from Carlisle went to Dunedin in 1848, nine months after the first ships arrived. He took his printing press and only a few weeks after arriving he published the first edition of the fortnightly *Otago News*. Henry Graham's effort in editing and printing the paper in his small wooden cottage has left a valuable insight into the first year of the new settlement. Unfortunately, his health was poor and he caused controversy with some of his views but he continued until the end of 1850 when he became ill and died a few weeks later.[46]

When the first emigrants arrived at Dunedin, 'town land' had been allocated but this was on hillsides or in swamp and not even temporary buildings existed. Streets were paths cut through thick bush. The hills were interspersed with deep gullies and the way from Port Chalmers to Dunedin was over steep hills by a narrow track, impassable in rain. Streams were crossed on stepping stones. The path led through 'flax, soft clay … over rocks, across hills and hollows' and 'a false step would precipitate the traveller into the waters of the bay.'[47] Settlers built simple cottages, made basic furniture and cultivated gardens. 'Houses, tents and primitive rustic dwellings [were] scattered over the landscape.' By the end of the first year, the town had about 140 buildings; 100 were mainly wattle and daub, 40 were 'more substantial' and two of these were of stone.[48]

The settlers in these new communities tried to maintain 'the social customs and manner of life to which they had been accustomed … and the future seemed assured.'[49] As elsewhere in New Zealand, Dunedin celebrated its first anniversary with a regatta, sports, horse races, church services and a ball in the Commercial Hotel. Gradually the central area was cleared, swampy land was drained, gardens were fenced and the stone or wooden public buildings included hotels, a combined church and school, shops, a saw mill and, a few months later, a library. Crops were harvested in gardens and on some suburban land but roads were nonexistent or inadequate and for years communication with other settlements was possible only by sea. A railway connected Christchurch with Lyttelton in 1867, Dunedin with Port Chalmers in 1872 and Christchurch with Dunedin in 1878. When the Powley family from Kirkby Stephen arrived in 1853 Dunedin was developing but it looked 'rather dilapidated' and the country around was still 'a desolate dreary wasteland.' Fifteen years later roads, bridges and houses had been built and farmers were rearing livestock and harvesting crops. As with Nelson and Wellington, progress was slowed by periodic supply problems, unemployment, lack of investment and isolation. However, by 1858, when Christopher Robinson (John Powley's brother in law) and his family arrived from Mallerstang, Westmorland, Dunedin was experiencing 'growing prosperity' and soon the 'bustle and turmoil of trade and commerce' reigned. [50]

When gold was discovered on the west coast if New Zealand's South Island, the 'rush' began.[51] Until 1861 the main focus of the economy had been agriculture. Gold attracted thousands to Otago as it had done in California and Victoria. The prospect of finding a fortune only a few days walk away sent Otago men in search of gold. Dunedin was almost deserted and soon thousands arrived by sea and to new west coast ports to join the trek to the diggings. Finds in other areas provoked new 'rushes' and the influx of thousands of hopeful migrants. Walter Irving from Little Corby near Carlisle searched for gold in British Columbia before moving to Dunedin in 1864. Other Cumbrians in the area were Joseph and William Mawson, Thomas and Elizabeth Fallowfield from north Westmorland and Hartley Dawson from the Duddon Valley. Several went to the west coast gold field but most moved on to other destinations and followed other occupations. John Ewart of Carlisle emigrated in the 1850s and after some time in Blenheim, went to the west coast gold field. Presumably he did not make a fortune because he joined the police force. Stephen Madgen from Nenthead followed gold from Australia to New Zealand – which he thought a 'very rough country.'[52] Eventually he returned Australia where he seems to have been at diggings in Queensland.

The ports of Greymouth and Hokitika on the west coast developed in the 1860s because of gold discoveries nearby and connected the diggings with the outside world. Both settlements were built on swampy ground, subject to flooding and as on other 'gold' fields, many prospectors lived in tents. Tented shops and inns were replaced by 'flimsy and ill-constructed' buildings. More than 15,000 diggers arrived at Hokitika by sea during 1865 when the town had only *c.*250 dwellings and hotels.[53] As new finds were made camps were abandoned and the diggers moved on. Kaniere attracted hundreds overnight and soon its population was similar to that of Hokitika. Arthur Head from Braithwaite went to join his brother in the Hokitika and Kaniere area in 1872. Skelton Head had run a hotel, possibly since the gold rush days. After working as a miner, Arthur also opened a hotel. When the Spedding family arrived at Greymouth harbour in 1908 low clouds covered the hills and 'the town looked rather grey.' But, the port was 'a hive of industry' and the town was 'brisk, business seemed to be flourishing.' The 'covered verandahs in front of all the shops over the footpaths seemed a wonderful idea.' and soon they 'rated [the town] very highly.'[54]

Several from West Cumberland followed gold to the Coromandel Peninsula area in the North Island. Not all were prospectors; there was employment in mines. James Richardson from Preston Patrick in south Westmorland went to the gold mines at Kuatona in the 1860s. William and Ann Sanderson from Harrington went to Thames because of gold but moved to Great Barrier Island and became farmers. Sim Dalgliesh Currie and his brother in law Frank Perkins were miners in Waikino, a gold town near Thames in 1906. Their families followed and within a few years other members of the family had joined them. As elsewhere, here there is evidence of clusters both of origin and destination. Others from West Cumberland were in the Coromandel and Thames area.[55]

Coal was also found on the west coast. Robert and Jane Troughear went to Dobson, near Greymouth in 1884. Robert was a civil engineer engaged in developing mines, he was not a hewer of coal. A major cluster of emigrant settlers in Runanga, a government township about five miles from Greymouth where a large group of miners and their families from West Cumberland had settled. The party of miners and their families who had emigrated together in 1908 settled in Runanga. In the early twentieth century the Spedding family's first home in Runanga, near Greymouth on New Zealand's South Island was a 'two roomed bach' (*sic*) with sacks on the floor in the midst of 'thick bush.' Runanga was so new that it was 'only just being laid out and streets formed but some West Cumberland families who arrived at the same time were able to move immediately into their permanent home. A builder was engaged to construct the Spedding's house – with three rooms and a large back verandah.'[29] However, descriptions of an emigrant's new home and everyday life are rare in the sources. Isaac Spedding's brother, Robert and others were already there. West Cumberland people included the Gainford, Ritson, Glover, Braithwaite, Lithgow, Hetherington, Brereton and Satterthwaite families 'and many others'.[56] The men worked in the coal mines. Fawcett Simpson from Egremont whose family followed in 1909 and two other West Cumberland miners were on a 'contract ticket.' The mines had been bought by the government in 1903 and employed 240 men with an output of 500 tons of bituminous coal daily.[58]

These West Cumberland miners chose a different destination from the hundreds who went to South Africa but they continued mining in the new country. Some later changed their occupation. After working in the Runanga mines William and John Simpson of Egremont became farmers near Huntly.[58] Christopher Thomas Kearton emigrated from Cleator but did not become a miner. He arrived at Wellington with his wife in 1909 and went by train to Studholme where they leased 50 acres of land and a large wooden house. Although they were near friends, Sarah found the change of life style and 'primitive conditions ... very degrading and hard to accept.' After a few years they moved to Christchurch.[59] Clusters of Cumbrians were in many locations in New Zealand. At least 10 were in or near Timaru in 1913.

Fewer in the sample went to the North Island, but the real total may have been greater. Henry Atkinson of Windermere was an engineer. He went to Auckland in 1863 to supervise the building of a gasworks, later becoming its manager. New Plymouth was founded in 1841 and became 'a quiet little community devoted to agriculture ... a minor settlement ... snugly situated near the beach.' Several Cumbrian families settled in the fertile hinterland, the Taranaki. James and Jane Turnbull and their children from Nichol Forest arrived during the Maori troubles in 1862 and became farmers. Gilbert and Edith Elliott from West Cumberland went first to Maryborough, Victoria (probably because of gold) but moved to Inglewood in the Taranaki *c.*1883. Philip C. Threlkeld also settled there and gave the name Inglewood to the community to remind him of the Inglewood Forest in Cumberland. Aaron Park who emigrated to New Plymouth from Egremont *c.*1913 had a grocery business. Mr and Mrs A. Gate moved south to Lyttelton in 1891 from the Taranaki area.

New Zealand lies on the edge of the 'Ring of Fire' and earthquakes have caused great damage on several occasions since British settlement began. For example, in 1842, 1848, 1855, 1888, 1929 and 1931 when Napier was destroyed and more than 250 people were killed. Wellington had a 'straggling appearance' in 1841, with a population of 3,000 and a further 700 in the surrounding area. Land was being cleared in the rural district and 'the whole Port Nicholson country would [soon] be open to the agriculturalist.'[60] But in October 1848 a violent earthquake followed by three months of after-shocks caused great destruction in Wellington and the surrounding district. Even across the sea, Nelson, the Wairau valley and Cloudy Bay areas in the South Island suffered damage. In Wellington 'the whole of that portion of the town deemed to be the most substantial and the most valuable of buildings both public and private [had been] either totally overthrown or reduced to a mass of dangerous ruins.' Stores, banks, the hospital, places of worship, government buildings, the gaol and houses were destroyed. A letter of appeal for help was sent to the Colonial Secretary in London in March

1849.[61] Charles R. Carter and his wife lived in a tent when they arrived in Wellington in 1850 until sufficient land could be cleared to build a house but they did not refer to the earthquake damage that must have been still evident.[62]

Seven years later, in January 1855 an even stronger earthquake, felt throughout the country, hit Wellington. Repaired buildings were destroyed and the coast rose by more than three feet. Farm buildings were damaged in rural districts. Landslides blocked roads. The Graham family from Appleby arrived in Wellington only three weeks later, intending to stay but they were so shocked by the damage that they moved on to Auckland.[63] When the Spedding family approached Wellington in 1908 after a voyage of almost 16,000 miles and saw their new country for the first time, they thought 'it looked very good to us.' The Speddings spent a few days there en route for Greymouth. Wellington was an attractive and busy city where electric trams, cabs and lorries moved 'in a perpetual procession.' They rode on trams 'to all the suburbs' and the shops were a great attraction.[64]

In 1888 a severe earthquake struck the Christchurch region. Buildings there and in the surrounding area were damaged and the quake was again felt throughout the island and in the southern part of the North Island. These violent but widely separated events and the many minor tremors felt at other times were unsettling but did not deter emigrants who may, of course, been unaware of New Zealand's geological history. There are also several volcanoes. Mount Ruapehu erupted more than 30 times from c.1840 to 1914 and Ngaruho had a similar level of activity but as active volcanoes in the Taupo region are far from settlements; they have not been a threat to life and property. William and Thomas Richardson from Culgaith and Hutton Troutbeck from Blencow went to Eskdale near Napier in 1860. At that time, less than 10 years after its foundation, Napier's population was 500 – no more than 1,500 in the whole Hawkes Bay area where only a few years later landholders had 850,000 sheep and 12,000 cattle. Napier was 'rather a dull place to vegetate in … [but was] … a healthy, steady-going prosperous little place with no great excitement.'[65] When Mount Tarawera erupted in 1886, Hutton Troutbeck had to move all his livestock back to Hawkes Bay. His land was covered by ash.[66]

During later years, letters from New Zealand still mention wild scenery densely covered by trees, fern or flax, dry ravines and impassable rocky or snow covered mountains such as Mount Egmont on the North Island or the Southern Alps. But, after more than 30 years of settlement much of the land in New Zealand had been 'tamed' by a committed and energetic population. The Colonist's Aid Corporation in conjunction with the New Zealand government gave free passages or free land in the late 1880s to emigrants who settled near Feilding. William Benson from Greystoke and several others went to Marton, only a few miles from Feilding in 1880. Gradually the whole area was transformed from impenetrable undergrowth and forest into good agricultural land and after four years of hard work, William's purchase of 250 acres near Marton was fenced, converted to grass and a house and farm buildings had been constructed. New Zealand was a thriving country.[67]

Australia

It is interesting that few letters written in the early years from New South Wales refer to convicts who must have been visible. They 'were marched through the town to and from work.' Of the 4,500 in the Sydney district in 1820 up to 2,000 lodged in barracks in Sydney itself. Others were in Parramatta, Windsor, Liverpool and Bathurst. The convicts either worked for the government or were assigned to settlers – the females as servants and the men as agricultural workers. Other females worked in a factory in Parramatta. Convicts built roads, bridges and buildings as well as clearing and cultivating land.[68] George Barrington from London seems to have been a 'higher class convict.' At Parramatta, he had 'a snug cottage' in a 'delightful situation ... in the midst of pleasant gardens' unlike convicts in barracks who undertook hard manual work. Skilled convicts were assigned to necessary crafts and trades or as agricultural labourers.[69] By 1835 20,000 convicts in New South Wales were assigned workers. More than 2,200 others worked on roads or were required to break stones. A further 6,475 convicts were in Van Diemen's Land.[70]

In 1819 Mrs Wood wrote from New South Wales that 'the prisoners must be kept down by worthy and respectable families but some are treated no better than slaves ... and this makes them worse not better.[71] Already, 'the investment John had brought out' had enabled them to buy 1,600 acres of which 130 acres had been cleared. Government papers dated 1822 state that John Wood had been given 1,500 areas at Bringelly; one of 48 grants made at that time.[72] Certainly it seems from Mrs Wood's letters that they had 3,000 acres and 24 servants in 1821. The land was thickly wooded and had to be 'burnt off.' They were building a house, trees were being felled and 'in a generation or two it will be a beautiful country.' They had more than 1,000 sheep, five horses, two carts and a gig. Thirty milch cows would soon arrive. All kinds of fruit including lemons were grown.[73] In 1820, only 333 free female settlers were in New South Wales, some of whom were the wives of convicts but most were wives of male emigrants.[74]

The 1828 Census shows that Mrs Wood had died and that Mr Wood's workforce was almost entirely composed of convicted men under sentence or ticket of leave.[75] Being granted a ticket of leave was, in effect, being placed on probation. But bushrangers and aborigines were a problem. In 1843 Mrs Wood's daughter, Mary wrote from Sidmouth Valley, New South Wales 'the aborigines are very troublesome in … parts of the Colony. The government will not give sufficient protection to the inhabitants. … It is dreadful to think how they destroy property and frequently human beings. … It is utterly impossible to civilise them.' In other letters she refers to the problem of alcohol among the aborigine population.[76] Bushrangers were outlaws – escaped convicts or others living rough because of destitution or fleeing from the authorities. They lived off the land or survived by robbery. Some rural settlers helped them but were more likely to be the target for their attacks. Bushrangers were a particular problem in Van Diemen's Land. In 1825, the *Cumberland Pacquet* contains a report of their activities and of the 'host of convicts' on the island. Pitt Water near Hobart had a population of 133 in 1822 of which only about 40 were not convicted men and women. Hobart's population had increased 'threefold in two years and bushrangers and natives with spears and dogs were nearby. Gangs were 'roaming the district.'[77] At least three Cumberland families were in or near Hobart at this time. Richard Downward, from Workington, had been a cooper in Cumberland but had a water mill at Iron Creek, near Pitt Water (Sorell) in the early 1820s. He moved to Sorell where he built a house, a windmill and associated buildings and acquired a large acreage of land.[78]

The *Australian* newspaper has many references to the activities of bushrangers and their numerous 'outrages.' The escape of prisoners from Port MacQuarrie, their recapture and punishment, was reported in November 1824 and, surprisingly, a column in that newspaper carried the report of a case at the Cumberland Quarter Sessions involving a Temple Sowerby man in a breach of promise action – the other side of the world.[79] The reality of bushranger activities is illustrated in Mrs Wood's letter to Miss Scott in Penrith, written in 1827. After family news and a request for the music she had left at home to be sent because they now had a piano she continued 'I must tell you what a warrior I have got to be.' While her husband was at his 'mountain station … bushrangers entered our farm and began plundering. … Our poor stockman [was] stripped [of] his boots' and threatened with a gun. He escaped and ran to the men who were ploughing. They came to the house for 'all the arms I had.' The engagement lasted an hour and 20 minutes. One was shot and the others gave themselves up to our men. … I hope I shall never witness such a scene again.' The men were taken to gaol.[80]

After Mrs Wood's death in 1827 her daughter, Mary continued to write to Miss Scott in Penrith. The many letters contain family news, mention others in New South Wales who would be known to Miss Scott and comment on life in Australia and events in England.'[81] By the late 1830s Mary Wood had married and was Mary Lowe. She was living in Sidmouth Valley where her nearest neighbours were seven miles away. She commented on the economy and religion in several letters and from *c.*1840, on drought, poor harvests, the Colony's economic problems and other farming difficulties. Money was 'very scarce and [there is] a great deal of distress. You cannot sell anything.' 'I fear it will be many years before the Colony recovers itself.'[82]

Melbourne, where so many emigrants arrived, was frequently mentioned in letters. In 1835 John Gibson stayed in a Wesleyan Hostel but 'work was very scarce and board high.' John was a stone mason which explains his request for letter patterns and his interest in the bricks and hard blue stone buildings in Melbourne and white freestone buildings in Sydney. After arrival he worked on the land then as a builder in Melbourne before going to the diggings. During the late 1830s John Gibson witnessed the effects of the economic depression. 'I am sorry to say that Australia at this time is worse than England ... thousands of people ... cannot get anything to do and their families are starving. ... Hundreds land every week.' All government work had ceased. 'Tradesmen of all sorts' were unemployed.'[83] John Gibson's letters from Sydney refer to tobacco, grapes, peaches, oranges and every sort of grain. One could eat 'new potatoes and peas all the year round.' Again, these comments convey a vivid impression of the climate and life in Australia to Cumbrians at home. After *c*.1840 John Gibson was in Parramatta, one of the last penal settlements where most of the 2,000 inhabitants were 'transports or their offspring' but he gives no more details. John was a builder and worked on government contracts.[84]

Four years later Melbourne was 'wonderful to see' but the problem of keeping pace with a rapidly increasing population was very real and there were labour shortages. In 1850, here and elsewhere in the colony, even before the rush to the goldfields, 'the operations of the settlers in New South Wales [were] completely paralysed for want of labour.' Two years later, gold brought thousands of migrants and immigrants and 'hundreds ... [were] living in tents.' Melbourne was 'a great sea of canvas ... [but was] ... a splendid town, far before Adelaide.' Both Victoria and New South Wales continued to suffer from lack of labour.'[85]

In 1908 Sarah Brunskill's letter from her home, Sandford, near Adelaide, is one of the few that contain descriptive details of the fauna in Australia. She comments on the great heat and dust and the flies. There were birds such as parrots, magpie, partridges and quails. 'Parrot pie is very good, very like pigeon.' Fish had a very different appearance from those at home. One, 'tasting of turbot is called a snapper' and 'smaller fish like mackerel taste like trout.' 'Kangaroo is very scarce' – she had not seen any but 'the meat is delicious.' Her husband had killed a snake. The country beyond Adelaide was beautiful, like a gentleman's park' with 'grass growing in tufts up to five feet tall ... and with cultivation we shall have lawns.'[86] In 1852, another writer thought Adelaide was 'a very fine town ... we were greatly surprised to find such a flourishing town [where] you can get everything ... the same as in England' and often 'a great deal cheaper.'[87]

Anthony Trollope commented on seeing kangaroos, hearing magpies, cockatoos and bull-frogs 'roaring' (a sound he disliked). The 'cheerful gobble' of the laughing jackass was heard as he rode through 'endless' forest and bush in 1871-2.[88] Hartley Dawson commented on hearing blackbirds and thrushes (that must have been introduced to New Zealand), fishing for trout and shooting pheasant, rabbits and wild pigeons near Dunedin.[89] Bedbugs, fleas, mosquitoes, locusts and flies are less endearing creatures mentioned in letters from all parts of the world. Jack Hudson wrote from the Transvaal that 'locusts are here' and South African fleas were 'rare fine ones.'[90]

Stephen Madgen went to Melbourne from Alston in 1854. He worked as a gardener and a quarryman before going to the 'diggings.' He wrote 'vegetables are dreadful scarce. I miss them very much.[91] In the same year, George Alderson wrote to his parents from Spring Vale in Fond du Lac County, Wisconsin in the United States. His experience was different. There were no apples, pears or gooseberries. Fruit was 'very scarce' but melons, cucumber, squash, pumpkins and tomatoes were doing well. He thought people in America ate 'a good deal of vegetables with every meal.'[92] Although of a later, North American-born generation, Lucy Anderson wrote to her relatives in Hilton that Oakville, Ontario, known for its strawberries, was a 'pretty little town.' Large maple trees lined the streets, the lake was blue, birds sang and the fragrance of flowers permeated the air.[93] In 1841 Penrith in New South Wales was described as 'a very pretty little place and is improving very much.'[94] In 1886, Robson and Mary Urwin wrote from Adelaide of their garden with grape vines, oranges, a fig tree and the vegetables that they grew in their garden, of trees and flowers and of the gum trees that lined the streets.[95]

Stephen Madgen advised his family and friends to emigrate and not 'kill yourselves in the mines' but they should 'bring a wife, for we all rough it so here.' He moved to the goldfields near Greymouth in New Zealand c.1864. Letters mention several of his friends who were also in New Zealand. In 1876 Stephen Madgen was back in Australia near Ipswich, Queensland and wrote to his family requesting that his inheritance should be sent to him at Dinner Camp via Samuel White, also from the Alston Moor area.[996] Samuel and Margaret White had been in Queensland since the mid-1860s. They had hoped to buy land, possibly with a Carlisle man, and to grow cotton but in 1866 Samuel was unemployed. A year later they had moved to Brickfields, where he found work sinking coal shafts. Later they did have a farm but by 1876 they were at Dinner Camp Diggings.

Several of Samuel and Margaret's letters contain thanks for money and books received from home and are the only examples that acknowledge regular payments although some refer to receiving inherited money. One possible reference to the need for money is in letters from Mr Molloy in the 1830s. He was first in the Swan River area of Western Australia then at Geographe Bay. He lacked resources. 'My means are not ample enough to expand the farm and the sheep flock. ... I have nothing to meet the expense' but they were able 'to scratch on amidst all [their] difficulties' even though building the house will 'rather screw my finances.' Were these subtle hints that a remittance would be acceptable? He did have a straightforward request for clothes to be sent comprising two pairs of strong milled cloth pantaloons, three good cloth waistcoats, some really good worsted socks, a dressing gown and 'good dark print for Georgy and the bairns.'[97]

Thomas Dent from Kirkby Stephen also went to Western Australia in the early 1830s to the Swan River Settlement. The Spark family from Alston did not arrive until 1912. They were met by friends and relatives at Fremantle where they stayed before travelling by train to Goomalling but were disappointed to find that their house was a two roomed corrugated zinc and wooden hut. Goomalling was 'nothing like towns at home.' Houses and shops were scattered amongst bush and scrub. There were no proper roads. Water was scarce but the air was dry, 'not dull and dreary.' They missed Cumberland.[98]

Such thoughts were common among emigrants in a strange environment but most were committed to making a success of their venture and to overcoming all the discomforts and difficulties in the new land. Not all were successful. Edward Rudd of north Westmorland was in the United States but after becoming unemployed in 1857 he moved to Canada to be near friends. His wife did not settle and they returned to the States. His friend, Joseph Hall remarked – 'nobody had worse luck than he had.'[99]

The Onward Journey

For the majority of emigrants the journey did not end at the port. Coastal shipping was important and in New Zealand was the only or the best means of communicating with other settlements in the early years. Steamships penetrated deep into North America via rivers, lakes and canals. In South Africa the focus of employment was far inland in the gold fields. The railway connected Cape Town with the Transvaal region by the time of the great expansion of the mines.

In 1818, the Alston Moor families who had sailed on the *Jason* from Whitehaven arrived at Port Hope, Upper Canada. The men went ahead to claim land in the 'remote wilderness' where the land was 'universally in a state of nature [with] thick and stately growth of trees [and] a perplexing cover of underwood.' Their families then joined them and this land was the beginning of Smith Township.[101] The first Cumberland men and women who went to the Vaudreuil district of Lower Canada *c.*1820 had a long journey by water and overland to Cote St Charles, near Montreal after a six weeks' voyage across the

Atlantic.[101] Relatives and other Cumbrians followed over the next 10 years. All emigrants who went to remote parts of new countries whether in forests, in bush country or on the prairies found a very different environment from that in their home country. Mrs Moodie was not a Cumbrian but her experience of travelling to her new home in Upper Canada and her feelings in such alien surroundings would be similar to those of many Cumbrian emigrants in Canada, in New Zealand or in parts of Australia. Mrs Moodie thought the Canadian forest was 'unlike anything' she had ever seen. 'The woods were frightful' and, after negotiating steep narrow tracks the family arrived at a rough 'clearing surrounded by dark forest.' Their home was to be 'a miserable hut.'[102] The Alston emigrants and others who claimed land in forests had found only large trees. The work of clearing, building a simple weather-proof hut or shanty and making furniture lay ahead. Trees had to be felled or ringed and left to die. Land was cultivated between the stumps. For early settlers in Upper or Lower Canada, for example, it was desirable to be within a day's journey of a mill, and soon clusters of settlers' holdings became the nuclei of small villages some of which developed into towns. Vast swathes of eastern Canada and in many other newly settled lands, was forest. In the Vaudreuil district families claimed their land, felled trees, built log cabins, burnt or grubbed out tree stumps and, after hand digging, planted their first crops in the clearings. These pioneers succeeded and the community of Hudson is their legacy.[103] In 1844 the Jackson family went to western Ontario from south Westmorland. Their experience would have been similar to that of their son in law's family who, after arriving at Port Hope, walked to Cavanville before turning west through the forest with 'only the blaze marks on the trees' to show the way to their destination. Robert Thexton, from Westmorland was already there and the Jacksons built a log house on his land.[105]

In 1825, Samuel Strickland went by water from Kingston to Whitby in Upper Canada then walked for two hours to join friends on their 200 acres at Darlington. Although the land had been cleared and a log house had been built, scrub, thistles and tree stumps had to be removed. Mr Strickland had a farming background and, a year later bought his own land near Peterborough. His friend was a Londoner, a retired Colonel – an example of a former professional or business man 'who knew nothing of agricultural operations' following a completely new occupation after emigrating. At that time bears were in the surrounding forest, roads were mud tracks with 'corduroy bridges' over some of the streams. Other watercourses had no bridges. It took three days to cover 50 miles. But there as elsewhere in North America and in other continents, 'the howling wilderness [was made] to blossom.[105]

In 1831 the Hodgson and Hall families from north Westmorland had a different destination; an urban environment. They disembarked in New Jersey

R.Hodgson

George Lancaster's original 1830s log house, Hudson, Quebec.

en route for Pittsburgh in the coalfield region of Pennsylvania. After sailing north to New York, they went by steamer up the Hudson River to Albany, a journey of more than two days but on a boat more comfortable than their trans-Atlantic ship. From Albany another boat took them 350 miles to Buffalo, NY. They continued by steamer to Erie on Lake Erie before the last lap of 130 miles by hired waggon to Pittsburgh where they were met by relatives. Several other north Westmorland emigrants were already living there and a house was waiting for them.[106] The Hodgson and Hall families (and others like them in a number of countries) had successfully completed a monumental journey involving several changes of transport, dealing in strange money and meeting people very different from those at home. Early emigrants were true pioneers but unfortunately we have few descriptions of their experiences.

In the United States it was possible to go from northern cities including Pittsburgh by road or waterways over vast distances to western and southern regions. One family travelled south from Pittsburgh mainly by water to St Louis before the overland journey into Illinois *c.*1840. In the late 1840s another family approached Illinois by a different route. From New Orleans they sailed more than 1,000 miles on a steamship northwards on the Mississippi then on a second river before reaching their destination.[107] Although these emigrants did not mention having friends in the area, it seems that they knew what to expect, how to travel

Eigenthum d. Verleger

*River steamer on the Missouri, c.1860 also showing
a ferry and a covered ox-drawn waggon.*

and found other English settlers nearby. Emigrants to North America journeyed over distances unimaginable in England. In Canada, the St Lawrence River, canals and the Great Lakes which also served travellers in the United States and rivers in that country meant that even early emigrants could penetrate deep into the continent along existing fur and other trade routes. Later in the century, travel was made easier by railways.

From the 1840s westward expansion continued apace. By the 1870s more than 300,000 men, women and children had crossed the continent, a journey of *c*.2,500 miles to California, Oregon and British Columbia. Lines of slow-moving ox-drawn waggons, often 100 or more in a 'train' were accompanied by herds of cattle, sheep and other livestock These waggon trains left collecting points in Missouri, crossed the Mississippi and journeyed west over plains, deserts and mountains. Although advertisements and publications suggested that the journey was simply one of slow steady progress towards a land 'flowing with milk and honey' the reality was very different. Hazards included lack of water in the dry lands and deserts, insufficient grass for animals, unfordable rivers or dry river beds that were too rough to cross. Sudden deluges, snow storms and impassable tracks in the high mountains slowed progress. Wheels broke, draught animals and livestock died, there were births, illness and death among the trekkers and many faced hostile native tribes. More realistic advice urged migrants 'not to be disheartened by ... the expansive desolation along the road; for in California as in Oregon, the country along the sea is very fertile ... cattle and horses are easily raised. ... Seek a good location for your farm and stick to it.'[108] It took approximately 150 days or more to reach Sacramento or destinations in Oregon by northerly routes through the mountains in the 1840s.[109]

William Workman from Clifton, Westmorland who had emigrated in 1822 took part in the 'opening up' of the west via a southerly route. His brother David had been in the United States for four years. William was 'an early traveller' on the Santa Fé Trail. In 1825 when the journey from Independence to Santa Fé in New Mexico usually took at least 45 days and from New Mexico to San Gabriel, California a further 40 days, William trekked from Missouri across the plains via the Santa Fé route to Los Angeles and in 1841 'led the first party of American settlers from New Mexico into southern California.'[110] A covered waggon train accompanied by livestock would have taken about seven weeks. William Workman would not have encountered high mountains but had to cross extensive deserts. Published accounts of overland travel from Missouri to Santa Fé in the 1840s and early 1850s tell of flowers on the plains, wild turkeys, buffalo, wild grapevines and rattlesnakes but also of hailstones 'larger than hen's eggs,' severe winds, days with no water, scarcity of bread, dust, gnats, mosquitoes, wild fires, sunburn, disease and both births and deaths.[111] California was a 'fine rich country' with a small white population and was attracting emigrants and migrants even before the twin events of its becoming an American possession and the discovery of gold.[112] At that time San Francisco had only a few buildings set beside an extensive bay among low hills.

From 1849, the 'gold rush' drew thousands of hopeful prospectors to California by all possible means and routes. Some sailed from New York to San Francisco via Cape Horn – a voyage of three to four months. The journey could be shortened by travelling overland across Mexico or by crossing the Panama Isthmus. Others crossed the continent. John Wilson of Soulby had arrived in the United States in the 1850s. He decided to join the search for gold in the north western Canada. From Indiana, he went to the coast, sailed to the Isthmus of Panama, crossed to the Pacific probably by small boat and mule or horse before continuing by sea to San Francisco. From California, he moved north to the Fraser River and Cariboo Trail regions of British Columbia. By 1864 he, as many others did, gave up the search for riches in gold. He and a partner bought cattle in Oregon, drove them north into Canada and settled near Kamloops as a rancher.[113] By the time William Nicholson went to the Klondike in the 1890s and James and Jonathan Taylor to California in 1904 the sea route was similar but railways now crossed the continent. James died after only three weeks in

California. Jonathan followed other occupations after he left the goldfield. He seems to have been in San Francisco in 1905.[114]

Others travelled for thousands of miles by water after arriving in the United States. Mr Buckingham, from London, sailed in 'sultry and oppressive heat.' from New Orleans to Natchez on the Mississippi in 1839. The scenery though flat was 'rich, luxuriant and interesting.' He saw plantations with magnificent houses and negro-quarters like 'soldiers' barracks.' After Baton Rouge the river banks were covered by woods and marshy land.[115] In 1835 John Gibson from near Kendal had arrived at New Orleans where he 'walked among the steam boats' before finding a temporary job unloading freight. He then sailed northwards on the Mississippi by the steamboat *Missourian*. He did not describe the scenery and the journey to Natchez was only part of the distance he and others covered. At St Lewis (Louis), where several routes and navigable rivers converged, he met friends – Edward Dixon and John Dowson. He found work but after suffering from 'fever and ague' for three months, moved to the Illinois side of the river, bought 15 acres and settled there.[116] In 1848 a Yorkshire farmer and his family had sailed from Liverpool to New Orleans then by steamboat to St Louis and on to a seemingly uninhabited part of Illinois. The boat deposited them at a jetty 'with no habitation in sight.' They 'found refuge in a log hut' for the night and made their home nearby. After only a few years, the wilderness had been cleared and farms and villages were dotted around.[117]

Families from Swaledale and Wensleydale (only a few miles from Kirkby Stephen), were in the Dubuque, Galena, Mineral Point and New Diggings region of the United States by the 1840s.[118] Some would be known or related to north Westmorland emigrants. Joseph Richardson and his wife joined her brother in 1851. They disembarked at New Orleans and sailed north to Galena in the north western corner of Illinois by river boat. Joseph's brother, George, went to the same area but seems to have travelled overland from Philadelphia via Cincinnati and St Louis before the 1,000 mile river journey to Dubuque and New Diggings where he opened a small shoe store.[119]

It was not only the early settlers that had to contend with 'raw nature' when the destination was in forests or on the prairies. After arrival, a home had to be built from local materials such as timber, or turf in the grasslands. This initial dwelling was probably not wind and waterproof with only earth floors until more pressing priorities had been dealt with. After the early years when journeys could be undertaken only on water or overland, railways transformed travelling across North America. The country was 'peopled by railroads' that cut through 'primeval forests and over prairies [and] created the value of the land.'[120] In 1848, Stephen Wilson Madgen wrote from near Philadelphia in the United States that 'the railroads are going on with us at a rapid rate.'[121] But initial enthusiasm could be tempered when the railroad was too close. In the 1850s Joseph Hodgson wrote from Charteris Creek, near Pittsburgh that the Columbus and Cincinnati railroad was to run within 100 yards of their house but in 1867, he wrote 'we have to be very careful about keeping everything off the track.' Although 'they had lost only one hog and a few chickens and turkeys ... in dry weather we have great difficulty in keeping it from burning our fences.' That railway carried passengers, freight and coal and its opening 'had led to a great increase in population in our neighbourhood. I cannot say that the change has been any benefit to us thus far. It is desirable to be a little out of the way of railroads and coal works for people engaged in farming.'[122]

Two Cumberland families who moved to Shelley County in Illinois in the 1860s or early 1870s from Ohio went overland in covered waggons – presumably their destination was not on a rail route.[123] And, in the 1870s another Cumberland family travelled 600 miles by rail from Quebec, 100 miles by steamer and walked many miles through forest to claim their portion of uncleared land.[124]

Settlers on the prairies faced different challenges from those in the forests of Ontario. Charles Dickens described a prairie as 'a vast expanse of level ground ... lonely and wild but oppressive in its barren monotony.'[125] Thousands went to the prairie lands in the United States and western Canada as homesteaders, living at first in turf shacks or, if there were trees, a wooden cabin. Such settlers were pioneers long after the land in other parts of the continent and other destination countries had been peopled, cleared and cultivated. Life for these emigrants was hard and could be lonely.

The first cross-continental railways lacked branch lines therefore, during the initial years of settlement in the west, migrant families had a long overland journey after leaving the train in order to reach their land. And, as migrants who trekked north from Utah in the United States to Alberta in the later nineteenth century had found, they had to become accustomed to differences in climate and conditions. They found 'a new country to subdue' with only 'land, water and sky' and possible clashes with the native Indians on whose vast open spaces the settlers planned to create their ranches and farms.[126]

In 1903, the Pinder family from Yorkshire had travelled to Saskatoon, Saskatchewan from New Brunswick by rail. They crossed the river by ferry and trekked across country until they found a suitable site on which to pitch a tent and establish their farm near New Battleford. In winter, journeys were by sleigh.[127] The Armistead family from Killington was among several in the sample who moved west after living in Ontario. They left their farm in Ontario and also settled near North Battleford in 1911.[128] James and Mary Brunskill and children, their parents and Mary's sister arrived at Halifax, Nova Scotia in 1883 but had to wait for 'the spring breakup' before sailing up the St Lawrence and on to

Wyoming, Ontario by train.[1129] After farming there for some years, James and his family decided to move to the prairies which James's son, Harry described in 1955 in his unpublished memoir as being 'one great carpet of grass on level land, hills or rolling country … just one great pasture from the North Saskatchewan clear down to the Mighty Missouri.' But he thought there had been a price to pay for settlement and farming there – much of 'its beauty and old-time grandeur has been lost.'[130] Mr Brunskill had travelled alone by train to join friends near Pense, 18 miles from Regina in Saskatchewan. The rest of the family took advantage of the special rates offered to new settlers by the railway company for transporting all their goods, livestock, fodder for the animals and timber for a house. 'The pony, four milk cows, chickens, turkeys, geese, pigeons, a dog and a cat' shared the rail car with furniture, household goods, implements and tools. One son travelled with the livestock. His brother and mother went separately to Pense.[131]

Edwin Ernest Hetherington from Greystoke, went to a homestead at Lumsden, Saskatchewan in 1905 and only later did his parents and four siblings join him.[132] In 1909 Bert and Jack Atkinson from north Westmorland had earned sufficient money in Ontario to establish a farm in the west. They bought 'necessary effects,' went by train to Saskatchewan but completed the journey in an ox-drawn waggon. It was only after three years of hard work that their mother and sisters joined them. They were taken to their new home in an ox-drawn cart from the nearest railhead.[133]

In the United States, George and Mary Calcott and their children spent one night in Castle Garden, New York after disembarking before travelling to Texas by train, a journey of 'four days and three nights' in 1885. It was a 'toilsome wearying trip' on wooden benches. Luggage filled the aisles.[134] After Christopher Gelder arrived in New York he 'took a train right away to the west.' It is clear that he had been in contact with friends in Chicago where he stayed. After continuing by rail to Bathgate, North Dakota, he was met by a friend.[135] In the early twentieth century Thomas Maxwell wrote that the completion of the railway had 'put us in connexion with the world.' Not only could his cotton crop be more easily transported but Mobile and New Orleans were only a two day journey and New York could be reached in three days.[136]

The self-sufficiency and life-style of settlers in rural North America is illustrated in a letter to the Salkeld family in north Westmorland. In 1857 Frances Bartlett was in Walpole, Ontario. She and her husband had 100 acres, all paid for, of which a few acres had been cleared and 30 acres were woods. They had a log house, a frame barn, seven horses, 12 cows and 30 sheep. Frances had produced 50 yards of cloth from the wool, made sugar, vinegar, syrup and soap. They were receiving 15-20 per cent on their savings. Clearly this was a family that, like so many others, used as many of their own resources as possible and they were in a solid financial position.[137]

During the 1890s and the years up to the outbreak of war Canada pursued a massive publicity and recruitment campaign aimed at persuading British emigrants, especially farmers or those prepared to become farmers to choose the western prairies as their destination. James Brunskill who had established a successful farm at Pense, Saskatchewan, was chosen to represent Canada on a six month tour of England in 1910 speaking about the opportunities that awaited prospective emigrants in that country.[138]

On other continents, onward journeys were also arduous and lengthy. John Gibson, John Hodgson and a friend had arrived at Melbourne in 1835. They walked into the interior (suffering much pain from blistered feet) and slept in the open before arriving at their destination – Hodgson's brother in law's slab hut which was 'at the end of the world for we saw nothing but mountains and rocky and wild bush [with] no roads.'[139] The Mundy family's 10 day journey from Melbourne to a sheep station at Muston's Creek, Victoria in 1844 was by bullock drawn carts. They camped at night and drove through swamps, across bush land and plains.[140]

When John Powley and his family moved from the Caversham and Dunedin area of New Zealand to the Tokomairiro Plain in the 1850s, it took two days by land and water to reach the place where they and other pioneering immigrants settled. His brother in law, Robert Robinson, bought land near Waipori Lake. Another brother in law, Christopher Robinson, also settled in the same area at what became known as Moneymore. Having walked from Dunedin, with the two cows and a bull he had brought from England and a cart laden with all their possessions drawn by the bull, the Robinson family reached the Plain. Arriving at a river with no obvious crossing point they decided to establish their farm there. But, it was hard work – they had to contend with 'floods, fire, rabbits, thistles, grassgrub [and] rampant nature had to be subdued.'[141] John Powley's mother in law and several other family members came to live nearby – yet another example of a 'Cumbrian cluster.'[142] In 1854 Michael Studholme, one of three Carlisle brothers, took land in the Canterbury region at Te Waimate. Michael and one man took several weeks to drive a bullock drawn waggon 100 miles to his land, over country with no roads and crossing un-bridged creeks and rivers. He lived in a tent until he built a small wood and clay house.[143] For some settlers in New Zealand, horse-drawn sledges were used for months or years before roads were made.

The Tinning family from Penruddock arrived in Melbourne in 1911 but their letters make no mention of their impressions. However, on their brief visit before sailing to New Zealand in 1908, the Spedding family remember riding on

Melbourne's 'cable cars' and the 'wonderful zoo.'[144] Mr and Mrs Tinning went to view prospective farm sites in the hinterland. After viewing land at Swan Hill, 214 miles away from Melbourne, at Bendigo, Echuca and Kyunga they decided on land at Tongala, c.130 miles from Melbourne. Clearly such journeys must have taken some time and even in 1911, travel over long distances was not easy or comfortable. A few months later Mr Tinning wrote to friends 'if you have any notion of coming there will be plenty of good land ready in the spring.[145]

In South Africa, George Clark Dickson, John Wilson Johnston and friends went from Pretoria, a 'pretty' town, to the mineral region in 1891. Rain and mud caused the waggons, some drawn by donkeys others by bullocks, to become stuck 'fast' many times. On the way they shot guinea fowl, duck and partridges and saw buck, hares, crocodiles and an iguana. They passed kaffir kraals, crossed several rivers including the Limpopo and journeyed through 'grand scenery.' Fires protected their overnight camps from predatory beasts. They had many setbacks including bouts of illness before eventually reaching Umtali where they found work 'sinking shafts.' The journey had taken several weeks. But their venture was not ultimately successful. George Dickson died from fever in 1894. His friend John W. Johnston returned home c.1896.[146] In the 1890s, Jack Nolan went by train from Cape Town to the gold fields near Johannesburg. He walked many miles and found work at the Glen Deep Mines where other Cumbrians were employed. He described scorpions, snakes, hares, rabbits, sand and hailstorms and, as Anthony Trollope had found in Australia, the frogs were very noisy. Nolan decided to return home in 1896 and tells of the death of a friend from miners' phthisis.[147] In 1904 Essie Metcalfe travelled by railway from Cape Town to Bulawayo. The train was 'very comfortable and 'passed through very interesting parts where the war was. ... Block houses and graves were visible.' It was a 'bare, hot dry country with rough stones, scrub and heat.' Having left Cape Town on Monday, she reached her destination, near the Victoria Falls on Sunday night.[148]

What occupation in the new land?

Some emigrants were 'foot-loose and adventurous' fortune seekers who went to find gold but many of these then settled into other occupations including farming. None in the sample became wealthy from prospecting although there is evidence that at least two took the opportunity to invest in mining and became mine owners. But for all, an unknown environment lay ahead. Only 914 adult males in the sample can be ascribed to an occupation. Table 5.1 shows the percentage of these who were engaged in broad categories of occupations in the major destination countries. Frequently the emigrant's occupation was not given in the sources. Relatives either did not know or failed to give these details and

Table 5.1   Percentage of adult males in occupations in selected countries

Category	Australia	Canada	N.Zealand	S.Africa	USA	All
Farming	34%	66.0%	48.0%	4.0%	38.4%	38.0%
Mining/gold	41.0%	4.0%	17.0%	89.0%	25.4%	36.0%
Other	25.0%	30.0%	35.0%	7.0%	36.2%	26.0%
Total	100.0%	100.0%	100.0%	100.0%	100.0%	100.0%

Source: *Collected information from named emigrants with known occupations.*

newspaper announcements of births, marriages and deaths were not helpful.

Only a handful of females had occupations including domestic service, as shop assistants or shopkeeper, weavers and teachers. Men too, found work as weavers in the United States. When William Shaw arrived in Philadelphia in 1841 he quickly found work as a weaver and wrote 'I can make 20 shillings here as easy as I could make 10 [shillings] in Cargo. ... Anybody that will work may do well enough, but they must work.'[149]

Table 5.1 highlights the importance of the South African gold and diamond mines as a destination for Cumbrian men most of whom went after *c.*1890. Many Cumbrian emigrants settled on land in rural Canada, the mid-west and prairie lands in the United States and rural New Zealand throughout the period up to 1914. Mining and farming were clearly dominant occupations but the substantial proportion that appear in the 'Other' category in every destination except South Africa is interesting and includes a wide range of craft and trade skills. Professional occupations include medical doctors and surgeons, clergymen, solicitors, civil and mechanical engineers, a stockbroker and teachers. The railway features in every country as an employer. Andrew Veitch, a young railway engineer who went to Illinois from Carlisle in 1907, spent his entire career working for railway companies. Having previously worked for four years on the railway at the Panama Canal construction site, he was employed by the Chicago-Alton Railroad Company at Bloomington, Illinois and eventually became the General Superintendent.[cl] William John Ellison from Whitehaven and his brother in law, William Warwick, were both employed on the Pennsylvania Railroad from 1911. John Suddart and his brother worked for the Cape Railway Company in South Africa during the 1890s. Others were road surveyors, hotel keepers, watchmakers and jewellers, chemists, policemen, a county treasurer, a jockey and several clerks. Henry Duston was chief engineer on a lake steamer at Queenstown, New Zealand. F.W. Knewstubb, a surveyor in Appleby, emigrated to Canada in 1908 and first worked on a dam project then as surveyor or engineer with the Grand Trunk Railway, for the Montreal Light and Power Company and the Canadian Pacific Railway. John Yeats combined his life as a homesteader at

Chinook, Alberta with employment on the Canadian Pacific Railway.[cli]
Evidence suggests that Cumbrian emigrants contributed to the economy of their destination country in a broad spread of occupations but the agricultural and mining sectors are the most frequently cited. William Atkinson who was in the eastern USA in 1831 and Robert Gibson in Iowa in the 1850s are two of the very few examples of agricultural or general labourers in the sample.[152] Although many emigrants continued in their previous occupations overseas others adopted new occupations especially on the land. George Calcott, a farmer in Texas, had been a railway signalman. Mr Threlkeld was a successful dairy farmer in New Zealand having been a printer in Cumberland.[153]

Farming

In North America Saskatchewan, Manitoba, California, Kansas, Wyoming, Texas and the Great Lakes region, for example, offered different challenges. South Africa, Australia and New Zealand had similar contrasts. Some emigrants spent years clearing land before they could grow crops; others had an easier path to farming. Some added other skills such as flour or timber milling. If they tried to continue with methods and crops as at home they often needed to adapt to new conditions. Some took thousands of acres where sheep and cattle grazed. Adequate rainfall, an equable climate and favourable conditions were experienced by fortunate settlers. Others faced drought, dust or hail storms, disease and other periodic disasters. Crops ranged from wheat, maize and other corn crops to citrus fruit, tobacco, vines, sugar and cotton. William Bell had a farm in Iowa. He wrote to his brother in north Westmorland in 1871 that 'a box of willows' sent from Wisconsin by Mr Richardson had all died in the dry summer. 'A farm looks so bare without timber around.' Was Mr. Richardson the brother of George Richardson the shoe manufacturer in Dubuque, both from Church Brough? Certainly he must have been known to William's family in Westmorland. The following year his letter reports on crop yields, prices and his orchard. He intended to plant a willow fence and he requested that 'you would send me a little of that big rhubarb bed' together with instructions 'how to raise it.'[154]

On new land buildings had to be constructed. Log cabins provided early homes where timber was plentiful. For some, tents were their first home and on the prairies or in parts of New Zealand, cabins were made from turf or brushwood. Other homes were made from 'wattle and daub.' It was possible to buy or to take prefabricated buildings from England but cost and transport meant that these were few. Family sized timber, brick or stone houses were built much later. Nathan and Sarah Rumney's first home on their 550 acres in New Zealand in the 1870s was a 'slab and mud' hut.[155] When Bert and Jack Atkinson settled in Saskatchewan in the early twentieth century they spent the first winter sharing the only shelter they had with their horses and only some years later was their cabin, made from sods and poles, improved by laying wooden floors.[156] Francis Jollie ceased to be 'a dweller in tents' once his large house had been built near Nelson in New Zealand in 1842-3.[157]

Some farmers moved to a larger holding which could be nearby or hundreds of miles away. Initially, John and Mary Brunskill had settled on a farm in Ontario but moved to Pense, Saskatchewan in 1889. John worked for a neighbour while preparing his own farm. In the first season 10 acres had been sown with oats. Their temporary shanty on their neighbour's land was moved to their own farm in 1891. A stable for the stock had been made from poles and 'spoiled hay' and a nearby ravine dammed to catch water – in winter, snow was melted on the stove. The following summer another 21 acres were' broken' and two yoke of oxen had been bought. The first wheat crop was in 1893 but 1894 was 'a complete failure' due to drought and heat. Only the rough 'prairie grass' saved their stock from starvation. It was not until 1896 that the Brunskill family had work-horses and their '20 by 24 ft house with three bedrooms upstairs' was built in 1897. But, like so many other settlers they kept the old shanty. In this case it became their kitchen.[158] There are several references in the sources for the original dwelling being used for a different purpose, for example, as a chicken house or for storage.

In 1906 Thomas Hetherington wrote from Lumsden, Saskatchewan, 'there are thousands of acres in the west almost like an ordinary lea field in Cumberland [but] the sod is tougher and [there are] more stones.' By then he owned four horses, some cattle, all necessary implements, a carriage, two waggons and a sleigh. About 70 of his 480 acres were cultivated growing oats, wheat, potatoes and garden produce. Horses or oxen could be bought on credit and if $100 or even half was available in capital then an emigrant 'would get on.'[159]

Some farmers excelled in breeding animals. To give only a few examples, William Fawcett of north Westmorland farmed near Melbourne. He won prizes with shorthorn cattle bred from those which he took to Australia.[160] In New Zealand, Jonathan Brown from Oughterside, was a noted breeder of Berkshire pigs, Leicester sheep, shorthorn cattle, horses and Aylesbury ducks on his Rangiora farm. Christopher Robinson of Moneymore and Hutton Troutbeck of Eskdale, near Napier were well respected breeders of Clydesdale horses. The Glencross brothers bred Shire horses, one in Manitoba, the other in Alberta. Richard Ellwood from Knock followed the gold rush to Ballarat but later became a farmer. He owned a large sheep run but was also a noted breeder of Clydesdale horses.

Elizabeth, William, John and Robert Allan, from the Appleby area were in Victoria, Australia in the 1850s. All had farms. William's was named Blencarn.[161]

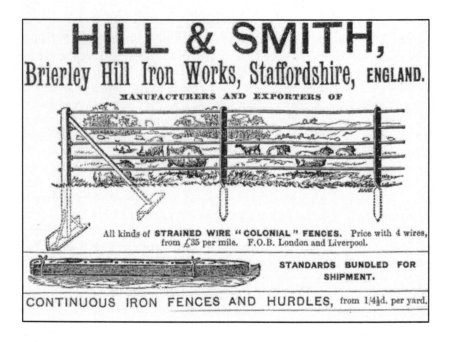

HILL & SMITH,
Brierley Hill Iron Works, Staffordshire, ENGLAND.

MANUFACTURERS AND EXPORTERS OF

All kinds of STRAINED WIRE "COLONIAL" FENCES. Price with 4 wires, from £35 per mile. F.O.B. London and Liverpool.

STANDARDS BUNDLED FOR SHIPMENT.

CONTINUOUS IRON FENCES AND HURDLES, from 1/4½d. per yard.

Wire fencing from England was advertised in Australia c.1895

Jabez and Andrew Holliday each farmed in Wagga Wagga, NSW in the 1880s. Other Cumbrians were there - another example of a cluster of relatives or friends settling in close proximity or within easy visiting distance. In New Zealand John Powley and his family, his brother in law Christopher Robinson and family, his mother in law and his wife's sister were all on the Tokomairiro Plain in the Moneymore area south of Dunedin. Several members of north Westmorland families who emigrated in the 1830s and corresponded with their relatives in Hilton over the next 30 years were in the Pittsburgh area of the United States. Others were near Humber and York (Toronto) in Canada.

William Lightburn was a 'very successful' farmer at Capron, Oklahoma in 1909. He had surrounded his farm with a four foot high 'hog-tight' wire fence and built a cyclone cave.[162] When The Tinning family from Penruddock emigrated to Australia c.1910 'ringed' trees were already dead on their land at Tongala and provided posts for fencing and firewood. In the first year, 10 acres were sown with oats and barley and 30 acres were 'ready for lucern.' They had 17 cows, poultry, and a horse but although there were good shorthorn bulls, horses were expensive. By 1911, he had cleared 50 acres, was creating an orange orchard and had fenced a quarter of a mile, all with wire and posts. Another quarter-mile was ready to fence.[163] Their four roomed house was among pine trees and they had 'plenty of neighbours. … Tongala station where we take our cream' and the school were three miles away. His wife thought the journey to the nearby town was more interesting than going to Penrith.[164] William Benson and friends, all from Cumbria, worked as bush clearers after arriving in New Zealand. William bought 210 acres of land at Waituna West in 1882. The bush was cleared; a farmhouse built and, after several years of work the farm, was ready – 'in grass.' A friend bought neighbouring land. [165]

From our evidence, the majority of emigrant farmers succeeded – even modestly but some had problems either because of illhealth, the weather, general economic conditions or from bush fires. After farming for 30 years, Thomas Ellwood of Knock, a farmer in Victoria became insolvent in the 1880s and in one of Mary Lowe's last letters from Sidmouth Valley, New South Wales she reported that her father's wealth had been so depleted that he had sold much of his land and property.[166] Those who did not survive bad times or failed for other reasons moved on. In Texas and Kansas many hundreds of farms were abandoned in the 1890s. The Ireland and Calcott families grew cotton at Rattlesnake Hill, Texas but the Irelands had to sell some of their land in the 1890s when the price of cotton fell and the rains failed. These were 'the worst of hard times.' By 1900 'the tide turned' and prospects improved.[167] William Barker from Crosby Garrett took a 500 acre farm in Kansas in 1889 just before that disastrous decade. His fate is unknown. Joseph Robson emigrated in 1885 and bought land in Kansas, planted crops but found he had been swindled. He lost everything including all the family's possessions when it emerged that he was not the owner.[164] Emigrants who settled on the land found that their new country was very different from the generally benign conditions in England where farming was only occasionally punctuated by outbreaks of disease, blight and bad weather. Worse still, George Thorburn, his wife and mother in law were all murdered in Saskatchewan by their farm worker in 1907.[169]

Immense tracts of land in North America, Australia and New Zealand were devoted to sheep and cattle grazing. After emigrating to the United States in the 1850s John Winter from Soulby, joined the search for gold in the west and in north western Canada before settling on a ranch near Kamloops, British Columbia where he kept several thousand cattle.[170] Several emigrants either owned or worked on huge ranches. In the early twentieth century the Threlkeld brothers from north Westmorland went to Wyoming. Two brothers moved north to Canada, bought 'several hundred sheep' in Edmonton which they took by train to their new homestead also near Kamloops.[171] John Balden from Appleby was in Wyoming in 1913 when Ernest Pilkington of Penrith went to work on his sheep ranch.[172] Another Appleby man, David Taylor was also in Wyoming on a sheep ranch at Big Horn Basin in 1910.[173] Isaac Handley of Ravenstonedale worked for a Cumbrian settler in Nebraska before he and his brother took their own ranch near Eureka, Nevada.[174] The Threlkeld brothers, Ernest Pilkington and John Balden were in Wyoming in the United States and John Wilson was near Kamloops, British Columbia where he owned 3,500 – 4,000 head of cattle.[175] William and Joseph Rogers had more than 3,500 sheep at Glenquoich, on New Zealand's South Island in 1862, William died in a boating accident but Joseph's flock had increased to 24,000 by 1906.[176] Hutton Troutbeck had extensive grazing lands in the Hawkes Bay region of the North Island.

Official literature advised prospective farmers to work for others first in order to become accustomed to the new conditions and the sources show that some Cumbrians had done so and though for many it was for the practical reason of earning money, they would have learnt about differences in methods and conditions.

Ambitious emigrants really could succeed. John Harrington of Drigg and Mr Atkinson of Wigton were two former farm workers who, by 1906 had their own farms in Canada. John Harrington farmed 1,000 acres in Saskatchewan and Mr Atkinson grew wheat and potatoes on his 160 acres near Winnipeg.[177] Aaron Gate reversed the usual trend. He went to New Zealand in 1891 and leased 107 acres in the North Island but the venture failed and he became an agricultural labourer.[178]

The search for gold and mining

References in newspapers or directories give some indication of the scale of gold production and of emigration to mining regions all over the world. During the ten years from 1862, for example, c.60,000 miners and quarrymen emigrated from Britain and this was before South Africa became a destination.[179] In 1855, the *Lightning* returned from Australia carrying 69,060 ounces of gold and the *Great Britain* carried almost £500,000 worth of gold bullion back to England on its return from Melbourne c.1860.[180]

Cumbrian emigrants were part of the 'gold rush' to California, Australia, New Zealand, to the Klondike, to Western Australia and to South Africa. It is clear that many hoped to make a fortune. At least 50 named emigrants seem to have followed the lure of gold. Eleven from north Cumberland were in the Bendigo area in 1853 and Samuel and George Furness from Kings Meaburn, Westmorland, were among Cumbrians in Victoria in the 1860s. William Atkinson from Staveley and Stephen Madgen from Alston were only two among many who went first to Victoria then to the New Zealand goldfields. Jonathan Brough from Bromfield settled in Nelson, New Zealand in 1867. He had not emigrated

A. Kohl

Sandhurst, Victoria (Bendigo), the centre of quartz reef mining, 1860s.

with the intention of prospecting but was 'one of the first explorers to [go inland] to search for gold.' Later he was engaged in building roads and bridges.[181]

Gold seeking emigrants sought instant wealth. Many who started as prospectors moved on to other occupations. Some continued in mineral extraction as employees not prospectors but Stephen Madgen tried to follow both paths. In 1859 he was employed at the quartz reefs, 200 miles from Melbourne. He earned £4 10s per week and paid a man £2 per week to continue prospecting.[182] The disillusioned returned home. William Nicholson returned penniless from North America and resumed his life in Brough.[183]

The majority seem to have passed through the 'gold phase' and settled into another occupation not necessarily in the same region or country and often after joining the 'rush' in more than one destination. Richard, Thomas and John Ellwood formerly of Knock, became farmers in Victoria after seeking gold in the 1850s. Thomas tried again and went to the Maryborough Diggings. Thomas Penny of Maryport also went to Maryborough but became a draper and from 1878 he was engaged in sugar cultivation.[184] John Johnston left his wife and son on the farm near Adelaide in the 1850s and went, probably on foot, 400 miles to the Victoria gold field.[185] In New Zealand, John Ewart of Carlisle became a policeman after trying his luck in the gold field.[186]

Stephen Madgen's letters to his family on Alston Moor tell of his travels in the Antipodes. He went to the Victoria gold rush in the 1850s, moved to the New

129

Zealand goldfields in the 1860s but by 1872 he was back in Australia, staying with a widow. 'She wanted me to marry but I told her I was getting too old and grey and she told me I looked fresh on it and how much better I would be.'[187] He does seem to have married in Australia but it is not known to whom. However, no wife was mentioned when he was staying with Samuel White, another Cumberland man at Dinner Camp, Queensland in 1876.[188]

After gold was discovered in the Rand, South Africa, thousands of prospectors flooded into the region. Kimberley and other towns grew because of gold and, after the first wave of prospectors either left or found employment in the gold and diamond mines, a stream of men continued to arrive to work as miners. In 1903, for example, 50 named men and many others whose names are unknown went to South Africa 'in parties' from West Cumberland and several deaths were reported.[189] The majority remained in contact with their family; some were accompanied by their wives and children. Others returned home for visits but Richard Robinson, an iron ore miner from Frizington made no contact with his family after leaving. He died while serving in the Rand Rifles during the war.[190]

Not all were actively digging, cutting or hewing in the mineral extraction industry. George Tyson of Eskdale was a surveyor in the Klondike.[191] William Little of Whitehaven was a mining engineer in South Africa.[192] James R. Wilson was the manager of a gold mine on the Coromandel Peninsula, New Zealand.[193] Robert Troughear was a civil engineer in the coal mines in or near Greymouth, New Zealand in the 1880s.[194] Joseph Kearney of Whitehaven was the manager of a coal mine in Southern Rhodesia.[195] John Metcalfe of Broughton founded the Ellenborough Hard Rock Company in Australia. He was very successful but died young, probably from silicosis.[196]

Some Cumbrians went to coal mines in Australia at Newcastle, Stockton and Swansea. James McClennan of St Bees worked in the Huntly coal mines in New Zealand in 1885 but later he became a farmer near Hamilton. Others went to gold mines in Victoria, Queensland or in the Coolgardie region in Western Australia. In 1909 a former farm servant in Westmorland was employed as a gold miner in Western Australia. He wrote that even the high wages 'are barely sufficient for the necessities of life.' He advised the readers not to go to the Western Australian mines because of noise, dust and 'many dangers.' 'Men here are soon worked to death.'[197] These dangers were real and caused many deaths. Copper was mined at Moonta, Burra Burra and other locations on the Yorke Peninsula in South Australia. In the United States, Joseph and Louise Allison were at the Sydney Mines, Cape Breton, in 1913 and John Fawkes from Rockcliffe was at the Great Bear Lake Uranium and Gold Mines in 1914.[198] Isaac Miller of Cleator Moor went to the United States in the late 1870s. At the time of his death in 1905 he was the Superintendent of the Western Mining Company at Leadville, Colorado.[199] Several Cumberland men were at the coal mines at Coleman Alta, Alberta in 1905.[200]

Newspaper reports of emigrants leaving and of visits home tell of the living but the announcements of the death of miners either from illness or accident have added dozens to the sample. In all, 60 named men and others whose names are not known, were killed in accidents or died from illness. Mr Foster of High Crosby died of tuberculosis in Bendigo, Victoria and James Taylor died from dysentery in California.[201] Joseph Allison from Cockermouth died in an explosion at the Union Mines, British Columbia in 1901.[202] James Kirkby of Cleator Moor was one of 23 men who died in an explosion at the Blue Canyon Coal Mines in the Pacific North West of the United States in 1895. Joseph Dixon and his wife had emigrated to Pennsylvania from Cleator Moor. He was killed in the mines at Pottsville in 1913.[203] Robert Megannon and Peter McCaffney who had worked in the South African mines for some years were killed in an accident in the Moyer and Charlton Mine, Johannesburg, in 1918.[204] Mr Jackson of Asby, Westmorland died at the Bingham mines in Utah in 1913.[205]

Deaths of Cumbrian emigrants were frequently reported from accidents in mines and also from illness. Working conditions in the British Columbian mines, for example, were described as 'dangerous if not lethal.' From 1879-1909 326 men died in 'calamities' underground and fatal illnesses. Tuberculosis exacerbated by working in damp conditions, outbreaks of typhoid fever and dust related diseases such as silicosis, killed many in the Nanaimo mines.[206] The evidence suggests that many Cumbrian men were working in coal mines on Vancouver Island, British Columbia in the 1880s. The names of some are known only because they died in mining accidents.[207] Explosions in the Nanaimo mines in 1887 and 1888 killed a total of 223 miners.[208] Five men from Aspatria were among several Cumberland men who were drowned in a mining accident at Nanaimo in 1915.[209]

But the most shocking statistic is the number of young West Cumberland men who died after working in the South African mines. Newspapers show that many dozens succumbed to 'the dreaded disease' abroad or at home after returning. The cause of death was sometimes stated to be pneumonia but all who worked in quartz mining risked developing lung disease. A Royal Commission reported in 1911 that 'gold miners in Victoria and Western Australia were dying in great numbers as were South African miners, Cornish tin miners and American metal miners.' Dynamite and the use of machinery had contributed to the problem. The report highlights the increase in the incidence of respiratory disease in the Charters Towers gold field following the replacement of hand working by machines. 'Quartz crystals enter the lungs' and lead to 'a painful and lingering death.' There was an 'urgent need to safeguard miners from dust' created by the use of machinery.[210] Stephen Madgen wrote to his father from Tarrangower Diggings, at Maldon, 85 miles north of Melbourne in 1855 telling him that others from Cumberland were in the same area. He told how working the quartz reefs was 'all the go now.' The rock was 'crush[ed] to powder' by machines.[211] In New Zealand too, similar dangers existed in the 120 quartz and 140 coal mines that were in operation in 1901.[212] It is not known if John Johnston's death in West Cumberland from miner's phthisis in 1908 was caused by his work in South Africa before he returned *c*.1896 or from mine work at home.[213] Both Mr Wilkinson of Moor Row and his son, Thomas died in South Africa of miners' phthisis and when William Cromwell died there in 1905, 35 named Cumberland men and 'many more' attended his funeral.[214] Alfred Armstrong of Moor Row and John Patterson died after returning home suffering from the disease. William J. Magee of Cleator Moor died only a few weeks after returning home – 'one of a long line of Cleator Moor victims of the dreaded miner's phthisis.'[215] An editorial comment stated 'the disease had carried off so many Cumberland men.'[216] Yet still they went in dozens; even hundreds. In 1909 several women were among a larger group who left Cleator Moor for South Africa. Presumably they were going to join their husbands.[217]

Cumbrian emigrants in the sample were in mines in many locations. In the 1830s, some of the young Westmorland men in Birmingham and Pittsburgh, Pennsylvania worked in the coal pits.[218] Others went to coal mining areas in Pennsylvania such as Pottsville, Mahanoy, Sewickley and in Schuylkill or Westmorland Counties. Isaac Miller was at Leadville, Colorado in 1905 and although the great days of silver production were waning, Leadville was still an important centre with several mines in the area. Bisbee in Arizona was only a few miles from the Mexican border. It was founded *c*.1880 in 'a region of cattle thieves and outlaws,' smugglers and train robbers. 'Hordes of desperadoes' gathered there intent on criminal activity. By 1900 the huge open pit copper mine was 'one of the largest in the world' and in 1906 the miners went on strike for higher wages. A 1908 photograph shows barren hills with buildings clustered in the foreground.[219] William Gibson and William Twentyman of Arlecdon were among the Cumbrians at the Bisbee mines. Several other ex-iron ore miners, their wives and families were at a number of mining communities in Arizona including Bisbee and at mines in California in the 1890s.[220] William Harvey, Felix Byrne and others were at the Butte Mines, Montana; a 'major industrial mining centre' in 1909. Felix Byrne's brother had died at Bisbee in the same year.[221] John Dawson was at the Ymire mines, British Columbia in 1910. Others were at mines in Ontario and other locations in eastern Canada. From family information it seems that more than 30 families from West Cumberland were in the coal mining area near Greymouth on New Zealand's South Island before 1914. Among these was Isaac Spedding from Egremont.

Anthony Clarke and J. C. Hudson were both connected with engineering or mining projects in the Transvaal and Rhodesia. Mr Hudson from Wasdale worked at a cyanide plant, part of the gold smelting process. His letters from Pilgrim's Rest near Sydenberg in 1894-6 tell of his lonely life, the plants and fruit grown, the developing troubles in southern Africa including the murder of 200 white people by the Matabele, swarms of locusts and outbreaks of rinderpest and pleuro-pneumonia in cattle. He expressed thanks for Cumberland newspapers, sent a photograph of a giraffe home but thought that 'the snuff here is not Kendal Brown.'[222] Anthony Clarke was an engineer with Pauling and Co. By 1904-5 was a farmer.[223] Although not a miner, at least one emigrant worked on a major construction project – the Roosevelt Dam where a Cumberland man fell to his death.[224]

Cultural and social life

Only a few comments in the letters and other sources refer to cultural and leisure activities. One of the earliest was from Sibella Crozier in 1819 when she visited her brother in Java. She thought that social life there was good. After a party she remarked that the 'beaux were numerous and agreeable' even though she 'detest[ed] the odious custom of waltzing.'[225] Clearly, emigrants who had settled in towns and cities had opportunities that a homesteader on the prairies, a farmer in Texas or in other destination countries such as New Zealand could not have. But even when work on the land dominated life, there must have been time for leisure. What evidence do we have that gives even a hint of the social life of Cumbrians overseas? While many letters reveal nothing of their religion, in others the church or chapel together with comments on religious practice are frequently mentioned. Some emigrants were Quakers, some were Presbyterians and others were members of the Church of England or Methodists. It is clear that for many their faith was an important part of life. In new settlements a church or chapel created a focus for both spiritual and social needs and helped to bind the community together. Of course, sometimes opposing doctrines could create division not cohesion but, nevertheless, each 'side' would be bound together. Emigrants writing to their families about their church or chapel may also have wished to assure relatives at home of their adherence to their faith and that they were leading a 'good life.'

As well as the spiritual welfare of its members, a church or chapel provided social contacts, perhaps a choir, women's meetings, a Sunday School, organised bazaars, picnics, concerts and children's 'treats.' We read in some letters of the hope that even if families were not reunited in this life, they would meet again in the hereafter. Joseph Hall wrote from Canada in the mid- nineteenth century that he was 'endeavouring to attend to things that pertain to my soul.'[226] For many Cumberland and Westmorland emigrants, the church or chapel had been the focus of community life at home before emigrating therefore the pattern was continuing.

It is clear from a letter written by William Crook in 1832 that the church was an important part of his life in New York. The nearest church was 'wealthy and respectable' with a 'fashionable and opulent congregation' but he preferred another – 'a beautiful building with a marble front and large ionic pillars where the minister was 'a very interesting young [man].' [227] Fifty years later, in 1888, Mr R. Harrison was unable to find the 'Talmages tabernacle' in Brooklyn, assured his family that he drank only lemonade not alcohol and commented on the many saloons. 'It is a great country for drink and wickedness.' Such views reflected his Methodist background in the Eden Valley and their principles.[228]

Thomas Hodgson from north Westmorland was in Pittsburgh in 1832-3. He wrote that 'there is no want of talent among preachers ... but ... their sincerity may be suspect.'[229] In the later nineteenth century, Christopher Gelder was a Methodist local preacher in North Dakota, taught in Sunday school and mentions a 10 day revival camp meeting held in 'a big tent' at Bathgate.[230] During these same years George Calcott was at Rattlesnake Hill in Texas where, until a small church was built a Circuit rider called once per month. The Calcotts were devoted to their faith and 'the family readily adjusted to the demands of puritanical living' with no dancing, no drinking, no card playing and no work on the Sabbath. The Gelder family's life was similar although their children were allowed to play some approved card games.[231] In 1908 the Revd J. Thompson, D.D. was 'one of the most prominent [Methodist Episcopalian] ministers in Chicago.' He had risen 'from the humble occupation of a lead miner' in Cumberland.[232]

One correspondent reported in 1853 that people had stood in the aisles in a Melbourne church. Mary Lowe's letters from New South Wales contain many references to the Episcopal Church. For example, in 1836 a church had recently been built within reach of her home in Sidmouth Valley. In 1837, the need for clergymen and the appointment of the former Archdeacon to be Bishop was reported. By 1840 Mary Lowe was concerned about the growth of the Roman Catholic faith in New South Wales. 'I sincerely hope and trust it will never be the fate of us to become converts to such superstition and idolatry as that professed by their church.' Five years later she wrote, 'Puseyism is on the increase here – many clergymen have embraced the doctrine' and 'I fear our Bishop has turned Puseyite.' In 1852, Mary Lowe's letter tells of the 'great field of labour' awaiting the two clergymen appointed to the gold mines near her home where a canvas church had been erected.[233]

In New Zealand, George Rigg (from Carlisle) and his wife were members of the Plymouth Brethren, Joseph Dowthwaite was a Methodist lay preacher, William Atkinson was a 'staunch' Methodist, James Parker was a missionary before becoming a Methodist minister and William Benson was 'an ardent Methodist.'[234] Thomas and William Slee, the Armistead family and Joseph Hodgson are examples of Methodist emigrants who settled in Canada. The Revd. Peter Addison was a Methodist minister who served his flock in southern Ontario on horseback in the later nineteenth century.[235] Joseph Hall wrote that there were several churches of different denominations within reach of his home in Ontario but he attended one of the two nearby Methodist chapels 'once or twice every Sunday' – a class meeting in the morning and circuit preaching or prayer meetings on alternate Sunday evenings.[236] The Revd. Wilkinson was a Methodist minister in Nanaimo, a mining community on Vancouver Island.

Societies and movements such as the Freemasons, the Oddfellows, Druids, Rechabites, Good Templars and other Friendly or Social Societies were represented in overseas destinations. Such societies for men, promoted particular ideals, for example, philanthropy, care of members and their families especially during times of illness or hardship and provided social contacts and convivial gatherings at regular meetings. William Slee, from Kirkby Stephen settled in Hamilton in 1880 as a carpenter. He was a member of the Oddfellows and the Ancient Order of Foresters. In New Zealand's South Island the Freemasons had Lodges in Christchurch, Lytellton, Hokitika, Greymouth, Kaiapoi, Nelson, Dunedin, Timaru and Oamaru by the 1860s. The Ancient Order of Foresters was in Christchurch by 1851 and the Druids from 1876. In North America, the Freemasons had been active from the mid-eighteenth century. Lodges were formed in Ontario from the 1830s and subsequently across the continent.

Concern about excessive drinking in England and overseas resulted in the growth of Temperance organisations; in Australia from the 1830s and from the 1860s in Canada. Stephen Madgen wrote about the quantity of spirits and liquor consumed at the Victoria Diggings but he only 'made use of one glass every night as the weather is so wet and cold.'[237] Correspondents commented on the drunkenness to be found in Hamilton and Toronto in Canada. Jeffrey Hodgson, a farmer near Pittsburgh who had emigrated from north Westmorland before 1832 was stated to 'like the whisky too well.'[238] A Total Abstinence Society was formed in Adelaide, South Australia in 1839 and The Women's Christian Temperance Union was active there from 1886.[239] In New Zealand, John Elliott from Workington was a staunch teetotaller and member of the Rechabites in Wellington. Andrew Graham from Appleby sang in choirs and was a Deacon of the Baptist church in Auckland. He was a member of the Band of Hope and of the I.O.A. Templars and was devoted to the cause of Total Abstinence. Christchurch was 'a stronghold' of the Temperance movement and the Rechabites were active there from 1877.

The population of the whole Hawke's Bay region in New Zealand's North Island was under 900 in 1857 when Napier, its small regional centre, was described as 'a rather dull place.' But Napier made swift progress. Social life included balls, horse races and sports. Even before the theatre opened in 1864, there had been concerts by visiting musicians and performances by a circus and by companies of actors. Groups of local people gave choral, dramatic and chamber music performances. There were regattas and sports. Horticultural, Philharmonic and other societies were formed and the Freemasons and Oddfellows were represented.[240] William and Thomas Richardson from Culgaith and Hutton Troutbeck were three Cumbrians living in the Esk Valley – in the Hawke's Bay area. They were farmers, land owners and had extensive sheep runs and even if they were not regular participants in the social life of Napier, Agricultural Shows and auction sales attract farmers everywhere. In 1875, an article in the *Hawke's Bay Herald* describes an excursion to the Esk Valley where the writer saw 'a store, two or three neat-looking cottages, the homestead of Messrs Richardson and Troutbeck embowered in trees ... a pretty feature of the landscape.'[241] Within 20 years of its foundation Napier, a small and, at that time, remote community on the coast of the North Island had a thriving social and cultural calendar and all the attributes of regionally important small town. Other communities and growing towns in New Zealand developed a similarly varied range of societies and activities.

In the South Island, the people who founded and developed the physical and business infrastructure in Nelson, Dunedin and Christchurch also formed associations and created their own communal identity through clubs, societies, membership of churches and other cultural and social activities. For example, in Dunedin by 1863 there were two Masonic and three Oddfellow's Lodges, a Gentleman's Club, a Garrick Club, a Debating Society, a Chess Club, a Mechanic's Institute, a Jockey Club, a Building Society, Regatta Club, a Library and three theatres. Caledonian Games were held and the Prince of Wales' marriage was celebrated. Joseph Braithwaite was 'a prominent Oddfellow' and of importance in the 'social and intellectual life' of Dunedin.[242] 'A host of entertainers' regularly visited the town and an English cricket team played there in 1864. Not only were Dunedin people concerned with their own welfare but they sent contributions to the distressed workers in Lancashire.[243]

Towns in New Zealand continued to develop in physical terms, in their quality of life and the opportunities for entertainment and leisure they offered. More societies were formed, new activities were introduced. Sullivan's *Patience* was performed in Dunedin only two years after its premiere.[244] Once the west coast gold rush was under way, new settlements such as Greymouth – 'a scene of gaiety and bustle' at the New Year in 1866 and Hokitika quickly grew from temporary tent and shanty strewn places filled by hopeful prospectors into permanent towns. Hokitika's second anniversary was celebrated for a week of 'roistering,' sports, a regatta, fireworks and entertainments such as Miss Palmerston's rendering of excerpts from Shakespeare that 'delighted rowdy audiences.'[245] Within three years Hokitika had several hotels, a Savings Bank, a Benevolent Society, at least one Temperance Society as attempts to discourage drunkenness gathered pace, Literary and Gymnastic Societies and had seen more than 37,000 people arriving at the port.[246] Nearby Kaniere made similar rapid growth. Two Cumbrian brothers, Arthur and Skelton Head from Braithwaite arrived on the west coast during the gold rush and became hotel keepers – Arthur in Hokitika and Skelton in Kaniere. Joseph Satterthwaite from Santon Bridge in south west Cumberland owned a store at the Hokitika Diggings. Some hotels there were also places of entertainment with dining rooms, billiards, gaming rooms, shooting galleries, skittles and held dances, balls and concerts. These and purpose built theatres and halls were the venues for visiting touring companies of musicians, singers, actors, music hall entertainers, gymnastic troupes and others. Entertainers were reported to visit the goldfields and remote communities in New Zealand, Australia and in North America. Any anniversary was cause for celebration, for example, St Patrick's Day, the New Year, Easter or American Independence and in Greymouth, an additional celebration was held when Louis Napoleon became Emperor of France.[247]

During the gold rush years Arrowtown was a mining settlement in Otago. By the 1870s it had grown into a small town where several denominations had churches – a meeting place for social contact as well as worship. Social life was simple. The arrival of the weekly *Otago Witness* newspaper from Dunedin was a major event and when collecting water from street pumps the women 'had a lovely chat together [which] broke the awful boredom that young wives endured.' By the 1890s the town had three hotels, a library, a Drill Hall and the Athenauem Hall where concerts, dances and other events took place. 'People made their own fun and community participation was high.' Outdoor activities included horse racing, rugby, hockey, athletic sports and wrestling (Cumberland and Westmorland style). Professional entertainers and a theatre companies visited the town 'as part of their Otago circuit.[248]

In the years from 1908-1911 Norman Spedding remembers the opening of the Miners' Hall in Runanga that was celebrated by three balls where they danced 'to the early hours of the morning,' the showing of the first silent films, the Sunday 'get-togethers' in the Hall, the 'good local talent,' the orchestra, the frequent concerts and the Minstrel Shows. In the gold rush days a Vaudeville Company had travelled to Greymouth from Australia and had later bought projection equipment, moving around the area showing films. Mr Spedding writes of celebrating Dominion Day, of a number of sports activities in the community, of membership of the army cadets, of shopping excursions into Greymouth and of visits from travelling shows such as Vaudeville, dramatic comedies, plays and the circus. Runanga grew into 'quite a nice little township' with shops, picture shows three times per week, and bicycle races on many Saturdays. Sports meetings there included Cumberland and Westmorland style wrestling.[249] In 1914, Cumbrians gathered together in Runanga for the 'ancient custom' of goose-carding. After the 'carding' there was a 'sumpuous spread' followed by songs and recitations.[249] These examples of activities in two small New Zealand communities illustrate life there at the end of the nineteenth century. Other places would have been similar. But for the farmers and those living in rural areas in New Zealand and in other destination countries the daily routine meant many hours of hard work. Social and community life revolved only within the family and neighbours, perhaps attending church or chapel on Sunday – or gathering together when a travelling minister called. Recreation and amusements had to be 'home made.' Christopher Gelder's accordion, Mrs Wood's piano, Joseph Hall's singing are examples of entertainment within the home or neighbourhood. But such 'home-made' entertainment and social life being centred on church or chapel was also part of Cumbrian life in the nineteenth century. In Canada, a correspondent wrote that the winter was a time for visiting friends and family and of recreation.[250]

In Australia, Melbourne had four theatres in 1882; Sydney and Adelaide both had two theatres and a number of concert halls. 'Hundreds of theatrical notables' visited Australia. Farming emigrants near Adelaide such George Brunskill or John Johnston were more likely to have visited the Agricultural Shows than theatrical performances but several, including Joseph Ladyman, Thomas Dixon and Robson and Mary Urwin were in the city. Sporting activities of all kinds were available. Adelaide had hosted the first inter-colonial cricket match against Perth in 1850. In 1874, W. G. Grace and his English Eleven played against South Australia at the Adelaide Oval and one of the first series of test matches against England was played there in 1891-2. Swimming, boating, hunting, racing, shooting, golf, croquet, tennis, cycling even roller skating football, and soccer from 1890 were all popular.[252]

New York was already a large and thriving city in the eighteenth century with theatres, musical performances, societies, churches of many denominations as well as other forms or entertainment and amusement but none of the letters refer to visits to the theatre. William Crook's letter suggests that he and others followed less formal social activities. For example, he had been to several parties in New York in 1832, one with more than 100 guests and had 'danced Quadrilles' until the early hours but had found 'more stiffness and formality than at home.'

His other main social contacts were through membership of his church.[252] Christopher Gelder wrote of baseball being played in North Dakota. Entertainers visited mining settlements at the goldfields. By the mid-1850s there were more than dozen theatres in San Francisco where entertainments included dancing, acrobatics, instrumental music and excerpts from opera.[253] Entertainers including singers offering popular ballads and operatic arias travelled throughout America.

In Canada, as elsewhere, theatres, public halls and even opera houses were built only a few years after many communities were founded. For example, Ottawa had a theatre from 1836 and by 1875 there was a 1,500 seat opera house and a music hall. Concerts were regularly held. Visiting companies performed plays and opera. *H.M.S. Pinafore* was performed in 1879, only a year after its premiere in England. Ottawa Choirs sang excerpts from choral works including Haydn's *Creation* in 1875. Although not in Ottawa, Joseph Hall was in Ontario in 1857 and thanked his relatives in north Westmorland for sending copies of Handel's *Messiah* and of *The Creation* which suggests that he sang in a local, possibly his chapel choir.[254] Singers, groups of entertainers, small groups of musicians and travelling players toured the country. From the end of the century Cumbrian emigrants on the western prairies in Calgary, Regina, Winnipeg and Vancouver formed Cumberland and Westmorland Societies and met at least once per year for celebratory dinners. It is possible that there were other such societies in other destinations. The sources suggest that many Cumbrian emigrants were within visiting distance of each other and letters frequently mention names that would be known to relatives at home therefore social life would have been on a more informal level especially for emigrants who had settled in rural areas. Summer sports with Cumberland and Westmorland Wrestling events were popular. In 1909 Frank Dobinson of Warcop, won a cup for wrestling at Winnipeg. A Penrithian, John Lester, visited England with the Philadelphian's cricket team from the United States in 1897, 1903 and 1908.[255]

In Manitoba, 'a very good place to live,' winter sports, football, baseball, cricket, tennis, hunting and fishing were mentioned in letters.[256] In New Zealand, Walter Irving from Corby near Carlisle was active in local sporting life as president of the Trotting Club and as a Cumberland and Westmorland style wrestler.[257] And in South Africa, 'a large gallery of Cumberland people from the Jumper's Deep area' were spectators at the Roodeport Sports in 1905 watching wrestling and other events and celebrating the participation and success of Cumbrians.[258] Essie Metcalfe's letters written during her visit to South Africa and Rhodesia from the site of the bridge over the Zambesi near the Victoria Falls tell of the progress in building the bridge and the railway, of social life among the engineers and their families, sports such as cricket, tennis, croquet, and athletic sports – 'a very good gathering for the wilds of Africa.' The New Year was celebrated in style. Guns and engine whistles sounded and fireworks lit up the sky. She wrote of the people she met some of whom were based there, others were distinguished visitors. In particular she described the grand celebrations at the opening of the bridge.[259]

Political and topical matters in England and overseas were occasionally discussed in letters. William Shaw was in Philadelphia but asked for news of the Chartists and Feargus O'Connor.[260] Several letters refer to the Civil war in the United States. Robert Rathnell described events in New York and Philadelphia during the War of Independence in 1778.[261] The Revd. Holme wrote of revolution in Peru, of a 'Romanish procession' in Lima and gave his opinion of the Roman Catholic religion in South America.[262] Mrs Wood, in New South Wales asked for news of English fashions in 1819.[263] In his letter to Hilton from Pittsburgh in 1867 Joseph Hodgson commented on the 'humbug' of Fenianism – 'The British government will have to use … more vigorous measures.' He also replied to comments in a letter from Hilton about the policy of the American President and stated 'the true principle of liberty will ultimately prevail and this country will become as free for the black man as it is for the white' – a situation not finally resolved for almost another hundred years.[264] Mary Lowe's letter from New South Wales in 1846 refers to her anxiety about the Queen. 'We hope it is only a rumour.'[265] James Walker wrote of his experience in the army during the Civil War in the United States.[2651] J.C. Hudson's letters from the Transvaal in 1896 included comments on 'the Boer situation' and problems with the Matabele people.[267] William Milner's letters refer to the Zulu wars and the war in Afghanistan in 1880.[264] Letters to relatives in Carlisle contain eye-witness accounts of the San Francisco earthquake in 1906.[269]

Many letters tell of nostalgia, homesickness, memories of home and concern over the welfare of family in Cumbria but were usually tempered with positive feelings about their new life. Christopher Gelder never forgot north Westmorland. He thought of the 'land where the fields are green' and where he 'would climb once more as in the days of yore … the mountain which … seems to touch the sky.[270] John Hodgson wrote to his uncle in Hilton from near Pittsburgh with similar sentiments. While he would not live anywhere else, he would like 'to be with you for two or three months' to visit friends and relations and to see Dufton, Murton, Hilton, Fell Dykes and his home again. Twenty three years after emigrating he wrote – 'Please send some little memorial … even a leaf from a tree or a bunch of cat posies.' 'My mind lingers around Burthwaite … my happy boyhood days among the mountains and dales of old Westmorland.' [271] Another correspondent thought the Bewcastle area of north Cumberland was 'the grandest country in the world.'[272] Edith Spark wrote soon after arriving in Western Australia in 1912. 'Dear old Garrigill. We wish we could be back with you all for a few hours. We feel we could be happy if only we had our own home and friends here. The country is promising ... one feel[s] very hopeful. ... We see the advantages of Australia [but] ... at present we feel unsettled and a bit homesick.'[273]

The Gelder family in North Dakota maintained their Cumbrian Christmas customs and ate goose, plum pudding and mincemeat pies. John Hodgson wished his relatives in north Westmorland a 'Happy New Year and plenty of roasted goose.'[274] Margaret White wrote from Ipswich, near Brisbane in 1869 that 'Easter is not much noticed here. There is [*sic*] no pace eggs or new clothes for the children.'[275] Norman Spedding refers to the 'quaint custom' [of making pace eggs] practised in Cumbria before 1914. Eggs were decorated often by coating them with onion skins before boiling them. This resulted in abstract patterning on the shells. The pace eggs were rolled 'down grassy slopes' – a custom that survived in Cumberland until at least the mid-twentieth century.[276]

Emigrants, whether in new communities or as recent members of established towns or cities tried to retain at least some customs of their homeland while settling into their new life. For the individual emigrant in a large cosmopolitan community, the task was to fit into local society and adopt their ways. But, wherever the emigrants whose names we know settled it is striking how often they tell of friends, relatives or fellow Cumbrians within visiting distance. Some even suggest that they prefer not to mix with others in the area apart from 'their own' people. But, the next generation was different. They were already men and women of the new land. While Christopher Gelder and his wife retained their Westmorland accents throughout their lives, their children were like their American neighbours and as such the melding of emigrants into true citizens of the destination country became a reality.

Chapter 6:
Returned emigrants and sojourners

Not all emigrants settled in their new surroundings. Many returned because of dissatisfaction, unemployment, failure, homesickness, ill health, bereavement or having made sufficient money to retire. Others returned home after serving abroad for a few years or an entire working life as administrators, in business, on military service or in the army. They were sojourners. It has been estimated that between one quarter and one third of all those who emigrated from Europe before 1914 returned. From c. 1870-1914, the proportion may have been as high as 40 per cent and to take just one year, 1871, 677 emigrants returned to England from New Zealand and 2,949 returned from Victoria.[1] In general, and for England in particular, published statistics are not helpful, as most fail to distinguish between passengers and immigrants. In 1902, government figures estimated that for every 100 British people who left – as passengers and emigrants, 51 returned, only some of whom would be emigrants. Others would be returning from business or other reasons for temporary visits abroad. For the English element which would include Cumbrians, (Table 6.1) the inward flow was substantial.[2]

From 1901-1915 the scale of movement was huge and not only to and from Britain. People moved between countries, for example from Australia to New Zealand and vice versa. A newspaper report in 1906 cited more than 200 English immigrants who had returned from Montreal – 'disgusted with the conditions of life. ... Early rising and the industrious life on a Canadian farm had proved entirely uncongenial [and] life was too lonely for the women.'[3] It has been estimated that 10 per cent of English emigrants who went to the United States in 1908 returned home and in that year more English passengers came to the United Kingdom from America than went to that country.[4] When immigrants were separated from passengers for the first time in British statistics in 1913, 35.5 per cent were returning emigrants.[5] But, total numbers mask many imponderables and the complexities in the currents of emigration make interpreting even the

Table 6.1   English Passengers - inward and outward, 1902

Country	OUT	IN
Canada	20.985	9,737
Australia & N.Z.	11,373	8,541
United States	58,382	32,479
South Africa	34,664	12.682

Source: *BPP 1903 LXXXII EIO Report English passengers only.p.762*

Table 6.2 (A) Passengers returning to Britain 1911 & 1912
(B) Returning emigrants 1912

Country (A)	1911	1912	(B) To England not visitors 1913	
Canada/Br.N.Am	50,095	52,654	B.N.America	18,803
Australia	12,305	14,511	Australia	10,293
New Zealand	2,696	2,562	New Zealand	1,901
United States	72,082	71,507	United States	10,998
South Africa	23,249	23,985	South Africa	8,418

Source: *EIOReports BPP 1913 XLV, LV p.865, 1912-13 LX p.633*

national statistics difficult; a task virtually impossible for a region.[6] Consequently, this chapter merely touches on the scale of return migration into Cumberland and Westmorland.

In the 1911 census, 161,502 people were recorded in England and Wales having been born in the Colonies or Dominions and this figure excludes all those who had a foreign birthplace – including the United States. Although some with an overseas birthplace would have been visitors, the majority were the offspring of parents who had returned. Most were in London, Cornwall, Lancashire, Yorkshire, County Durham and Staffordshire. While visitors may have predominated in London, the inclusion of industrial and mining regions strongly suggests returning emigrants.[7] The only evidence of emigrants returning to Cumbria is from the overseas birthplace of children enumerated in the census. Single emigrants and families with no children born overseas who returned are invisible unless family information fills in details therefore only minimum levels of return are known.

Distance and cost were inhibiting factors for returning emigrants or visitors from Australia and New Zealand but government papers indicate that in 1844 72 adults and children left Adelaide for the United Kingdom. In only one quarter in 1849, less than 10 years after the first colonies in New Zealand were established, 16 men, women and children returned home. During the first six months of 1850, 176 including freed convicts, men on military service and others returned to London from Van Diemens's land.[8] In 1871, 2,949 passengers from Victoria and 677 from New Zealand sailed to Britain.[9] Some of these would be disillusioned gold seekers. Approximately 1,300 of the 4,665 with a New Zealand birthplace who were in England and Wales in 1911 were visitors therefore more than 3,300 were children of returned emigrants.[10] From 1861-70, an average of 25,000 emigrants per year returned home.[11]

How many (if any) of the emigrants returning to England in 1913 (Table 6.2 (B)) were Cumbrians is unknown. In the wake of gold rushes across the world, for example in the 1850s and mid-1860s, many gold seekers returned from

California, Australia and New Zealand; often penniless. In 1861, during the Victoria gold rush, 5,909 left Australia and returned to Britain.[12] Emigrants returned from the United States, especially during economic crises such as those in 1873, 1877, 1894 and 1908. They had found 'the streets were not paved with gold but were very hard with real stones.'[13]

Clearly, those who emigrated had intended to settle or at least to stay until they had earned sufficient money to return to a better standard of life than that which they had left. Single men and women had perhaps more freedom to move, to stay or to return. The majority of emigrants were able to earn good wages or work for themselves in the new country giving at least a reasonable standard of living and a 'life-style' which although often more simple than at home especially for farmers and homesteaders, they hoped would be preferable to life in England. Those who had emigrated with free or assisted passages would have found the cost of returning so challenging that their decision must have seemed irrevocable. Letters frequently tell of the emigrant's desire to return for a visit, to see family and friends again even if that were an impossible dream but not to abandon their new life in spite of feelings of nostalgia, even homesickness.

Some emigrants found it impossible to adapt to life abroad. One correspondent told of both sets of grandparents who had found that 'the grass was not greener' and returned to Cumberland. In 1859 John and Rebecca Fearon and their children, then living in Liverpool went to Canada having moved there from Cockermouth two years previously. Their destination was Bonne Chère River, Ontario, where a relative was living. They found that their new home was to be in the forest. Trees and undergrowth had to be cleared, a log cabin built and farming land created. Eventually John Fearon owned more than one farm and employed two other Cumbrian families to run them which suggests evidence of chain migration and clusters of origin and destination. John Fearon then opened a store but financial problems and his wife's desire to return home led to their returning to Cockermouth in 1868 having lost all their savings.[14]

A visit to the home country became a realistic proposition from the mid-nineteenth century and the sample includes several who visited their home county more than once. James Woodward of Dubuque, Iowa visited Kirkby Stephen on several occasions. In the 1860s Mr P.C. Threlkeld was in England and John Airey returned twice – in 1878 and 1898, both from New Zealand. Visitors came in increasing numbers. Although some passengers on ships from Australasia were returnees, others were not. Australians visited the Colonial and Indian Exhibition in London in 1886 and in 1911, 23,000 with an Australian birthplace were in England and Wales. Only some of these would be visitors.[15] Some emigrants, for example Anthony Tyson, returned briefly in order to escort elderly parents or siblings to the new country. In 1906, he took his mother and sister to Manitoba where they joined his family and other siblings.[16]

'Some steerage passengers to the United States stayed three days, some three months, others went home on the same ship. Some had sold everything including clothes to pay for the return home [and were] even poorer than before they left.'[17] When Thomas and Jonty Lambert from Brough were not met by their sponsor or friend at the docks in New York they returned home immediately.[18] John Yeats from Alston went to Canada in 1883 but did not stay. Jonathan Gelder and his brother went to North Dakota. Jonathan returned to Westmorland to marry in 1896, took his wife to America but in 1902 he sold his farm, returned home and settled in Long Marton, Westmorland. After about four years in the United States, Susanna Barnfather went home during the Great War to marry and remained in Carlisle.[19] Thompson Park from Crosby Ravensworth was in Illinois for about four years before returning home.[20] Mr Hethorne of Melmerby went to Australia in the mid-nineteenth century taking his household with him. After his death two of his servants stayed for four years before returning home.[21] It seems that Christopher Monkhouse and his family had been in New Brunswick in the 1820s when his daughter was born but was in Brough in 1849. Benjamin Simpson and his wife had been in New York at the time of their daughter's birth in the early 1850s. Mr Simpson was stationmaster at Warcop in 1871.[22]

While some whose aim had been to seek gold stayed and took other occupations, others returned home but not all were content to remain in England. Giles Walker and George Park (Thompson Park's brother) later re-emigrated to Australia and Ohio respectively. John Elliott of Workington went to Valparaiso, Chile in 1862, was in Workington in 1866 but went to New Zealand with his wife and son in 1872. William Herd went to New Zealand in 1884 from Cumberland. He returned in 1892 and farmed in Northamptonshire for several years before re-emigrating to New Zealand in 1906.[23] The Spedding family went to New Zealand in 1908, moved to Australia but did not like it and returned to Egremont only to re-emigrate some time later to the same small coal mining town in South Island, New Zealand where they stayed.[24]

Several families in the sample returned after the wage-earner died. Mary Ann Ormandy was a young widow living in Kirkby Stephen in 1861. Her young son had been born in the western Canada. Frances Tuer was in Drybeck in 1861. Her three year old son had also been born in western Canada.[25] Colonial governments gave financial help to assist some to return. Alice Fraser, a domestic servant was found to be unfit for work on arrival in Australia and sent home to Carlisle.[26] While assistance might be seen as a philanthropic gesture, it also avoided the cost of supporting such people in the new country. Regular travellers would enter the statistics annually and thus distort total numbers. Harry Park of Crosby Ravensworth went to the United States 11 times to sell horses.[27] In the

145

later nineteenth and early twentieth centuries many migrant workers went abroad, some, for example seasonal construction workers, crossed the Atlantic on a regular basis. These temporary emigrants and others such as craftsmen or miners intended to return after saving their wages in order to support a better life at home. Other emigrants went for a trial period and were prepared either to return or stay depending on circumstances. In 1870, for example, emigrants who had worked in mines in Arizona or California could return home after about 10 years with 'well-lined pockets' which would enable them to live in comfort. But often they went back to earn more.[28] By c.1900 the 'tidal flow' of young men from West Cumberland to South Africa included many who made repeated journeys to the gold, copper and diamond mines. However, South Africa did not fulfil the expectations of all. In 1891 Esme Howard had met many emigrants 'leaving [South Africa] ... in disgust.' They were 'ex-policemen, pioneers, prospectors, and others.' South Africa had been promoted as an 'earthly paradise' but was 'a land of fever, privation and want.'[29]

Returnees and visitors had a significant influence within their local community. Many returned for personal reasons having no complaints against the destination but even if the reason for return were negative, the effect on prospective emigrants might be only to change the destination rather than to decide that 'home was best.' Newspaper reports of emigrant groups often include the names of previous emigrants who after visiting home accompanied the new leavers.

Overseas birthplaces

The 1851-1901 census enumerations for the two counties show that the number of Cumbrian residents with an overseas birthplace increased decade by decade. (Table 6.3) A high proportion of the Cumberland returnees were enumerated in the industrial areas of Carlisle and West Cumberland which although reflecting the distribution of population, was also influenced by the economy and the overall level of emigration. (Map 6.1) Fewer with an overseas

Table 6.3   Overseas birthplaces* and returned emigrants 1851-1901

Category	1851 Cumb	1851 West	1861 Cumb	1861 West	1881 Cumb	1881 West	1901 Cumb	1901 West
Returned emigrants	20	-	93	15	317	49	386	50
Adults born abroad	24	9	37	7	117	21	115	26
Children born abroad	12	8	56	18	205	41	263	41
Total	56	17	186	40	639	111	764	117

Source: *Census enumerations. *Excluding Europe*
Children born abroad include pupils in boarding schools and young adults living with parents.
'Returned emigrants' includes older siblings born in Britain who emigrated with parents.

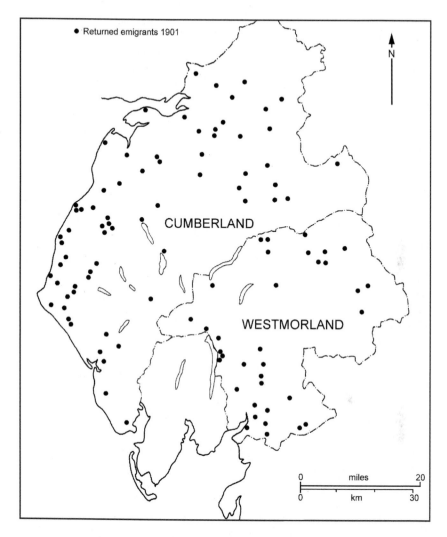

6.1 Location of known returned emigrants in 1901.

birthplace were in Westmorland, but as the population was so much smaller than that of Cumberland and the numbers that emigrated were lower, this is entirely predictable. The data in Table 6.3 showing known returned emigrants comprises those families who had at least one child born abroad but how many emigrated and returned without a child being born overseas? So much is missing and anomalies abound. Consequently this analysis must be treated with caution and

Table 6.4   Absent or dead parents 1851-1901

Category	1851	1851	1861	1861	1881	1881	1901	1901
	Cumb	Westm	Cumb	Westm	Cumb	Westm	Cumb	Westm
Dead	2	-	5	-	32	1	22	1
Absent or dead	5	-	12	3	42	9	108	11
Total	7	-	17	3	74	10	130	12

Source: *Census enumerations.*

Table 6.5   Overseas birthplaces including returned emigrants 1851-1901

Category	1851	1851	1861	1861	1881	1881	1901	1901
	Cumb	Westm	Cumb	Westm	Cumb	Westm	Cumb	Westm
Australia	4	1	27	14	113	19	82	26
Canada	16	-	61	6	87	19	95	28
N. Zealand	-	1	-	-	10	13	36	14
S.Africa	-	-	-	-	17	-	169	10
USA	33	7	87	20	353	59	352	25
W. Indies	3	1	-	-	40	-	-	-
Total	56	10	175	40	620	110	734	103

Source: *Census enumerations. These numbers include all with birthplaces in the selected counties*

indicates only approximate levels.

Many with overseas birthplaces were adults with no family attachments or were married to a British-born spouse with no evidence to indicate if the partner was a returnee or if the marriage had been abroad. Often the spouse would be the adult child of an unidentified returned emigrant. In some families, we are able to follow a migration pattern – where the family had been at the time of the birth, approximate dates and length of stay. Increasing numbers had returned but as emigration had increased so greatly the proportion is unknown.

There are many examples of families where a parent had died but did the death occur before or after returning? If the family included younger children born in Cumbria, then the return would have been before death but if only the last child was born locally, the mother could have returned while pregnant. Another group comprises children or young adults living with grandparents or other relatives with no indication of family circumstances. Were their parents dead or overseas? Pupils in boarding schools have been omitted from Table 6.4 because it is possible (but unknown) that at least one parent would be alive, perhaps overseas or, if in Britain, unidentifiable as the parent. Any of uncertain status is included in the 'absent or dead?' category.

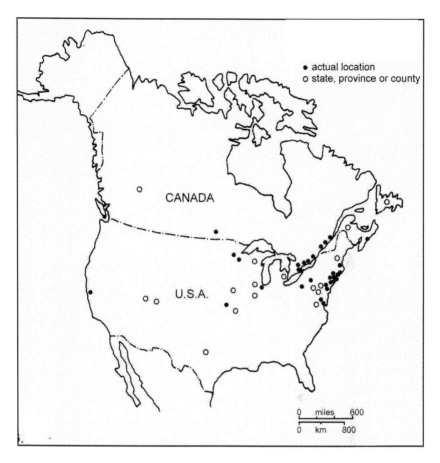

6.2 North America showing where residents in Cumbria had been

Country from which the emigrants returned

Where were the emigrants returning from and when? The first question is easier to answer than the second. Table 6.5 shows only the countries under examination in this project from which the returnees had come.

Fewer returned emigrants had a birthplace in Australia and New Zealand than in North America partly because the distance meant fewer returns but also because fewer emigrants went to Australasia. Although some emigrants to South Africa became farmers or worked in other capacities, the majority went after the development of gold and diamond mining in the late nineteenth century. Some children born in South Africa seem to have been with their mother in Cumbria.

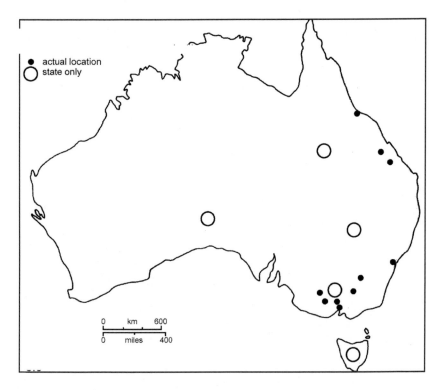

6.3 Australia showing where residents in Cumbria had been

There is no indication in the census (apart from a handful of women described as widows) if the father had died or was still in South Africa as a regular 'commuter' between the mines and home.

Destinations within an overseas country are known only if stated and that may be only one of several in which the emigrants had resided. An overseas town or county within the country was mentioned for only approximately 40 per cent in 1851, 32 per cent in 1861, 39 per cent in 1881 and 44 per cent in 1901. Maps 6.2 and 6.3 show known destinations of the returnees in North America and Australia in 1901. Montreal, Quebec and Toronto in Canada occur in each enumeration. By 1901 it is clear that Cumbrians had spread across the continent. Birthplaces ranged from Halifax, Nova Scotia and Prince Edward Island in the east to Winnipeg and British Columbia in the west. In 1851, although birthplaces of returned emigrants in the United States were only in the east, the parents could have travelled farther into the interior before or after the birth. It is known that Cumbrian emigrants did settle in other destinations in the first half of the

150

nineteenth century. In 1881 birthplaces include Seattle, Rhode Island, Wisconsin, Texas and New Orleans and in 1901, Oakland in California, Iowa, Colorado, Chicago and Washington.

Identified birthplaces in South Africa were all in the mining region apart from Cape Town, Stellenbosch and Port Elizabeth. Kimberley and surrounding mining communities occur most often. Similarly, several in Australia were in mining regions, for example, Ballarat, Sandhurst, Bendigo, Maldon, Townsville and Newcastle. But returned emigrants had been in other locations including Ipswich, Sydney, Brisbane, Adelaide and Melbourne. Several islands in the West Indies were mentioned but in New Zealand, only Hokitika, Blenheim, Flat Bush which seems to be near Auckland and Kumara, a gold mining centre south of Greymouth are birthplaces named in the enumerations.

Occupations after return

Table 6.6 shows only the occupations of fathers of children with overseas birthplaces as recorded in the census enumerations. Other known returned emigrants, for example, those in the sample are not included.

In 1881 the iron ore miners in Hensingham and Cleator Moor (Table 6.6) had returned from Australia; those from the USA were in Millom, Egremont, Cleator Moor and Arlecdon which suggests clusters of both origin and destination. All the returned coalminers had been to the United States and were enumerated in Great Clifton, Cleator, Aspatria, Flimby and Greysouthen. In 1901, two iron ore miners had returned from Australia. Both were in Millom. Iron ore miners who had returned from the USA were in Cleator and Egremont. South African returnees were in Arlecdon and Egremont. Coal miners from the USA were in Aspatria, Maryport, Flimby and Whitehaven, and four from Canada or New Zealand were in Bolton, Workington, Brigham and Ellenborough. At least some of the returnees had been to destinations to which others had emigrated. How many did not return is unknown.

Few of the known returning emigrants were from or returned to eastern Cumberland or north Westmorland where there was little prospect of finding work in a limited rural economy. Paradoxically, several had returned to the central Lake District which was also a rural economy. John Grieves of Keswick sold a secrétaire to fund his emigration costs to the United States in 1851. Some years later, on returning home he re-purchased his piece of furniture but at a higher price.[30] Returned emigrants in the Kendal area worked in brewing, in gunpowder, shoe, carpet or cloth manufacture, as an income tax collector, a poultry dealer, a chemist and on the railway.

Some young returnees may have lost their parents. In 1871, Elizabeth Richardson, birthplace Adelong, Australia was with her uncle in Crackenthorpe,

Table 6.6 Selected occupations of emigrant fathers after reurn, 1851-1901

Occupation	1851	1861	1881	1901
Farmer	-	3	3	7
Landowner	-	2	-	1
Agric. Labourer	--	2	-	1
Crafts	1	4	14	12
Mining	-	-	8 Coal/9 Iron	8 Coal/10 Iron
Quarry	-	1	1	-
Army	2	3	5	-
Professional	1	2	5	6
Textiles	1	2	5 (1 unempl.)	2
General Labourer	-	3	7	11
Retail/shops	-	3	10	8
Mariner	-	3	4	1
Railway	-	1	9	8
Innkeeper	-	2	4	1
Steel	-	-	2	4
Clerk	-	-	1	2
Journalist	-	-	-	1
Photographer	-	-	-	1
Comm. Traveller	-	-	-	1
Carrier/van driver	-	-	1	1

Source: *Census enumerations. Only returned emigrant fathers identified by their children's birth-places and having a stated occupation in Cumbria after return have been counted here.*

north Westmorland. She had lost both her parents in Australia. Also in the 1871 census John Scott, birthplace America, was with his uncle, and Henrietta Lane, birthplace Melbourne was with her uncle, both in Kirkby Stephen. Elizabeth Evans, birthplace New York, was with her grandparents in Alston and Joseph Millican, a young lead ore dresser born in America was also in Alston with an unmarried aunt. While it is possible that these and other young returnees were with family members while their parents remained abroad or were elsewhere on the night of the census, it does suggest that they may have been orphaned. In 1881 Sarah and Mary Carter, birthplace Queensland, were with their grandfather in Castle Sowerby and Agnes Fox, birthplace Quebec, was in an orphanage in Wigton.

West Cumberland and Carlisle were major sources of emigrants and, as Table 6.7 shows, a high proportion of the known returnees were enumerated there. They were not unemployed. In 1881, of all the returned emigrants of working age in

Table 6.7 Number and location of those with overseas birthplaces, 1851-1901

Location	1851	1861	1881	1901
Carlisle Area	25	57	109	105
West Cumberland	18	75	350	444
East Cumberland	4	22	59	27
North Westmorland	2	6	29	32
South Westmorland	11	24	41	47
Central Lakes	1	16	42	73
Total	61	200	630	728

Source: *Census enumerations.*

the two counties only three were stated to be unemployed. Mr Rolandson of Appleby and Fred Percival of Ambleside were unemployed clerks and Henry Walton of Penrith was a cotton carder. No returned emigrants were identified as unemployed in 1851, 1861 or 1901. In West Cumberland Millom had been a growing town before 1900. Furness was nearby. New iron ore mines were opening even if some were short-lived. The iron and steel and coal mining industries suffered both cyclical and long term problems but the returnees had found work which raises a question about reasons for emigration. If returned emigrants were in work did the decadal censuses reflect an untypical set of circumstances? Were the stated occupations indicating an employed status inaccurately or were opportunities for all returnees to be employed due to the huge outflow that had removed a surplus workforce? Certainly, returnees and those who had stayed had a better chance of finding permanent employment in the wake of migration or emigration. By the late nineteenth century Carlisle had developed a range of industries offering good employment opportunities. Although insecurity and uncertain employment prospects were likely reasons for considering emigration, higher wages abroad were a powerful incentive for persuading miners and others to be part of the 'flood' that left.

As neither the total number of emigrants nor of returnees is known we cannot calculate what percentage returned to Cumbria but it is clear that of the substantial outflow which increased each decade especially from the western part of the region, an increasing number returned. Birthplace evidence in the census enumerations show that Cumbrian families had been in many countries, among which were India, Burma, Ceylon, Brazil, Argentina, Chile, Peru, China, Egypt, Australia, France, Italy, Belgium, Germany, as well as the United States, Canada, South Africa and New Zealand. (Map 3.1)

The male totals in the 1901 census may be affected by the Boer War. In the context of this investigation, the large number of wives whose husbands were absent and had returned from South Africa with at least one child may have returned home to avoid the war, leaving their husbands in Africa. While some were widows, it is likely that some of the 40 absent husbands were still working there. A number of children with South African birthplaces were with relatives. Some may have been orphans but the mother could have stayed in South Africa with her husband.

Table 6.7 shows the number and location of returned emigrants. Map 6.1 indicates their locations in 1901. A significant number of West Cumberland returnees, especially in Cleator, Cleator Moor, Arlecdon, Workington and Millom had Irish, Cornish or Scottish roots.

How long were they abroad?

It is difficult to determine how long emigrants stayed before returning but when a child born in Cumbria emigrated with the parents and a younger child was born after returning, the length of time can be roughly calculated. On this basis, and only from families whose dates give clear date 'windows,' a tentative statement can be offered that the majority who returned had stayed no more than five years, some for only two years. More than 10 years before returning was rare. Mr Cousins from Carlisle, a handloom weaver had two children, born in the USA, in 1849 and 1851. He and his wife had emigrated before 1849 but had returned to Carlisle before the census date in 1851. Mr Cartmell, a schoolmaster in Carlisle had emigrated before 1834. His two older children aged 17 and 16 were born in Philadelphia, the two younger children were born in Carlisle after 1838. Giles Walker and his family were in Gosforth in 1871. He was a West Cumberland man, his wife was from Alston. It seems the family went to Australia before 1860. Three older children were born in Maldon, Victoria, but the four year old was born in Gosforth suggesting that they returned after 1854, before 1867. They re-emigrated in the early 1870s. Maldon was a gold mining centre and others who had been there included Hannah Bray who was in Wigton in 1871. Her two children were born in Maldon. As no father is recorded Hannah may have returned after her husband's death. Another gold mining centre, Sandhurst, renamed Bendigo in 1891, was the birthplace of Ida Mills in 1859. The family was in Millom in 1871. Four children of Joseph Matthews had an Argentina birthplace but the youngest aged two was born in Whitehaven where their father was a firewood merchant in 1891.

A number of overseas births in the enumerations were to army families who should be classified as sojourners but others are less clear. John Pennington was born in Quebec in 1825. In 1851 his father (birthplace Kendal) was a Captain in the army and the family was in Whitehaven. This seems a clear example of army service being responsible for the overseas birth. Ex-Sergeant Flynn had been in the Royal Cumberland Militia. His five year old daughter was born in Melbourne. Did Mr Flynn go to Australia after leaving the army? Did he go to the goldfields? Whatever the reason for the family's emigration, his son John was born off Cape Horn on the way home in 1857. They were in Whitehaven in 1861.

Surprisingly few with an overseas birthplace can be followed through succeeding censuses which could indicate migration or re-emigration. Women may have married and are therefore difficult to trace but Jane Nagel did not marry. Her parents had returned to Carlisle from Australia after 1841 but before 1851. She was still there in 1901 as a retired music teacher. In 1861 Mr Pugmire was an agricultural labourer in Plumpton. His son, Thomas and an older daughter had been born in Canada. The family seems to have returned after about six years abroad. Twenty years later, Thomas was a farm servant in Great Salkeld.

Some emigrants married overseas before returning. Stephen Green, a farmer near Cockermouth married his American wife in the USA before 1848. They returned after 1857. James Philips, a Cumberland commercial traveller married in Ontario where his wife and four year old daughter were born. They had returned before 1881. Ralph Lowis, a joiner in Kirkby Stephen had married in Canada before 1881. He, his wife and three children returned after 1891. Similarly, Forster Wilson of Kendal, a Commission Agent in 1891 and Income Tax Collector in 1901 had married in Tasmania before 1877. The family had returned with two daughters before 1886. Dr Denny of Arthuret had married in the USA before 1888. He returned to Cumberland after 1897; a stay of approximately 10 years.

Several widowed families are in the return lists. The death may have precipitated the return or may have occurred after arrival. In 1881 Mrs Harris was alone in Egremont with three children. Two aged three and two were born in Australia but an infant was born in Cumberland. Mrs Harris may have been widowed and returned while pregnant. Mrs Bray was a widow in Wigton in 1881. Her two daughters had been born in Victoria during the 1860s. Mrs Robinson was a widowed ironmonger in Wigton. Two children aged 12 and 10 had a Wigton birthplace. Her seven and four year old sons were born in Canada suggesting that the family had emigrated after 1871 and returned after 1877, probably following her husband's death. Similarly Mrs Thompson was a widowed grocer in Penrith in 1881. Her three older children had a Penrith birthplace but the two youngest children aged eight and six were born in Canada. Again, it seems likely that they had emigrated with three children but she had returned from Canada after her husband's death.

Many miners and skilled craftsmen in the building or related trades were regular travellers and we have evidence that others emigrated or, alternatively, followed a regular pattern of moving overseas for short periods of work. It is

155

difficult to follow their movements in the sources but family letters and items in newspapers are helpful. Occasionally repeat emigration can be traced in the enumerations. In 1881, Mrs Selby was a widow in Workington. Her 18 year old son had a South African birthplace, the second son was born in Workington but the 12 year old had the same birthplace as the eldest son, Cadoch, South Africa which suggests that she had made at least two journeys to South Africa and that Mr Selby had been employed there.

Some family made several journeys overseas which may or may not indicate emigration. In 1881 James Dunlop was a grocer in Workington. Three of his children were born at sea. His daughter was born off the Cape of Good Hope, in 1867. One son was born on the way to New Orleans in 1868; a younger son was born off Baker Island which seems to be in the Pacific Ocean. Had Mr Dunlop recently become a grocer after years at sea as a mariner? Thirty nine residents in Cumberland and Westmorland in 1881 were 'born at sea.' Most were adults. Several had a military or colonial service background or their father was a master mariner. However, Sarah Caffrey of Cleator aged 11 who was born 'off the Cape of Good Hope' had a nine year old sister whose birthplace was 'near St Helena.' Were they perhaps born on the outward and return journey to the Antipodes? Lillian Sherwood was born while sailing through the Suez Canal in 1876. Two older siblings were born in Whitehaven. In 1881 they and their mother (a widow) were in their grandparents' household in Cumberland. They may have been returning home after Mr Sherwood's death.

Some returned emigrants had not been in Cumbria either before or immediately after their return but had arrived as migrants from other parts of Britain later. Several were from Cornwall, Scotland, Ireland or Wales and had been in Australia or the United States. A number of Irish people were in Cumberland after returning from overseas. At least some of these had emigrated from Cumbria. Mr Flynn and his wife were Irish. In 1901 he was a furnace-man at an iron works in Harrington where he had lived before emigrating. Four children were born in Harrington but the fifth aged seven had a USA birthplace. They had returned by 1897. It is not known if Mr Killen, a lawyer and his wife (both Irish) who went to Canada in 1857 and were in Workington in 1861, and Mr and Mrs Heald who were in St Bees in 1861 with their daughter, born in the USA in 1853, had emigrated from Cumbria or had arrived only after their return.

Ill health could be a reason for emigrating or for returning. Joseph Kilvington of Brough emigrated because of poor health and died in Australia. Richard Gelder, a joiner in Warcop returned from Melbourne in 1892 after five years because of illness. A family with seven children returned from the USA in 1909 because of the mother's ill health and one correspondent reported that several of her relatives emigrated but some 'came back within a year or two to die.' William and Rachel Little of Bowness on Solway returned after nine years in New Brunswick in 1916. He died the following year. For William this was a second emigration. He had previously been a mining engineer in South Africa. William Russell was a mining engineer in Rhodesia in the 1890s. After the Boer War he returned to England, married and went to Saskatchewan but his health soon brought the family home. These mining examples are particularly interesting. Work in hard rock mines caused hundreds of men to contract lung disease and death for many.[31] Robert McAffney took his brother home to West Cumberland from South Africa after he had been almost blinded in an accident. Robert returned to the mines but died soon afterwards in another accident.[32]

John Moser went to Canada as a young solicitor in 1912. Injuries sustained while on military service during the war caused his early discharge. He returned to Canada but came home to Kendal in 1919, married his Canadian fiancée and resumed his law career in Westmorland. The Kearton family had moved from Brough to Cleator Moor. One son, Ralph, went to Boston, USA but, after an accident he returned home and became a grocer's assistant. Many other examples could be given, only some of which indicate the reason for returning. Some may have retired; others returned because of health. Some had simply got the wanderlust urge 'out of their system.'

Several older parents emigrated to join their adult children and stayed in the new country but Mrs Lewis of Milburn who went to Canada with her three sons eventually returned to Milburn. Death overtook at least three emigrants during a visit to England. John Yates died in 1851 while visiting his Cumberland home after 59 years in the USA. Robert A. Ponsonby Brooke of Haile, died in 1885 during a visit from New Zealand. Thomas Richardson died in Culgaith aged 42 in 1877. It is not known if this was during a visit or if he intended to stay.

The majority of emigrants did not return but, increasingly, especially during the late Victorian and the Edwardian years, ex-Cumbrians visited their relatives at home – some on more than one occasion. It is clear from census evidence and from the sample that many from Cumberland and Westmorland did return and re-settled in their native county. In the later years, it is possible that some had emigrated simply to see what living overseas was like, and if home seemed better then it was easy to return. No longer was crossing the ocean a lifetime commitment and such attitudes may have contributed to the increasing numbers of returnees. William Willan went to South Africa as a prospector. He worked as a miner, mining engineer and mine manager in South Africa and Rhodesia. After returning home to marry in 1911 he and his wife went to Canada and visited South Africa before settling in Brough, Westmorland in 1914 where he became a partner in a quarrying business.[33] John Balmer returned to north Westmorland after some years abroad

Only a few returned emigrants can be identified and intriguing questions arise. After John Lilly died in a mining accident in Whitehaven in 1909 his widow returned to Australia. Had he previously emigrated and married there?[34] Some emigrants like the sojourners who set out to serve time abroad before returning home, came back to Cumbria after years of work abroad or to retire. Philip Harrison, born at Brough Sowerby was one of these. He retired to Church Brough after many years in North America.

Willing and Unwilling Sojourners

Sojourners usually returned home after their term of service, in order to retire or, in the case of convicts, at the end of their sentence if that was permitted and if the now freed convict wished to do so. Sojourners therefore need to be discussed separately from emigrants but, on leaving the country they would have been included as passengers or emigrants in the statistics. For thousands of men, women and children, the temporary or sometimes permanent stay in far distant countries was not of their choosing. Convicts were sent to the American colonies until Independence then, from 1788, to Australia. By 1842 more than 80,000 had been sent to New South Wales to serve a sentence lasting a lifetime or a period of years. About two thirds of these were from England and approximately 15 per cent were females. Because of a severe labour shortage and by request, more than 10,000 convicts were sent to Western Australia before transportation finally ended in 1868. Only a small number returned to Britain after serving their sentence. Ex-convicts started a new life in Australia and they, together with free emigrants who went in increasing numbers, were the foundation of the Australian nation.

Other sojourners served overseas in the army, in the Civil Service, as clergymen or missionaries, in medicine, as engineers, in business or on plantations. Many were accompanied by their dependents. These men and women always intended to return home. Some had amassed considerable wealth and were able to live comfortably as 'country gentlemen.' Others retired in modest circumstances. Some clergymen took parishes in England. Engineers and others on shorter contracts perhaps moved on to other projects.

Transportation

The first convicts sailed to New South Wales in 1787. Conditions in early convict ships were 'truly deplorable.'[35] A Carlisle prisoner, awaiting transportation in 1832, stated that he had liked Carlisle Gaol but preferred Millbank, London where the food was better and there was more instruction.[36] Convicts were given lessons in reading, writing and arithmetic before departure and, in later years, during the voyage and, whereas 20 per cent had no knowledge

Hobart, Van Diemen's Land, c.1850.

of arithmetic before embarkation, all had at least some proficiency on arrival.[37] When the *Sir George Seymour* arrived in New South Wales in 1845 85 per cent of the 345 convicts could read 'well or tolerably,' 34 per cent could write 'well or tolerably.' Some commentators have suggested that because literacy was a necessary skill in the new colony, literate convicts or those who were deemed to be 'teachable' were chosen for transportation before the rest.[38]

Appeals were made to the highest authority asking for pardon or leniency. For example, in 1822 the Town Clerk of Carlisle wrote to the Home Secretary begging that a woman with four children convicted of receiving stolen goods be pardoned and 'restored to her husband who is a very honest working man.'[39] There are conflicting views about transportation – was it for first or repeated offences? One study suggests that most were first time offenders whereas another writer calculated that between half and two thirds had previous convictions. Eighty per cent were thieves; few were from rural areas and most were of the 'labouring class.'[40] Both sides of the argument agree that the majority were young, male, mainly from towns and were literate or had skills necessary to build the new colony but very few had any experience in agriculture. Because of the extreme gender imbalance it has been suggested that more females were sent after a first offence 'to be the wives and mothers of the future.'[41] As the years passed and news of Australia reached home, some convicted men and women welcomed transportation rather than being incarcerated in Britain.

In 1830, about 90 per cent of Australia's white population (*c.*63,000) had been transported. Sixty per cent of the convicts were English but 'fringe counties' including the four northern counties of which Cumberland and Westmorland were two, were 'under-represented.'[42] The proportion of convicts in the population would have been even greater when John Wood and his family from near Penrith arrived in New South Wales as free settlers in 1818. By 1847 by which time many had become ex-convicts, large numbers of free emigrants had arrived and only three per cent of the New South Wales population was then serving a sentence.

Similarly, when Richard Downward and his family from Workington arrived in Van Diemen's Land in 1819, convicts formed the overwhelming majority of the population. The 1822 census shows that 102 of the 133 people in Pitt Water (near Hobart later named Sorell) where the Downward family settled were convicts or ex-convicts and they still constituted more than one third of the population in Van Diemen's Land in 1847.[43]

Newspaper accounts of trials at Quarter Sessions and Assizes in Cumberland and Westmorland show that a sentence of transportation for seven years could be for stealing money, or a pony and horse gear, geese, potatoes, clothing or the property of their employer. Stealing sheep or assault and robbery could carry a sentence of transportation for seven years or even for life, probably depending on whether the offence was the first.

It is not clear how many of those sentenced to transportation by the courts were sent to Australia. Estimates suggest that only about two thirds to three quarters actually left England.[44] For the purposes of this investigation, the names of *c.*120 men and women who were sentenced to transportation after being convicted of a crime in the Cumbrian courts have been included in the calculations as well as those known to be in Australia. The Australian Convict Index 1788-1868 contains at least 75 names with a Cumberland reference between 1785 and 1840.[45] James Black and William Cooper had been transported for seven years in 1821 for stealing four and three geese respectively. Mr Christopherson of Carlisle had committed arson.[46] Eleanor Sandwith was transported for receiving stolen cloth. Her children remained in Carlisle.[47] In 1844 and 1845 Isaac Milburn and 12 year old Thomas Rudd were sentenced to be transported for 10 years and John Sewell and John Gillespie for life.[48] In a single year, 1849, after transportation to New South Wales had ceased, Cumberland and Westmorland courts sentenced 27 to transportation but, unless they were sent to Western Australia, they would not have served their sentence abroad. Three men, convicted in Cumberland, went to Western Australia in the *Edwin Fox* in 1858. Patrick Davey had been sentenced at Carlisle for robbery with violence and John Lowes stood trial at Whitehaven for theft. Both received six year sentences. William Graham received a life sentence at Carlisle for manslaughter.[49]

An attempt to find the names of those sentenced in the 1820s in the Cumbrian courts in the New South Wales Census of 1828, the only one to be published, has yielded few matches. Some may have died. Others were perhaps in prison at home or had been sent to Van Diemen's Land. Possible mis-spelling, the use of aliases, the number of common names and possible non-arrival made searching for Cumbrian connections very difficult. However, the 1828 census gives interesting details of settlers and of the employment of convicts in New South Wales. In 1818 John Wood, accompanied by his wife and children arrived at Sydney. Mrs Wood who was from north Westmorland, had died by 1828 when the census reveals that there were four children. Letters sent by Mrs Wood and later by her daughter to a Penrith family tell of the family's life in Australia.[50] John Wood named one of his estates Lowther after the village only a few miles from Penrith, which suggests he was also from north Westmorland. In 1828, ten years after his arrival, he owned 4,840 acres at Chipping near Bringelly, at Lowther, Bathurst and Cox River and had 26 horses, 1,029 cattle and 1,283 sheep. John Wood employed a number of men but only Peter Workman, his 'superintendent' who had accompanied him from Cumbria was a free settler. For the first few decades, until the number of free settlers reached a useful total, convicts underpinned the economy and contributed to the development of Australia. The need for more free immigrants who were experienced agricultural workers and female domestic servants continued for many years.

Convicts were employed directly by the authorities in construction, road building and other schemes but most worked for the settlers. All of John Wood's workers apart from Peter Workman were 'assigned' by the government.[51] At least six had been transported for life. One was in a road gang near Lowther. Others included a stockman, a shepherd and two bullock drivers. Those transported for seven years included a gardener, a shoemaker, a cook and a stockman at Bringelly, all of whom had been freed after serving their sentence. A watchman, a stockman and a labourer at Lowther and a fencer and shepherd at Cox River were serving seven year sentences. Three and possibly four, 'government servants' serving 14 years were employed at Cox River and Bringelly. One had been given a 'ticket of leave.' From this example it is clear that John Wood was a successful emigrant. He owned three estates and employed at least 22 men, only one of whom had emigrated as a free man. In 1828 the population of the Bringelly district was *c.*670 of whom only 44 male and 15 female residents (including children) were free settlers. In New South Wales and in Van Diemen's Land, runaway convicts lived in the bush and survived by living off the land or from the results of robbery. *The Australian* and the Wood family letters contain references to robberies and violence caused by 'bush rangers.' In Van Diemen's Land they represented a real challenge to the authorities and to the free population.[52]

Another probable Cumbrian in the census was John Earl, an innkeeper and farmer who owned an estate called Glenridden (*sic*).[53] He had 1,500 acres and employed two men, both sentenced to seven years, one of whom had completed his sentence by 1828. T. W. M. Winder whose estate was named Windermere was also probably a Cumbrian unless the name is a play on words. He had 7,400 acres and employed 11 government servants still under sentence (including life), two freed by servitude and one with a 'ticket of leave.' Other names common in Cumbria raise questions but their origins cannot be ascertained. For example, was G. T. Savage, a merchant in Sydney and a landholder at Bringelly, from Cumbria? He had emigrated as a free settler and was John Wood's neighbour. William Lawson, another Cumberland name, had emigrated before 1800. In 1828 he had 7,000 acres at Prospect with 1,250 acres under cultivation and owned 10,000 sheep. Isaac Nelson was a farmer and ex-convict. His 100 acre farm was called Ulverstone which, although then in Lancashire, has been in Cumbria since 1974.

Others identified in the 1828 census include Christopher Robley from Cumberland, a 41 year old blacksmith. The census shows that he had served a seven year sentence and, after conditional discharge, was a Sheriff's Officer in Sydney. Lowther Jefferson was also Cumbrian, sentenced to 14 years *c*.1818. He had a ticket of leave and was a shoemaker in Sydney. Local newspapers show that after almost every session of the higher courts in Cumberland and Westmorland men and women were sentenced to transportation during the years 1825 to the late 1840s but even if all went which is unlikely, they formed only a very small proportion of the total sent from England. Apart from incorrigible offenders who continued a life of crime or violence and the few who chose to return to Britain after completing their sentence, thousands of transported men and women may have been unwilling immigrants but as settlers played their part alongside the increasing numbers of free immigrants, in creating the nation of Australia.

Military, administrative and business sojourners

Few went to Asia, Africa (apart from South Africa) or to the West Indies as emigrants but many went to these and other parts of the world for a period of time. Sojourners in the sample have been identified in census enumerations, from correspondence and from newspapers and family records. Cumbrian men served in India with the Honourable East India Company, the British Army and the Civil Service. The East India Company, with bases in Bombay, Madras and Bengal employed several thousand men as civil servants or in other capacities for example, as medical staff, lawyers, chaplains, captains of company ships, cadets, military or naval men and workers. All trade, revenue and military or maritime operations were in the hands of the Company until *c*.1858 when the British government took direct control. Although powerful and nominally independent, the Company had been ultimately answerable to the British government for its actions. Bombay and Madras retained their own armies until the end of the century but other Company forces had become the Indian Army.[54]

In the early nineteenth century Thomas Pattinson, the son of the Rector of Kirklinton, near Carlisle was accepted as a cadet by the Company. Cadets spent two years at Addiscombe Military Academy at Croydon which served a similar purpose in training young potential officers as Sandhurst. Here they studied drill, gun and sword skills and academic subjects. In the 12 years following 1809 almost 400 Addiscombe cadets went to India. After a further period of training in college in Bengal where Hindustani and relevant military skills were taught, the cadet was seconded to a regiment. Promotion in the Company's army was strictly by seniority. In principle, this was a fair system unlike the British army where commissions could be purchased, but as advancement depended solely on a vacancy after death, removal or retirement, young officers lived for many years on low pay which was a cause of dissatisfaction. It could take 30 years to attain the rank of major.[55]

Thomas Pattinson went to India in 1805. A neighbour of the family, Mr Watts of Kirklinton Hall, had spent 10 years there so the family would have had some knowledge of what lay ahead. Thomas's letters mention a number of Cumbrians who either sailed with him or who were already there including General Bellasis, Colonel Holmes, George, James and Brisco Graham, Eliza Howell (nee Graham) wife of a naval officer, Charles Dacre, Edward Pearson, George Scott's sister (married to a naval officer), Mr. Palmer and Thomas Davidson. Thomas described the journey during which he changed his shirt weekly, wished he had thinner jackets because of the heat and how he intended to wear 'a blue coat, white waistcoat, nankeen smalls, silk stockings and thin shoes' when he arrived in Bombay.[56] By 1807 he had left College with a 'creditable pass' in Hindustani; an 'honour to myself and to the advantage of the Service.' He hoped to be sent to Bombay as an Acting Ensign.

As always, health in India was of concern. Thomas refers to being in Dhollerah where 'all the officers were getting fevers.' George Graham was sent to China for health reasons. In 1808 Thomas was an Ensign in Gujerat, more than six feet tall in good health and 'very stout.' He tells of keeping locks of hair of family members and wished to have 'a little of Jack's hair.' At a time when there was no means of exchanging visual images, locks of hair were a precious keepsake. He also promised to have a portrait painted for his parents. During the years of correspondence Thomas requested that his family should order boots and boot stockings to be sent to him. Shoes and silk stockings were worn 'only at a dance.' In 1810, Thomas was in Poona, still an Ensign but hoped to be a Lieutenant in two years. Home leave could not be for at least five years – 10 years after leaving home. He thanked his mother for sending £20 and reported that 'all the Cumberland young men' were well. He was an Adjutant in 1815 and wrote that home leave was likely to be postponed until 1818 or 1820. Thomas never saw his family again. He died in action in January 1818 aged 29.[58]

More than 50 residents in Cumberland and 25 in Westmorland had an Indian birthplace in 1881. Twenty years later the Cumberland total had more than doubled but in Westmorland it had increased by only two. It is almost certain that the parents of an adult with a birthplace in India had been sojourners, not emigrants. It is interesting that the most of these adults were clergymen or were in the army which may indicate that a family tradition had been followed. The Revd. John Lowther had been born in Benares, Canon W. H. Taylor and Alfred Wagentuber, a student at St Bees Theology College had been born in Bengal and Emily McCall, a Vicar's wife, had a Madras birthplace. Two army captains in or near Carlisle, James Hutton and Thomas Irwin had been born in India. In 1881, several children with an Indian birthplace were boarders in Cumbrian schools, possibly sent home for their education. Henry Lowe of Carlisle, birthplace India, and aged four years had two brothers aged seven and two, both born in Carlisle which suggests that Private Lowe had served in India but that his tour of duty in India had lasted less than six years.

While it was customary for officers to be accompanied by their families, by the later nineteenth century the families of some NCOs and private soldiers were sent abroad at official expense. It was believed that a normal family life would reduce the incidence of venereal disease which affected *c*. 10 per cent of soldiers serving overseas. In 1900 1,629 military personnel were distributed throughout the two counties but most were in Carlisle. Warrant Officer Kelly had retired from the Bengal Establishment. The birthplaces of his children indicate some of his postings in India – Barrockpore, Calcutta, Mowgong and Mooltan. Both the wife and daughter of Second Master Frederick Lewis of the 13th Hussars had been born at sea. As their second child was born in India it is likely that the daughter's birth coincided with the outward voyage. Other adults in Cumberland whose birthplace was India were in a variety of occupations. It is probable that the fathers of James Anderson and John Corbett had served in the army. James was a farm servant at Bowness on Solway in 1881 and, although John Corbett's father was then a general labourer in Carlisle, he had probably left the army.

Many died from disease in India and others were invalided home. From

1825-44, an average of 6,327 members of the East India Company's forces per year were admitted to hospital. Of these 217 died and 116 were sent home. In some years, for example 1841, more than 11,200 were admitted to hospital, 107 died from cholera and 298 from other causes. In the same year, 200 were sent home from Bombay. A sample survey of newspapers and memorials in churches and graveyards confirms that many Cumbrians including servicemen died in India from illness or injury. Captain Thornbury's wife (from Cockermouth) died in Poona in 1842, Sergeant Lockwood of Penrith died in 1905 and Captain C. Chamley of Warcop died in Bengal in 1911.[58] After c.1860, the total number in the new Indian Army increased and so did the number of those suffering from illness. From 1861-73 there were more than 90,000 admissions to hospital per year, each for approximately two to three weeks. It is clear from the statistics that some must have been ill more than once. In 1862 alone, 110,584 were admitted to hospital and in 1869, approximately 2,000 died.[59] Other tropical countries held similar risks to health especially the West Indies and West Africa. William Robinson of Penrith died in Demerara from yellow fever in 1838-9 and four Cumberland men died from illness in the West Indies in 1842. Captain Strickland died in West Africa in 1909.[60]

Birthplace evidence in the census indicates that other military families had been to Hong Kong, Shanghai, Singapore, Egypt, Aden, Gibraltar, Jamaica and Malta. Among these were Colour Sergeant McKee and his family from Carlisle who had served in China and Singapore. Bugle Major Riley of Carlisle had served in Malta. Charles Coaton was a Paymaster Sergeant in Carlisle. His eldest daughter was born in India, the second in Aden and the younger children in southern England. Emma Gillies, wife of a Brevet Major of the 55th Foot regiment had been born in Calcutta; her daughter in Aden.

The Church: clergy and missionaries

Cumbrians served the church in many parts of the world. Dr W. Gardiner, from Cumberland, was minister to the British Factory in Danzig in 1790.[61] William Thwaites of Kendal, Joseph Henderson of Dufton and the Revd. Greenwood of Cockermouth were among several who had been in India.[62] The Rt. Revd. Robert Tucker of Langdale was Bishop of Uganda from 1899-1911 and in 1909, the Rt. Revd. W.R. Mounsey, the new Bishop of Borneo spoke about his work there at a meeting in Penrith, his home town.[63]

In the eighteenth and early nineteenth centuries several clergymen from the two counties were in the West Indies. Thomas Falcon of Workington, Mark Nicolson of Barton and Thomas Allison were all in Barbados and associated with Codrington College. Members of a later generation of Nicolsons returned to live in Penrith. Joseph Helliwell, a Congregational minister from Whitehaven died in Barbados *c.*1840.[64] Percival Bewsher of Penrith was Rector of Hanover, Jamaica for 11 years. The Revd. Peter McPhion had been in British Guiana before becoming the incumbent at Langwathby in the first half of the nineteenth century and the Revd. Bunting had been a Wesleyan minister in Jamaica before 1881.

Some were missionaries working to spread the Gospel as ordained clergymen or as lay men and women. By the nineteenth century societies sent their missionaries across the world. George Woodley of Martindale had been an SPCK missionary overseas for 21 years before his death in 1845. Arthur Birkett of Keswick served for 29 years as a CMS worker in India and died there in 1916. Thomas Blamire of Carlisle and his wife from Whitehaven, and James Wigstone of Penrith went to Madrid as protestant missionaries *c.*1870. The Revd. R. Hutchinson of Winton and Miss Ferguson of Penrith were missionaries in China *c.*1906. William L. Knipe, Vicar of Great Strickland had been in China, probably as a missionary for 40 years up to 1930.

Others who served the church were, or became emigrants. Thomas Woodrow, a clergyman in Carlisle, took his family to Canada in 1836. He moved to the United States where a later member of the family became President. Henry E. Fell went to New Zealand to open a Seamen's Mission in Auckland in 1882. He continued to pursue his missionary work after he became a farmer at Waihutu where he 'serv[ed] God as a preacher and teacher travelling all around the north on horseback. [65]

Other sojourners

James Lowther was Governor of Barbados in the eighteenth century. His family and other West Cumberland men owned plantations and estates abroad. Cumbrians were employed as managers or workers on these estates. Coffee and tea were important export crops from India and Ceylon. By 1900, more than 350,000 acres were devoted to tea plantations in Ceylon. Rubber plantations were being established in Malaya by the early twentieth century. Cumbrians were engaged as planters or managers in these countries.[66] Several in the sample had lived in Ceylon. Matthew Thomas, of Underskiddaw near Keswick, had been a supervisor in coffee plantations. His wife and four children all had a Ceylon birthplace. Thomas Steele, a retired member of the Ceylon Civil Service and living at Walton, Cumberland had three children born on the island but as his eldest and youngest were born in England his tour of duty may have been only about seven years. Henry Larkum a retired government factory engineer in Ceylon was in Brough in 1881. Three of his four children had been born in Ceylon. But, in this case the family had been there more than once. The eldest daughter and the two youngest children were born in Ceylon; the second child had a West Hartlepool birthplace.

Sibella Crozier's brother was with a shipbuilding company in Java in 1819 when she went from Cumberland to visit him.[67] Henry Hobson of Workington went to Hanyang, China in 1890 to build and manage an iron and steel works – clearly marked on early twentieth century maps. Henry Taylor was sent to Smyrna in 1901 to represent his firm for several years.[68] Norris Dent of Sleagill, Westmorland was in Lagos, Nigeria working for the British Cotton-growing Association in 1906. His cousin was in Egypt in a similar capacity.[69] Mr Forrest of Ravenstonedale went to Manilla in 1906 as an electrical engineer for the railway. Anthony Clarke was an engineer in the Rhodesian mines before becoming a farmer but had he not died it seems probable that he would have stayed there.[70] Richard Lapsage whose relatives were in Carlisle had been a civil engineer in Buenos Aires for at least four years. R. Cramond was an engineer in Cleator but his daughters aged from 11 to 15 had a South African birthplace.

The Cleveland Bridge and Engineering Company won the contract to build a bridge over the Zambesi at the Victoria Falls; part of the railway that was intended to link Cape Town with Cairo. An extra imperative was the discovery of minerals in the region. Cumbrian engineers including Mr Woods, Essie Metcalfe's brother in law, worked on this project. The 635 ft long steel suspension bridge was made in England, exported in sections and 'thrown across from either side on the cantilever principle.'[71] Essie Metcalfe wrote to her Carlisle family about life there, about her sister and brother in law, the progress of the construction work, the social life in the surrounding area, the visits by eminent people to view the project, the first crossing by a small vehicle and the opening celebrations in 1905 when spectators and visitors were brought in several special trains.[72]

The majority of those recruited to the Civil Service and the Colonial Service as administrators of the British Colonies and overseas territories were men who had graduated from Oxford, Cambridge or London Universities. Selected candidates underwent further training and, while the men who went to India and Ceylon were recruited for those countries, Colonial Service men were sent to many distant parts of the Colonial Empire, often to inhospitable and isolated places where they represented the Crown and government. They were required to transmit the imperial and colonial policy of the home country to people in a land with a very different cultural background and were responsible for administration, supervising agriculture and justice and for the general well-being of the people. In 1900, for example, 261 were employed in Nigeria, 47 in the Gold Coast, 82 in Kenya and 125 in Malaya. Richard Breeks served in India. Mr H.P. Chamley, a retired District Commissioner in Nigeria died in Warcop in 1913. Unfortunately no other clear examples were found apart from two men from the Penrith area who were in Nigeria in the 1930s.

William Sharp of Orton was Vice Principal of Victoria College, Gwalior, India. He died there in 1914. Isaac Miller of Cleator Moor was Superintendent of the Western Mining Company at Leadville, Colorado at the time of his death in 1905. Dr R. Hutchinson of Mallerstang, Westmorland, had worked as a medical missionary in Canada for more than 50 years before his death in 1908. These men were therefore emigrants even if that had not been their original intention. The country in which sojourners and others worked seems to have had an influence on whether they returned or stayed. Climate and health concerns in the Far East, West Africa and the West Indies did not encourage permanent settlement. Sojourners were more likely to remain permanently and therefore became emigrants in countries with a more favourable climate.

Visitors

Although not strictly relevant to an emigration discussion, Cumbrians travelled long distances as visitors. Jackson Rodgers of Lamplugh visited Paris in 1798. After crossing the Channel, he went by coach to Abbeville, by boat on the Somme to Amiens with the final stretch to Paris by coach.[73] Following the end of war in 1815 Britain controlled the Dutch East Indies. Sibella Crozier from Longtown went to visit her brother, a shipbuilder in Java in 1819. She suffered greatly in the oppressive heat and was ill during her visit to the 'beautiful' area around Batavia with its 'many fine gentlemen's residences.' A remarkable outgoing spirit is demonstrated by this Cumberland young woman who sailed to the Far East only four years after the end of the war.[74]

Many years later, in 1889, Mr Braithwaite of Kirkby Stephen travelled across the United States by train to California visiting several towns and cities including Los Angeles, Sacramento and San Gabriel. He visited The Revd. Grant, who had been the Baptist minister in Kirkby Stephen, saw deserts, vineyards, orange groves, oil wells, silver mines, Indians and describes travelling through the snowy Sierra Mountains on the way home.[75]

Perhaps the most extensive travels described in the sample were those by Essie Metcalfe who was in Africa and America in the early twentieth century. Essie met her brother, Anthony Clarke, then a farmer at Eagle's Nest during her visit to South Africa and Rhodesia in 1904. Her journey from Bulawayo to the Victoria Falls Hotel at Livingstone was by railway and carrier's cart to the river which was crossed in a canoe. She stayed with her sister and brother in law at the camp where the men employed by the Cleveland Company were based while they built a bridge over the Zambesi. The roar of the Victoria Falls could be clearly heard in the camp. Accommodation was in tin houses but a hotel was built nearby for visitors who would come by rail to view the Falls. 'All the accompaniments of civilisation [had been] deposited [there].'[76] Essie was present during a Royal visit and at the grand opening of the bridge in 1905. Other letters tell of Essie Metcalfe's visit to relatives in San Francisco and of a voyage to Japan and China.[77]

The travels of visitors and their accounts of their experiences abroad may seem out of place in an investigation into levels of emigration from Cumberland and Westmorland but, apart from the Jackson Rodgers example, all those quoted here either went to visit relatives or friends who worked and lived overseas or met with emigrants from Cumbria during their visit. Even if few details are known, those contacts have added to the total number of emigrants and further demonstrated the spread of Cumbrians across the world.

Chapter 7
Conclusion

The sample of approximately 4,000 named emigrants represents an unknown proportion of the thousands who emigrated from Cumberland and Westmorland before 1914 but it shows the enterprising and outgoing resolve of the men and women who left all parts of the two counties and went to all parts of the world taking their skills with them. They were engaged in many different occupations and their endeavours helped to promote the wellbeing and progress of new colonies, of newly settled regions and contributed to developing industries in a number of destinations not forgetting the many who went to already thriving towns and cities. It is clear that the outflow was substantial. Some worked or served overseas as sojourners. Others set down their roots, raised families, supported themselves and became actively engaged in their local communities whether in remote rural areas or in long established cities.

This investigation has demonstrated the wide spread of origins, destinations and dates of leaving. The themes of sojourners and returned emigrants have been explored. Cumberland and Westmorland had a long tradition of migration, emigration and trading overseas. As others have concluded, by the later nineteenth century emigrants made a 'rational choice based on a considerable amount of information ... and [were] going to parts of the world they knew something about.'[1] Unfortunately we know little about the initial pioneers who crossed the oceans in tiny ships but their, perhaps annual, letters began a chain of information that linked those overseas with their families and friends at home. Newspapers, letters and in later years visits from emigrants to their home communities reinforced links between home and overseas and conveyed information that increased as communications improved. It is also clear that in spite of 'push' factors at work in some parts of Cumbria, in specific occupations and at particular times, the 'attracting forces [were at least as potent as] the propelling forces'.[2] A high percentage of emigrants were not 'fleeing from problems at home.' At different times and in different parts of the region there were problems to flee from, and some chose to leave. But, why emigrate? There were opportunities in England and many took that path.

If more general studies have concluded that emigrants were not mainly from rural districts, then Cumbria was different. Apart from West Cumberland, Carlisle and, to a lesser degree, Kendal, this was a region with a largely rural economy. The sample shows that the outflow from communities in the Upper Eden Valley, from the Bewcastle area and from the central Lake District was significant and there may have been other substantial clusters of origin or destination about which we know nothing. Clusters of Cumbrians some of whom were related, others were from neighbouring communities, have been observed in all destination countries. The families at Wagga Wagga in New South Wales, the miners in Nanaimo, B.C. and the mining families from West Cumberland in Runanga, New Zealand are only three of many examples that could be cited. In 1830, Joseph Dover mentioned six north Westmorland families in his letter from Pittsburgh and, four years later when he had moved to Humber, near York in Upper Canada, he gave the names of ten local people and 'a great many others that I have not room to mention all live within a few miles.'[3] John Atkinson wrote from Walpole, Ontario in 1852 that two brothers and their families had visited him and other relatives lived less than 100 miles away.[4] George Alderson's farm in Wisconsin was 2½ miles from one brother, 20 miles from his sister and 24 miles from his brother at Oshkosh.[5]

The very large numbers who left Alston Moor in the 1830s (and again in the 1870s) and West Cumberland after about 1880 were leaving failing industries or those with an uncertain future. The Alston emigrants in the 1830s escaped from poverty, unemployment and distress. Many were under similar stress in Carlisle in the 1840s and the threat of unemployment was at least partly responsible for West Cumberland men going to South African mines. Even those who were not unemployed feared the future and could see little prospect of improvement. In Aspatria, for example, the population fell by 14 per cent 1901-11 and in the east of the region Penrith (urban and rural) lost 3 per cent, Brampton, 10 per cent and Shap, 21 per cent during the same decade. Emigration to overseas mines presented an opportunity for more stable and lucrative employment notwithstanding the toll on health which led to the death of so many. Although not all went overseas, there was 'no finality to emigration' evident in 1905 and, in 1913, the 'ravenous British colonies' were said to be 'skimming off the cream of labour.'[6]

Only a few letters have survived but from these and from family information, a picture has emerged of emigrants building a new life in urban or rural destinations far from home. It is clear from their comments, from their interest in their family in Cumberland or Westmorland, in their home communities and in England more generally that at least the first generation did not forget, and took pride in their Cumbrian roots. The Cumberland and Westmorland societies in so many places are evidence of this. Emigrant letters also emphasise how important maintaining contact with home was by writing and by exchanging newspapers. Repeatedly, we find in letters, in the press, in emigration publications, from family information and in advertisements the necessity for emigrants to be prepared to work hard, to have a difficult time at first, to be

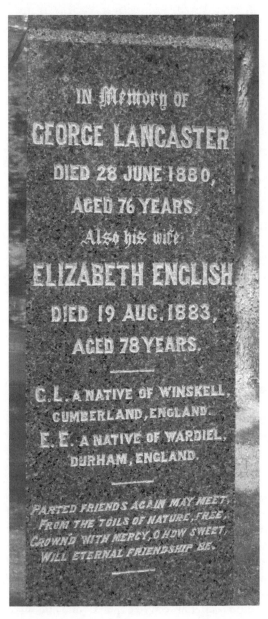

George Lancaster's tombstone, Hudson, Quebec.

determined to succeed and to commit themselves wholeheartedly to that end but that life would be freer and they could 'get on.' For those intending to settle in towns, especially in North America letters contained warnings about unemployment during severe winter weather and during economic downturns in several destinations. It was essential to be an optimist.[7]

Gravestones and memorials in the home parish and overseas, mark the death of emigrants. Many memorials overseas like those in the West Indies, in Tenerife, in New Zealand, in Canada and other countries record the deceased's Cumbrian origins for example, the almost illegible memorial in the Alte Friedhof, Bonn where a Cumberland visitor or resident died from consumption in 1831 and George Lancaster's gravestone in Hudson near Montreal. Memorials to James Irving and Edward Jollie are in Christchurch Cathedral, New Zealand and numerous memorials in Cumbrian churches and churchyards are testament to the fact that emigrants or sojourners were not forgotten.[8]

Mississippi River Museum , Dubuque

George Richardson's boot and shoe factory and workers,
in Dubuque, Iowa.

What did they become?

Cumbrian emigrants went to New Brunswick and others were in Nova Scotia especially during the years after the end of war in 1815. For example, two families were in New Brunswick before about 1820. Thomas Garnett, son of a corn miller from Bowness on Windermere was a gardener. Although it is not clear if Thomas had served in the army, he and his wife went to New Brunswick under a scheme for ex-army personnel in 1818. They took 300 acres of Crown land and established Garnett Settlement near St John. The settlement was a success. Labour was provided by former African slaves who had settled nearby and the family prospered.[9] Richard Smith, his wife and children of Whitehaven also settled in New Brunswick. Richard was a stone mason and is credited with building at least one of the few stone houses in St John.[10] Almost a century later, J.R. Warwick of Kirkby Stephen was there. He had emigrated to Canada as a carpenter, owned a furniture business, was an acting magistrate and was a member of the Imperial Board of Trade.[11]

William Workman from Clifton, Westmorland emigrated in 1822. After pioneering travels across the United States he made money in California, owning land at San Francisco and Alcatraz Island. He was a cattle rancher and banker who eventually was 'a leading city maker in Los Angeles' where he owned the land that became Beverley Hills.[12] Joseph Scott of Penrith who went to the United

173

States in 1889, became Mayor of Los Angeles, was 'a civic leader, distinguished lawyer, spellbinding orator … was awarded four honorary doctorates and was decorated by three popes.' His statue stands near the Los Angeles Court building.[13] Mr Lancaster of Temple Sowerby was County Treasurer of Traverse County, Minnesota. James Woodward of Kirkby Stephen became a successful business man in Dubuque and was a generous benefactor of Kirkby Stephen Wesleyan Chapel.[14] George Richardson also achieved success. He became a boot and shoe manufacturer first in Galena then in Dubuque where he employed more than 300 workers.[15] Hugh Thomas Bell went to New York as a bricklayer in 1856 but moved on, became a farmer and eventually owned an extensive estate in California where he was a prominent Freemason and a 'highly respected citizen' of Chico.[16] George Rumney of Brough was a successful merchant in Chicago for 35 years.[17] Andrew Veitch from Carlisle was a young railway engineer and emigrated to Bloomington, Illinois with his wife in 1907. Other Carlisle emigrants known to the family were there. Andrew Veitch became the General Superintendent of the Chicago-Alton Railroad.[18] Jonathan Taylor of Waitby in north Westmorland was an apprentice carpenter before emigrating. He went first to the Californian goldfield then to San Francisco in 1905. He worked as a carpenter.He was there in 1906 at the time of the earthquake and his purchase of a 'planing mill' was a profitable venture. He sold the mill and studied to become an engineer eventually becoming superintendent of the railway in the San Francisco to Salt Lake City region. In 1911 he was to be based in Albuquerque, superintending the reconstruction of the railway in New Mexico.[19]

Early emigrants to New Zealand tended to be 'the class best fitted to break a raw new country and make it a home of civilization and comfort. … Many were men and women of education and culture who gave a lead in the shaping of colonial life.' The majority were 'yeomen farmers and land-bred men.'[20] Not all had a farming background. Philip C. Threlkeld and the Jollie brothers were the sons of Cumbrian clergymen. Philip Threlkeld, from Milburn, died in 1907 more than 50 years after emigrating to New Zealand. He named the small town of Inglewood near New Plymouth, in the Taranaki on the North Island, after the Inglewood Forest in Cumberland. Later, his farm at Flaxton north of Christchurch in the South Island and near to Wetheral (a Cumberland village near Carlisle),was 'among the best' in the country. He was President of the Canterbury Agricultural and Pastoral Society in 1882, was prominent in Colonial affairs and was a noted shorthorn breeder. He visited England on several occasions to buy sheep, horses and cattle.[21] Francis Jollie was a member of the House of Representatives in New Zealand from 1861-70 and Colonial Treasurer in 1866. His brother, Edward, who was originally employed as a surveyor at Nelson and Christchurch, became a farmer, was a member of the Provincial Council and, after years in the South

Island, bought land in the Taranaki. Anthony Metcalf from Stainmore went to New Zealand in 1869. He was a successful farmer and became a J.P. Was this the same man who was sentenced to six months in gaol for debt in 1858-9?[22] Joseph Braithwaite was taken as a young child to Australia in 1852. The family, from north Westmorland, moved to Dunedin in 1860. Eventually, Joseph's business published a newspaper and books, was the largest wholesale and retail book selling business in New Zealand and had diversified into many other fields. He was a member of the church synod, Grand Master of the Oddfellows, a Commissioner of the Peace and Mayor of Dunedin. He visited his home county in 1899.[23] According to family information, could Isaac Martin, a successful businessman in Dunedin and 'a pillar of society' have been the Isaac Martin of Penrith who with his brother had been convicted of larceny and sentenced to transportation many years earlier? This remains an unanswered question.

John Studholme of Carlisle was a Canterbury magistrate, a member of the Provincial Council and a racing enthusiast. Joseph Lowthian of Penrith was manager of the Kaiapoi Building Society, a J.P., Councillor and Mayor of Kaiapoi. William Watson of Lorton was first a farm worker before having his own farm at Brookside. He was a respected judge of cattle and shorthorn breeder, active in local affairs and a member of his local Wesleyan church.[24] Many other examples of Cumbrians who actively participated in the life of their community in New Zealand could be cited. Several were magistrates and served on local councils.[25] Charles Rooking Carter, a Kendal man, founded the first Building Society in Wellington, became a stockbroker, built bridges, analysed earthquake damage and had many business interests. He introduced red deer into New Zealand, founded a library and observatory, was a J.P. and active in local politics. Carterton is named after him.[26]

Fisher Thwaites of Keswick began life in Australia as a fencer, became a farmer and in 1909 had an extensive sheep run which he called Newlands to remind him of home. He was a Commissioner of the Peace in Roma, Queensland.[27] Richard Downward went to Van Diemen's Land in 1819. He established a water powered flour mill at Iron Creek in 1824. He was also a brewer, a land owner and built a windmill, house and granary in Sorell in 1831.[28] John Twentyman had a successful tailor's business in Ballarat. He was a President of the Benevolent Asylum, was connected with the Town Council and served on the Public Library Committee and was an active member of his local church before his death in 1899.[29] William Collins was a teacher for many years in South Africa after emigrating in 1826. On retirement in 1873, when he was living in the Orange Free State, he was given a farm in recognition of his service 'in many spheres of Free State life.' He named the farm St Bees.[30] Henry Richardson of Penrith became Town Clerk and Treasurer of Springs in the Transvaal.

From the information so generously supplied by hundreds of correspondents and from other sources it is clear that Cumberland and Westmorland men and women and, in due time, their children, contributed much to their adopted country. They went to different countries, different environments and, although farming and mining are dominant occupations in the sample, and are likely to have been so among the countless unknown emigrants, there is almost a complete spectrum; urban and rural, craft and trade, professional and military. Successful emigrants could have had any background in England. They may have been poor or privileged and some who had been transported achieved freedom and a stable life. Some were active in public life. Others may have been equally successful but quietly anonymous. Many were not noteworthy for any reason but made a new life and created circumstances that enabled their children to benefit and contributed to the advancement of their communities in the new country. Inevitably some may have persevered in a lowly capacity and others may have been failures who sank into 'bad ways' and there is evidence that men, possibly from Cumberland were in Australian gaols in the mid nineteenth century. Many emigrants died from disease or accident. Some returned home. Bereavement, ill-health, unhappiness or simply the recognition that perhaps emigration had been a mistake were the most common reasons for return.

Clusters of origin and destination are very evident and it must have been a great comfort to find fellow Cumbrians or, at the very least, fellow north-country folk after arrival. Nevertheless, nostalgia and an initial sense of feeling adrift in a strange environment far from the security of home are implicit if not explicit in letters however optimistic and confident the words of the writer. William Bell's request for rhubarb to be sent to Iowa tells that he hoped to cultivate it in America.'[31] Joseph Hodgson wrote in 1866 'Please excuse blunders and write soon.' Other letters to Hilton from the United States and Canada expressed nostalgia and reveal the vivid memories of the local area retained by members of Joseph Salkeld's emigrant family. A writer from West Cumberland stated 'If God spares us ... we will be back again as we can never like this country as we like the old one.'[32]

The sample indicates that all who kept in touch with their families at home after emigrating or whose names are known through publications or newspapers were determined to succeed and were at least modestly successful even if they lived quietly and contributed only to the wellbeing of their family and their local community. Matthew Hall, writing to the *Penrith Observer* in 1865 stated 'the majority ... better themselves ... some make fortunes.' But most were like him, content to make 'a good living' and were like the Gelders in Carlisle, North Dakota who became 'not rich but had a comfortable and rewarding life,' eating well and they were satisfied with what they had.[33]

What conclusion can be drawn from this study? Clearly the outflow was very large as even this limited sample shows. Some went to cities, many took virgin land. There is little evidence of unskilled general labourers in Cumbria emigrating in the sample but this may be a deficiency in these particular data. Similarly, the huge excess of emigrants to the United States found by others is not borne out from our evidence. Canada and the South African mines attracted hundreds of emigrants. Convicted men and women played their part in the building of Australia. Cumbrians were sojourners in a variety of occupations across the world. The 'tide of emigration' continued to all destinations up to the outbreak of war. But 1914 brought a different exodus. Countries in the British Empire supported the 'mother country' by sending their young men to fight in Europe which gave some emigrants or their sons or grandsons an opportunity to visit Cumbria. Servicemen from all parts of the Empire served in France, in Flanders and Gallipoli and other fields of battle. Men with Cumbrian roots whether still living in the two counties or in other parts of the world, were among the thousands for whom that exodus ended in death.

NOTES

Chapter One: Introduction

1   R. Lawton in R.A. Dodgshon and R.A. Butlin, (eds.), *An Historical Geography of England and Wales*, 2nd ed., p. 293, Table 11.3.
2   BPP 1826-7 V, Select Committee (hereafter SC) Report on Emigration, pp. 4-5.
3   C.J. Erickson,   *Invisible immigrants: the adaptation of English & Scottish immigrants in nineteenth century America* (Cornell, 1972).The title suggests this.
4   D. Baines, *Migration in a mature economy: emigration and internal migration in England and Wales 1861-1900* (Cambridge, 1985), p.48.
5   C.J. Erickson, *Leaving England: essays on British emigration in the nineteenth century* Cornell, 1994).p. 20. M.A.Jones, 'The background to emigration from Great Britain in the nineteenth century.' *Perspectives in American History* 7 (1973) pp. 3-94, p. 23.
6   Baines, *Migration in a mature economy*, pp. 301-3, 47-51.
7   BPP 1904 LIX, Emigrant's Information Office (hereafter EIO) Report. pp. 837-46.
8   Baines, *Migration in a mature economy*, p. 59. BPP 1914 LXIX, EIO Report. pp. 946-9.
9   For example, Jones, 'The background to emigration from Great Britain' pp. 3-94.
10 Erickson, *Leaving England*, p. 32.
11 Baines, *Migration in a mature economy*, p. 4.
12 C.R. Pooley and I.D. Whyte, *Migrants, emigrants and immigrants: a social history of migration* (London, 1991), p. 12.
13 *C & W Advertiser* 19 October 1880.
14 D. Clarke, *This other Eden* (Milburn, 1985) p.52. CRO, Kendal, WDFC/M1, 55, 69-71. Wesleyan and Primitive Methodist records,
15 Baines, *Migration in a mature economy*, p. 46.
16 Pooley & Whyte (eds.) *Migrants, emigrants and immigrants*, p. 4.
17 M.E. Shepherd, *From Hellgill to Bridge End: aspects of economic and social change in the Upper Eden Valley 1840-1895* (Hatfield 2003). (Hereafter *Hellgill*). See pp. 15-18 for a summary of the Cumbrian region.
18 Jones, 'The background to emigration', pp. 3-94, p. 26. BPP 1912-13 111 Census Report, pp. 11, 13-14.
19 Erickson, *Leaving England* Table 1.1, p. 38.
20 Baines, *Migration in a mature economy*, p. 161.
21 D. Fitzpatrick, *Oceans of Consolation* (Cork, 1994) pp. 469, 472. See for example, Erickson, *Leaving England* pp. 16-17, Fitzpatrick, *Oceans of Consolation*, p. 20, D.A. Gerber, *Authors of their lives,* pp. 1-6 , A. McCarthy, 'Personal letters, oral testimony and Scottish migration to New Zealand in the 1950s: the case of Lorna Carter' in *Immigrants and Minorities* Vol 23 (2005), pp. 59-79, p. 75. T. Bueltmann, 'Where the measureless ocean between us will roar: Scottish emigration to New Zealand, personal correspondence and epistolary practices, c.1850-1920, pp. 242-257.
22 *Letters from settlers and labouring emigrants in the New Zealand Company's settlements of Wellington, Nelson & New Plymouth* (London, 1843), pp. 90-2, 116-7, 122-9.
23 CRO, Carlisle, D/BS/Scott. CRO, Kendal, WDX 822.
24 Dover letters – family information. CRO Carlisle, DX301/7.
25 CRO, Carlisle, DX 249/14.
26 C.J. Erickson, *Invisible Immigrants*, pp. 4-5. D. Fitzpatrick *Oceans of consolation*, pp. vii-viii, p.3.
27 CRO Carlisle, DX67/37/1.
28 CRO Carlisle, DX67/37/1, D/BS/Scott.
29 For example, Gerber, Fitzpatrick, Richards, Erickson., Gerber, *Authors of their lives*, p. 81, Richards, in *Letters across borders: the epistolary practices of international migrants*, Elliott, Gerber, Sinke (eds.) (Basingstoke, 2006), p. 65, 59.
30 BPP 1842 XVII Report on the employment of children and young persons in mines, p. 16.

Shepherd, *Hellgill*, pp. 227-42, especially 229, 231-3.
Literacy levels calculated from Registrar General's Annual Reports.

	Cumbd		Westmd		Herts,		Cambs.	
	M	F	M	F	M	F	M	F.
1840	86%	66%	81%	65%	48%	43%	55%	48%
1851	84%	66%	83%	69%	52%	52%	59%	50%

[31] *Westmorland Gazette* 1818, *Cumberland Pacquet* 1774, *Carlisle Journal* 1801, *West Cumberland Times* 1874, *Cumberland & Westmorland Advertiser* 1854. *Westmorland Gazette* 1818, *Cumberland Pacquet* 1774, *Carlisle Journal* 1801, *West Cumberland Times* 1874, *Cumberland & Westmorland Advertiser* 1854.

[32] CRO, Carlisle, DX/67/37/1.

[33] See F. Crouzet, *The Victorian Economy*, (London, 1982) and J. Langton & R.J Morris, *Atlas of Industrialising Britain 1780-1914* (London, 1986). E. Pawson, 'The framework of industrial change 1730-1900,' in Dodgshon and Butlin, (eds.), *An Historical Geography,* 1st ed., p. 272.

[34] Jones, 'The background to emigration ,' p. 38.

[35] Jones, 'The background to emigration,' p. 40. Only the Pennines separated north Westmorland from the North Riding of Yorkshire.

[36] See BPP 1833 V, SC. on the state of agriculture, William Blamire's evidence. pp. 303-26. J.L. and B. Hammond, *The Village Labourer 1760-1832: a study in the government of England before the Reform Bill* (London. 1911, Gloucester, 1987), pp. 98-9. H.C. Prince, 'The changing rural landscape,' in J.Thirsk (ed.), *The Agrarian History of England and Wales, 1750-1850* Vol. 6, p.12. And, as agricultural difficulties re-emerged in the later nineteenth century see BPP 1881 XVII, Royal Commission (hereafter RC) on the depressed condition of the agricultural interest. Mr Coleman's report and Mr Swan's evidence. For example, pp. 234-49. BPP 1895 XVII, RC on agricultural depression. Mr Wilson Fox re Cumberland, especially p.22.

[37] BPP 1843 XXXIV, Emigration Report, p. 28.

[38] J.R. Walton in Dodgshon and Butlin, (eds.), *An Historical Geography*, 2nd ed., p. 342.

[39] BPP 1843 XXXIV, Emigration Report, p. 19.

[40] BPP 1852 XXXIV, Emigration Report, p. 534.

[41] *Post Office Directory of Westmorland and Cumberland* (London 1858, Kendal 2009), pp. 1, 101.

[42] See also Shepherd, *Hellgill*, pp. 19-24, 40-5.

[43] See J.V. Beckett, *Coal and tobacco: the Lowthers and the economic development of west Cumberland 1660-1760* (Cambridge, 1981).

[44] Brocklebank and Ismay transferred to Liverpool.

[45] BPP 1881 XVII RC on the depressed condition of the agricultural interest, p. 248 BPP 1895 XVII RC on agricultural depression, p. 22.

[46] Calculated from C. Hallas, 'The northern region,' in *Agrarian History* Vol. 7, Part 1, pp. 403-5.

[47] W. Marshall, *The Review and Abstract of the county reports to the Board of Agriculture: northern department,* Vol. 1, (York, 1818, New York, 1968), p. 172.

[48] E. Hughes, *North Country life in the eighteenth century: Cumberland and Westmorland 1700-1830*, Vol. 2 (Oxford 1965), pp. 365-6. See J.D. Marshall and J.K. Walton, *The Lake Counties from 1830 to the mid-twentieth century* (Manchester, 1981).

[49] J.D. Marshall, 'Kendal in the late seventeenth & eighteenth centuries,' *TCWAAS,* 75, 1975, pp. 188-257.

[50] L. Ashcroft, (ed.) *Vital Statistics: the Westmorland 'census' of 1787* (Kendal, 1992).J. Thirsk, (ed.) *Agrarian History,* Vol. 6 (Cambridge, 1989), p. 717. J.D. Marshall, 'Kendal in the late seventeenth and eighteenth centuries,' pp. 188-257.

[51] W. Marshall, *Review and abstracts,* p. 170. Parson & White, *History, Directory and Gazetteer of Cumberland and Westmorland* (Leeds, 1829, Beckermet, 1976).

[52] *Jollie's Cumberland Guide and Directory* (Carlisle, 1811, Whitehaven, 1995).

[53] BPP 1826-7V, SC Report on emigration, pp. 4-5.
[54] Parson & White, *History, Directory and Gazetteer of Cumberland and Westmorland* (Leeds, 1829, Beckermet,1976).
[55] *Ibid,* Kendal and Carlisle entries.
[56] *Ibid,* p. 187.
[57] BPP 1826-7 V, SC Report on Emigration. Mr Hunton's evidence, pp. 502-9.
[58] R.N. Thompson, 'The working of the Poor Law Amendment Act,' *Northern History* 15 (1979), pp. 117-37.
[59] BPP 1843 XXXIV, Report on emigration to Canada, p. 19.
[60] BPP 1840 XXIV, Report on the condition of handloom weavers. Mr Muggeridge's evidence, pp. 586-7.
[61] *Carlisle Journal* 14 March 1865.
[62] *C & W Advertiser* 3 March 1868.
[63] See Bulmer's *Directories.*
[64] J. Wilson, (ed.), *The Victoria History of the county of Cumberland,* Vol. 2 (London, 1905/1968), p. 345.
[65] *Jollie's Guide,* p. 19. Parson and White, *Directory,* p. 244.
[66] *Jollie's Guide,* p. 15.
[67] *C & W Advertiser* 28 July 1868.
[68] *C & W Advertiser* 25 August 1891.
[69] *West Cumberland Times* 2 March 1901.
[70] *Maryport News* 22 April 1905, *Cumberland Pacquet* 18 December 1913.
[71] *West Cumberland Times* 30 January 1907.
[72] *Cumberland Pacquet* 28 January 1909.
[73] *Kelly's Directory of Cumberland and Westmorland* (London, 1906). BPP 1917-18 XXXV, Census Report 1911, pp. 524-8
[74] *C & W Herald* 17 June 1911. BPP 1917-18. Census Report 1911. pp. 524-8.
[75] *Carlisle Journal* June 4 1842. BPP XV 1842, SC Report on the employment of children and young persons in mines. p. 99.
[76] *Victoria County History,* Vol. 2. p. 384.
[77] Baines, *Migration in a mature economy,* p. 204. Westmorland is not mentioned.
[78] BPP 1834 XXVII, Poor Law Report. Captain Pringle's report. pp. 314-36, p. 324.
[79] N.S. Spedding, *Footsteps in retrospect* (unpub.), p. 4.
[80] *C & W Advertiser* 21 January 1886. In Penrith soup kitchens were again active in 1910, *C & W Herald* 5 February 1910.
[81] *C & W Advertiser* 25 August 1891.
[82] *C & W Herald* 22 March 1913.
[83] Erickson, *Invisible immigrants,* pp. 25, 29.
[84] Transcript of letter from Isabel Archer
[85] CRO, Kendal, WDX 822.

Chapter Two: Origins: who went where and where from
[1] BPP 1840 XXIV, Report on Handloom Weavers, Mr W.E. Hickson's evidence, p. 693.
[2] Shepherd, *Hellgill,* p. 229. BPP 1851 XL, Registrar General's Annual Report, pp. 4-5.
[3] See Note 32, Chapter 1.
[4] BPP 1883 LIV, Election Report, pp. 294-6, 1906 XCVI, Election Report, pp. 2-4.
[5] See J. Rose, 'Willingly to school: the working class response to elementary education in Britain, 1875-1918' in *Journal of British Studies* 32 (1993) pp. 114-138, p. 126. From the transcript 'Thy Kingdom *did* come' (6) in Brunel University Library.
[6] Shepherd, *Hellgill,* p. 143.
[7] *Ibid.* p. 141.
[8] BPP 1874 XXIII Part II, RC Friendly and Benefit Building Societies. Mr Culley's report re Cumberland. pp. 144-52. Farm servants who lived with the farmer had few expenses and were still numerous in the two counties into the twentieth century. See A. Howkins,

'Overview,' in *Agrarian History* Vol. 7, Pt. 2, p. 1508.

[9] R. Haines, 'Indigent misfits or shrewd operators: government assisted emigrants from the United Kingdom to Australia 1831- 60.' *Population Studies* 48 (1994), p. 246.

[10] CRO, Kendal, WD/AG/Box 3. J.A. Ferguson, 'A journey with Captain Wood,' *CFHS Newsletter* 117, (2005), pp. 6, 9.

[11] B. Bailyn, *Voyagers to the West* (New York, 1987), pp. 78,

[12] *Cumberland Pacquet* 3 Feb, 31 May 1825, 18 April 1826.
Cumberland Pacquet 7 June 1836.

[13] C.J. Erickson, 'Emigration from the British Isles to the USA in 1831,' *Population Studies* 35 (1981), pp. 175-97.

[14] *Ibid.* p. 191.

[15] Baines, *Migration in a mature economy*, p.74.

[16] *Carlisle Patriot* 1 May 1830.

[17] *Whitehaven News* 2, 9, 23 *January*, 13, 20 February, 6, 27 March, 17 April 1879.

[18] *Whitehaven News* 27 February, 13 March, 1, 15 May, 19 June, 18, 25 September 1879 and frequent references in this and the *Cumberland Pacquet* up to 1914.

[19] Spedding, *Footseps in Retrospect*, p.4.

[20] *C & W Advertiser* 16 June 1891.

[21] *Maryport News* 8 April 1905.

[22] Family information.

[23] S. Lancaster, (ed.), Thompson, J., *Hudson: the early years up to 1867* (Hudson, 2004), pp. 78-96.

[24] Thompson, *Hudson,* pp. 8-9.

[25] Erickson, 'Emigration from the British Isles to the USA in 1831,' pp. 175-97, pp. 175-6 refer to 1880.

[26] B. Short, 'Rural Demography' in *Agrarian History* Vol. 7, Part 2, p. 1295.

[27] *Maryport News* 5 August 1905.

[28] *Whitehaven News* 24 January, 14 February, 7, 24 March 1895.

[29] *C & W Herald* 13 October 1906.

[30] Baines, *Migration in a mature economy,* pp. 100-01. In 1881 45.3 per cent of all migrants were aged 15-24 and 38.6 per cent were under 15. Presumably the latter would be part of family groups. However, Baines states 'no attempt has been made to examine emigration.' p. 123.

[31] Erickson, *Leaving England,* p. 115. (re the United States).

[32] Family information.

[33] Family information.

[34] *C & W Herald* 15 March 1913.

Chapter Three: Destinations

[1] *Carlisle Patriot* 10 May, 28 June 1828. CRO, Kendal WDX 822.

[2] BPP 1826 XXVI, SC Report on Emigration, pp. 4-5.

[3] E. Richards 'How did poor people emigrate from the British Isles in the nineteenth century' in *Journal of British Studies* 32 (1993) pp. 250-79, pp. 251-2.

[4] *Cumberland Pacquet* 2 February 1836.

[5] G. Howells, 'Emigration and the new Poor Law: Norfolk emigration fever of 1836' in *Rural History* 11 (2000), pp. 145-64, Tables 1 and 2, p. 148-9

[6] *Carlisle Journal*, 30 March 1832.

[7] Information from Mrs M Russell.

[8] Howells, 'Emigration and the new Poor Law' pp. 157-8.

[9] BPP 1847-8 XL, Poor Law Report, pp. 695, 703.

[10] Family information.

[11] S. Strickland, *Twenty-seven years in Canada West,* Vol. 2 (London 1853, Michigan 2009), p. 32.

[12] BPP 1837-8 XL, Report on Emigration, p. 4.
[13] C.J. Erickson *Emigration from Europe 1815-1914: select documents* (London, 1976), p. 248. Document 38, *Morning Chronicle* 15 July 1850.
[14] Haines, 'Indigent misfits or shrewd operators?' pp. 223-47. Richards, 'How did poor people emigrate ...' pp. 256, 277.
[15] Family information.
[16] P.S. Hudson, 'English emigrants to New Zealand 1839-1850: an analysis of the work of the New Zealand Company' (Ph.D. thesis, Lancaster 1996), p. 116.
[17] BPP 1843 XXXIV, Emigration Report, pp. 59, 92.
[18] BPP 1851 XL, Emigration Report, p. 447.
[19] Baines, *Migration in a mature economy*, p. 72.
[20] Richards, 'How did poor people emigrate ...', p. 275. The 1861 figure in Table 3.1 refers only to the English.
[21] BPP 1837 XLII, Annual Report from Agent for Emigration to Canada 1836, p. 19.
[22] BPP 1904 LIX, Emigrant's Information Office Report (hereafter EIO) Report. p. 841.
[23] *Daily Telegraph and Courier* 29 June 1855.
[24] *The Australian Handbook and Almanac* (Sydney, 1877).
[25] *C & W Herald* 24 March, 27 January 1912.
[26] BPP 1888 LXXIII, EIO Report, pp. 25-34, pp. 33-4.
[27] BPP 1899 LVIII, EIO Report, pp. 135-43.
[28] BPP 1908 LXX, EIO Report, pp. 901-15.
[29] BPP 1909 LIX, EIO Report, pp. 305-18.
[30] BPP 1908 LXX, EIO Report, p. 913.
[31] BPP 1908 LXX, EIO Report, p. 905, 1912-13 XVI, RC Report on the Dominions, Appendix, pp. 203-4.
[32] *C & W Herald* May 16 1914.
[33] BPP 1904 LIX, EIO Report. pp. 837-46, p. 842.
[34] *Carlisle Journal* 25 February 1853.
[35] *C & W Advertiser* 17 March 1872, 2 February 1874.
[36] *C & W Advertiser* 9 February 1875.
[37] BPP 1895 LXX, Report on Canada, pp. 41-53.
[38] *Murang's Annual Register of Canadian Affairs*, pp. 424-5.
[39] BPP 1895 LXX, Report on Canada, pp. 41-53. *Cumberland Pacquet* 7 January 1909.
[40] *C & W Herald* 16 November 1907.
[41] *C & W Herald* 24 February 1906, 16 February, 16 March 1907, 13 February 1909, 19 March, 1 October 1910, 1 February, 11 October 1913.
[42] *C & W Herald* 19 January, 16 February, 13 July, 10, 17 August 1907.
[43] *C & W Herald* 13 February, 20 March 1909.
[44] Family information, quoting Harry Brunskill's memories of his father. *C & W Herald* 7 March, 2 February 1907.
[45] *C & W Herald* 10 January 1914.
[46] CRO, Carlisle, DX/46/5.
[47] CRO, Carlisle, D/BT/6/209/1.
[48] *Carlisle Journal* 25 March 1853. CRO, Carlisle, D/67/37//1.
[49] CRO, Kendal, WDX 822.
[50] C. Dickens, *American Notes* (London, 1842). A. Trollope, *North America,* Vols. 1 and 2 (London, 1862).
[51] W.S. Shepperson, *British emigration to North America: projects and opinions in the early Victorian period,* (Oxford, 1957), pp. 165-6. J. Caird, 'On the agricultural statistics of the United Kingdom,' *Journal of the Statistical Society of London* (hereafter *JSS*), 31, 1868, pp. 127-45. pp. 136-7.
[52] Trollope, *North America*, pp. 61, 63.
[53] E. Thompson (ed.). R. MacDougall, *The emigrant's guide to North America,* (Ottawa, 1998), p. xxii.

[54] Dickens, *American Notes*, p. 340.
[55] *Post Office Directory of Lancashire* (London, 1858), *Kelly's Directory of Liverpool and Birkenhead* (London, 1893).
[56] *Post Office Directory of Cumberland and Westmorland* (London, 1894).
[57] *Kelly's Directory of Cumberland and Westmorland* (London, 1905, 1906). Margaret Crosby, article in *Whitehaven News* 12 April 2007.
[58] *C & W Advertiser* 14 March 1891.
[59] B. Bailyn, *Voyagers to the west: a passage in the peopling of America on the eve of the Revolution* (New York, 1987), pp. 26, 92, 96. Rigg, *Cumbria, slavery and the textile industrial revolution*, pp. 38-9.
[60] CRO Kendal, WD/AG/Box 3.
[61] *Cumberland Pacquet* 7 June 1842.
[62] *Sidney's Emigrant's Journal* 14, 28 June 1849.
[63] Family information.
[64] CRO Kendal, WDX 822.
[65] CRO Kendal, WDY33/1.
[66] CRO, Kendal, WDX 822. Trollope, *North America,* Vol. 2, p. 80.
[67] *Sidney's Emigrant's Journal* 3 May 1849.
[68] *C & W Advertiser* 10 July 1855.
[69] *The Population of the USA 1860*, 8th Census Report.
[70] J. Hayward, *Gazeteer of the United States of America* (Philadelphia, 1854). J. Newhall, *A glimpse of Iowa in 1846* (Iowa, 1846), p. 72.
[71] W.E. Wilkie, *Dubuque on the Mississippi, 1788-1988* (Wisconsin, 1987), p. 276.
[72] Trollope, *North America*, p. 183.
[73] *C & W Advertiser* 25 December 1880.
[74] *Maryport News* 8 July 1905. *Cumberland Pacquet* 2 March 1905.
[75] *Cumberland Pacquet* 25 May 1905.
[76] *C & W Advertiser* 28 November 1871.
[77] *C & W Herald* 21 April 1906. BPP 1908 LXX, EIO Report, pp. 901-15.
[78] *Cumberland Pacquet* 30 August 1842.
[79] *Sidney's Emigrant's Journal* 12 October 1848.
[80] *Cumberland Pacquet* 8 March 1842.
[81] *Sidney's Emigrant's Journal,* 11 January 1849.
[82] *Canada and the Western States Handbook 1859*, pp. 35-6.
[83] *C & W Herald* 6 May 1909.
[84] *C & W Herald* 2, 23 August 1913.
[85] *C & W Herald* 19 September 1909, 22 February 1913. Shepherd, *Hellgill*, p. 286.
[86] *C & W Herald.* 30 December 1911, 6 July 1912.
[87] *Ibid.* 27 January 1912, 19 April 1913.
[88] *Ibid.* 22 February, 27 March 1913, *Cumberland Pacquet* 27 March 1913. Shepherd, *Hellgill, p.* 286.
[89] J.G. MacGregor, *A History of Alberta* (Edmonton, 1972), p. 134.
[90] *C & W Herald* 3 January 1914.
[91] C. Stuart, *The Emigrant's Guide to Upper Canada* (London, 1820), p. 390.
[92] Trollope, North *America* Vol. 2, pp. 141-3.
[93] *C & W Herald* 9 May 1908.
[94] BPP 1903 XLIV, EIO Report, pp. 61-70, p. 65.
[95] *C & W Herald* 24 October 1908.
[96] *C & W Herald,* 26 November 1906.
[97] *Maryport News* 29 April 1905.
[98] J Irving's letter in *C & W Herald* 2 February 1908.
[99] *West Cumberland Times* 16 March 1901.
[101] *Cumberland Pacquet* 30 November 1905, *Maryport News* 18 March 1905, *C & W Herald* 20 June 1908.

[101] *Stanford's Emigrant's Guide* (London, 1854), p. 15.
[102] J.D. Belshaw, *Colonisation and community: the Vancouver Island coalfield and the making of the British Columbia working class* (Montreal, 2002), p. 62.
[103] Belshaw, *Colonisation and community*, p. 52.
[105] D.T. Hawkings, *Bound for Australia* (Chichester, 1987), pp. 158-9. CRO, Carlisle, D/Ken.3/28/2.
[105] *The Australian* January 1825.
[106] CRO, Carlisle, D/BS/Scott.
[107] BPP 1843 XXXIV, Emigration report, pp. 59, 92.
[108] BPP 1851 XL, Emigration Report. Appendix. pp. 445-9. Table showing counties from which bounty emigrants were sent 1846-50.
[109] BPP 1852-3 XL, Emigration report, p. 84.
[110] J. Whitaker, *An Almanack for the year of our Lord 1869* (London, 1869).
[111] *Carlisle Journal* 5 August 1853.
[112] *Cumberland Pacquet* 20 September 1842.
[113] *Carlisle Journal* 23 September 1853. *Australian Handbook and Almanac,* 1877.
[114] BPP 1873 XVIII, Emigration Report, p. 316.
[115] *C & W Advertiser* 3 February 1872. Registrar General's Report 1874. BPP 1873 XVIII, Emigration report. pp. 295-520, pp. 315-6.
[116] *Australian Handbook and Almanac,* 1877.
[117] M. Muir (ed.) *Anthony Trollope in Australia,* (Adelaide, 1949), pp. 69-70.
[118] *Keswick Reminder* 26 October 1907.
[119] *C & W Herald* 22 February 1908.
[120] BPP 1847-8 XXVI, Emigration Report, pp. 8, 47.
[121] *C & W Herald* 9 November 1907.
[122] *Keswick Reminder* 26 October 1907. *Australian Handbook,* Queensland section, 1910.
[123] R.M. Allan, *Nelson: a history of early settlement* (Wellington, 1965). W.D. Borrie, *Immigration to New Zealand 1854-1938* (Canberra, 1991), pp. 1-12. J.S. Marais, The *Colonisation of New Zealand* (London, 1968). Hudson, 'English emigrants to New Zealand 1838-50.'
[124] Allan, *Nelson,* p. 47.
[125] Hudson, 'English emigrants to New Zealand 1838-50,' Appendix 5 and Map 14.
[126] TNA CO208/272 and 273, New Zealand Company records. Hudson, 'English emigrants to New Zealand 1838-50,' pp. 122,164.
[127] *Letters from settlers and labouring emigrants,* 1843, Nelson section, p.64. Letter from Francis Jollie to William Blamire, June 1842 and from the Chief Surveyor, February 1842. *Nelson Examiner,* various dates, 1842-3.
[128] *Carlisle Journal* 4 June, 8 October 1842.
[129] *Sidney's Emigrant's Journal* 30 November 1848.
[130] C. Terry *'New Zealand: its advantages and prospects as a British Colony,* 1842.' Quoted in Borrie, *Immigration to New Zealand 1854-1938,* p. 10.
[131] Borrie, *Immigration to New Zealand 1854-1938,* p. 11. Quotation from J.H. Burton, *Emigration in its practical application to individuals and communities* (1851).
[132] *Sidney's Emigrant's Journal,* 31 May, 7 June 1849.
[133] *Ibid.*
[134] A.H. Reed, *The Story of early Dunedin* (Wellington, 1956), p.20.
[135] *Ibid.* p. 68.
[136] 'A caution to Canterbury Colonists' in *Sidney's Emigrant's Journal,* 1850, p. 252.
[137] Borrie, *Immigration to New Zealand 1854-1938,* p. 111.
[138] *The Cyclopaedia of New Zealand: industrial, descriptive, historical, biographical, facts, figures, illustrations,* Volumes 1-6, (Wellington, 1897-1908).
[139] Family information.
[140] Family information.
[141] *West Cumberland Times* 19 January 1901.

[142] *C & W Herald* 17 April 1909.
[143] Quoted in *Daily Telegraph,* 30 July 2005.
[144] *Maryport News* 5 August 1905.
[145] *West Cumberland Times* 2 February 1901, *C & W Herald* 2 February 1915.
[146] CRO, Carlisle, DX 301/87.
[147] *Cumberland Pacquet* 7 January 1909.
[148] *Maryport News,* 9 September 1905.
[149] *General Directory South Africa 1890-1* (Cape Town, 1890).
[150] A.N. Rigg, *Cumbria, slavery and the textile industrial revolution* (Kirkby Stephen, 1994), pp. 38-52. *Carlisle Journal* 16 July 1842. Report of lecture by Dr D. Rushworth, 'Family networks and migration links between Cumbria and the Caribbean in the eighteenth and nineteenth centuries' in the *Keswick Reminder* 27 March 2009. *Carlisle Patriot* 27 January 1843.
[151] CRO, Carlisle, DX/249/23.
[152] BPP 1842 XXXI, Return of Emigrants 1841, p. 421.
[153] BPP 1849 XXII, EIO Report, p. 35.
[154] BPP 1899 LVIII, EIO Report, pp. 135-43, p.140.
[155] BPP 1899 LVIII, EIO Report, pp. 135-43, p. 140, 1909 LIX, EIO Report, pp. 305-18, p. 310.
[156] *Cumberland Pacquet* 12 July 1842.
[157] *Carlisle Patriot* 12 November 1830, *Carlisle Journal* 16 July 1842.
[158] BPP 1897 LXI, EIO Report, pp. 95-104, p. 100.
[159] *C & W Herald* 28 July 1906.
[160] *Cumberland Pacquet* 5 January 1905, *C & W Herald* 17 October 1914.
[161] *C & W Advertiser* 4 April 1871. BPP 1890 XLIX, EIO Report. pp. 79-84, p. 82.
[162] *Cumberland Pacquet* 21 August 1913.
[163] Dr B. Callaghan, Report of lecture, *Whitehaven News* 1 January 2007.
[164] H. Summerson, *An Ancient Squire's Family: the history of the Aglionbys c.1130-2002* (Carlisle, 2007).
[165] CRO, Carlisle, D/BS/Scott.

Chapter Four: The Journey

[1] D. Hollett, *From Cumberland to Cape Horn: the sailing fleet of Thomas and John Brocklebank of Whitehaven and Liverpool 1770-1900* (London, 1984), pp. 37-43, 153.
[2] CRO, Whitehaven, YDX 481.
[3] *Jollie's Guide 1811* (Otley, 1995).
[4] C. Smith, *Carlisle to Canada* (Carlisle, 2006), p. 54. *Carlisle Journal* 2 February 1842.
[5] A. Robertson, *A History of Alston Moor,* (Alston, 2002), p. 42.
[6] D. Morris, *The Dalesmen of the Mississippi River* (York, 1989), pp. 17-19.
[7] *Carlisle Journal* 30 March 1832.
[8] CRO, Carlisle, D/Ken/3/28/2.
[9] CRO, Kendal, WDY 159.
[10] Spedding, *Footsteps in retrospect,* p. 5.
[11] A.B. Granville, *The Spas of England and principal sea-bathing places* (London, 1841, Bath 1971), pp. 29-31.
[xii] *Bradshaw's Guide,* 1843.
[13] *Bradshaw, 1843.*
[14] *Bradshaw,* 1849, 1852-3. Shepherd, *Hellgill,* Chapter 4, pp. 174-223.
[15] *Bradshaw,* 1849.
[16] *Bradshaw,* 1852-3, 1858.
[17] CRO, Whitehaven, YDX 481.
[18] T. Coleman, *Passage to America: a history of emigrants from Great Britain to America in the mid-nineteenth century* (London, 1972), p. 62.

[19] C. Erickson, *Emigration from Europe*, Document 26b. Extract from the *Newcastle Chronicle*, 22 March 1865, pp. 248, 250-1.
[20] *Post Office Directory, Lancashire*, (London,1858).
[21] N. Fogg, *The Voyages of the Great Britain: life at sea in the world's first liner* (London 2002), pp. 114-5.
[22] *Post Office Directory, Lancashire*, (London,1858).
[23] L. Hughes, *Henry Mundy:a young Australian Pioneer* (Leighton Buzzard, 2003), p. 62.
[24] Quoted from Thomas Hetherington's diary, courtesy of John Hetherington.
[25] Hollett, *From Cumberland to Cape Horn*, p. 34.
[26] Robertson, *History of Alston Moor*, p. 42.
[27] *Carlisle Patriot* 26 January, 2, 15 February, 22 March, 27 April, 10, 17 May, 21, 28 June 1828.
[28] *Cumberland Pacquet* 3 February, 31 May 1825.
[29] *Cumberland Pacquet* 28 March 1826.
[30] *Carlisle Patriot* 27 March, 1 May 1830.
[31] *Cumberland Pacquet* 4 January, 12 April, 20 September, 1 October 1842.
[32] BPP 1847-8 XLVII, Passenger returns, p. 393.
[33] *Carlisle Patriot* 27 March, 1 May 1830. Hollett, *From Cumberland to Cape Horn*, p. 153.
[34] *Carlisle Journal* 12 February, 7 May 1842.
[35] *Carlisle Journal* 4 June 1842. Hudson, 'English emigrants to New Zealand.' TNA, CO 208/266-9, 272-5, NZ Company records.
[36] *Carlisle Journal* 8 May 1841.
[37] C. Petrowski, *A bride's passage: Susan Hathorn's year under sail* (Boston, 1997), p. 57.
[38] Dickens, *American Notes*, p. 2.
[39] D. Charlwood, The *Long Farewell,* (London, 1981), p. 6.
[40] *Post Office Directory, Lancashire*, 1858.
[41] Spedding, *Footsteps in retrospect*, pp. 6-12.
[42] Dr. K Hornsby. Quotation from family memoirs.
[43] E. Spark, *Outward Bound: my diary (Alston, 2002),* pp. 7-9.
[44] Fogg, *Great Britain,* pp. 26, 56.
[45] M. Muir, *Anthony Trollope in Australia*, p. 2.
[46] D. Savill, *Sail to New Zealand*, (London, 1986), pp. 43-4.
[47] T. Coleman, *The Liners: a history of the north Atlantic crossing* (London, 1976), p. 35.
[48] *Whitehaven News* 2 January 1879.
[49] F. Barnes, *Barrow and District* (Barrow in Furness, 1968), pp. 93-4.
[50] *C & W Advertiser* 20 July 1880.
[51] *Whitaker's Almanack*, 1900.
[52] Fogg, *Great Britain*, p. 127.
[53] *Australian Handbook and Almanac,* (Sydney, 1877).
[54] CRO, Kendal WDX 190, from *Kirkby Stephen & Appleby Monthly Messenger* 1891.
[55] *Whitaker's Almanack*, 1885, pp. 18-19.
[56] Spedding, *Footsteps in retrospect,* pp. 9-11.
[57] *Canada and the Western States,* 1859, p. 26.
[58] *Australian Handbook and Almanac,* (London, 1877).
[59] *C & W Advertiser* 15 November 1880.
[60] Fogg, *Great Britain*, p. 116.
[61] Family information.
[62] Shepherd, *Hellgill*, p. 273. CRO, Kendal, WDX 190, *Kirkby Stephen and Appleby Monthly Messenger,* March-June 1891, January 1892. CRO, Kendal, WDX 822.
[63] Thomas Hetherington's diary, courtesy of John Hetherington.
[64] CRO,Carlisle, DX 249/14.
[65] CRO, Carlisle, DX 451.
[66] Spedding, *Footsteps in retrospect,* p. 6.
[67] Family information.

[68] CRO,Carlisle, D/Ken/3/28/2.
[69] Spedding, *Footsteps in retrospect*, pp. 6-12. *General Directory of South Africa,* 1889. pp. 545-6. Gold and diamond export value also increased. By 1908 gold exports totalled more than £24.4 million and diamonds, £9.25 million but feathers were not quoted in that year.
[70] CRO, Kendal, WDX 822.
[71] CRO, Carlisle, DX 1755/1/4.
[72] CRO, Carlisle, DX/1070/1.
[73] CRO, Carlisle, DX 1755/1/4.
[74] N. Fogg, *Great Britain,* p. 55.
[75] Family information.
[76] CRO, Kendal, WPR 9/257.
[77] Fogg *Great Britain,* p. 124
[78] Hart, *The Powley Connection,* p. 61.
[79] Fogg, *Great Britain* pp. 140, 144.
[80] Thomas Hetherington's diary, courtesy of John Hetherington.
[81] *The Press* 24 December 1968.
[82] CRO, Carlisle, DX/46/7.
[83] Family information.
[84] This would be Gough Island with its high cliffs, south of Tristan da Cunha.
[85] Hughes, *Henry Mundy,* p. 75.
[86] Dickens, *American Notes,* p. 18.
[87] CRO, Carlisle, DX/249/23.
[88] CRO, Kendal, WRX 259.
[89] J.Y. Lancaster, 'The Wreck of the Geltwood' in *Harrington through the years,* Vol. 2, pp. 8-10.
[90] Family information.
[91] CRO, Kendal, WDX 848/7.
[92] Family information.
[93] V. Addison, *Black Sheep and Diamonds: a true family story* (Carlisle, 2003), p. 8.
[94] Information from John Hetherington.
[95] CRO, Carlisle, DX 1755/1/4.
[96] Family information.
[97] R. Arnold, *The Farthest Promised Land: English villagers, NZ immigrants of the 1870s* (Wellington, 1981), p. 239.
[98] D. Charlwood, *The Long Farewell,* p. 251.

Chapter Five: Arrival: first steps in a new land

[1] J. Fowler, *Journal of a Tour through the State of New York* (London, 1931, New York, 1970), pp. 21, 221-2.
[2] J.S. Buckingham, *A journey through the Slave States of the United States* (London, 1842, 2006), p. 10.
[3] Buckingham, *A journey through the Slave States,* pp. 153-8.
[4] Dickens, *American Notes,* p. 156.
[5] CRO, Kendal, WDX 1005. Dickens, *American Notes,* p. 72.
[6] CRO, Kendal, WDX 1005.
[7] *Sidney's Emigrant's Journal* 10 October 1848.
[8] S. Strickland, *Twenty seven years in Canada West or the experience of an early settler* Vol. 1. (London 1853, Bibliolife 2009), pp. 5-7.
[9] E. Thompson, (ed.) *The Emigrant's Guide to North America* (Ontario, 1841, 1998), p. 26. Trollope, *Notes from America,* p. 61. Strickland, *Twenty seven years in Canada West* Vol. 1, p. 9.
[10] Strickland, *Twenty seven years in Canada West* Vol. 1, p. 11. Thompson, *Emigrant's Guide to North America,* p. 42. C. Gray, *Sisters in the Wilderness: the lives of Susanna Moodie and Catherine Traill* (London, 2001), p. 64.

[11] Dickens, *American Notes*, p. 189.
[12] CRO, Carlisle, DX/249/23.
[13] BPP 1851 XL Emigration report. p. 324.
[14] CRO, Carlisle, D/Mg/224/8.
[15] Rickard (ed.), *George Barrington's voyage to Botany Bay*, pp. 75, 78.
[16] CRO, Carlisle, D/BS/Scott.
[17] CRO, Carlisle, DX/46/5.
[18] Hughes, *Henry Mundy*, pp 78-85.
[19] CRO, Kendal, WDX 948.
[20] Haines, *Life and death in the age of sail*, pp. 211-2.
[21] CRO, Carlisle, D/Ken/3/28/2.
[22] CRO, Kendal, WDX 822. Family information.
[23] Transcript of letter from Isobel Archer.
[24] CRO, Kendal, WDX 822.
[25] CRO, Kendal, WDX 1005.
[26] CRO, Carlisle, DX 1755/1/4.
[27] CRO, Kendal, WDX 169.
[28] Dr K. Hornsby. Quoting from family memoir.
[29] Spedding, *Footsteps in retrospect*, pp. 12, 13.
[30] *C & W Herald* 13 July, 10 August 1907.
[31] *C & W Herald* 22 November 1913.
[32] Allan, *Nelson*, pp. 138-9, 135, 101-2.
[33] *Letters from settlers and labouring emigrants*, 1843, Nelson section, p.64. Letter from Francis Jollie to William Blamire, June 1842 and from the Chief Surveyor, February 1842. *Nelson Examiner*, various dates, 1842-3.
[34] Letter to William Blamire, June 17 1842 in *'Letters,'* (1843), p. 90.
[35] Allan, *Nelson*, pp. 138, 204. Letter to William Blamire 20 December 1843 in *'Letters'* (1843).
[36] *Lyttelton Times,* 11, 18 January, 1 March, 10 June, 13, September, 8 November, 20 December 1851.
[37] *Lyttelton Times,* 25 January 1851.
[38] *Cyclopaedia NZ,* Vol. 3, Canterbury, pp. 68-9.
[39] C.W. Adams, *A Spring in Canterbury Settlement* (London, 1853, Christchurch, 1971), pp. 18, 24, 24-35, 85-6. A.H. Reed, *The Story of Canterbury: the last Wakefield settlement* (Wellington, 1949), pp. 250-7.
[40] 'Blind Guide' in *Sidney's Emigrant's Journal,* 1850, pp. 250-7.
[41] Adams, *A Spring in Canterbury*, p. 25.
[42] Reed, *The Story of Canterbury*, pp. 37-8, 40. *Cyclopaedia NZ*, Vol. 3, Canterbury, p. 68.
[43] *Carlisle Patriot* 4 February 1857.
[44] *Cyclopaedia of NZ, Vol. 3,* p. 255.
[45] Family information.
[46] A. H. Reed, *The Story of early Dunedin* (Wellington, 1956), pp. 86-9.
[47] *Otago News* 14 November 1850.
[48] Reed, *Dunedin,* p. 51.
[49] *Ibid.* pp. 40, 44-5, 53.
[50] Dart, *The Powley connection*, p.115. Reed, *Dunedin*, pp. 44-5, 53.
[51] Reed, *Dunedin,* pp. 138, 146, 148, 156.
[52] CRO, Carlisle, DX/67/37/1.
[53] P.R. May, *The west coast gold rushes* (Christchurch, 1962/7), p.125.
[54] Spedding, *Footsteps in retrospect*, pp. 11-12.
[55] Family information.
[56] Spedding, *Footsteps in retrospect*, pp. 13-17.
[57] *Cyclopaedia of NZ*, Vol. 5, Nelson.
[58] Family information.

[59] Family information.
[60] *New Zealand Guide,* p. 67.
[61] BPP 1850 XXXVII, Colonies: New Zealand, pp. 21-2.
[62] A. Bloxham in *Westmorland Gazette* 19 March 2004. Family information.
[63] Family information.
[64] Spedding, *Footsteps in retrospect,* p. 11.
[65] A. H. Reed, *The Story of Hawkes Bay* (Wellington, 1958), pp. 300, 116, 118-9.
[66] Family information.
[67] Family information.
[68] BPP 1822 XX, Report on the State of New South Wales, pp. 556, 563.
[69] Rickard (ed.), *George Barrington's voyage to Botany Bay,* pp. 75, 78.
[70] BPP 1837-8 Report on Transportation, pp. iv, vii, 10.
[71] CRO Carlisle, D/BS/Scott.
[72] BPP 1822 XX, Report on the State of New South Wales, p. 536.
[73] CRO, Carlisle, D/BS/Scott.
[74] CRO, Carlisle, D/BS/Scott. M. Perrott, *A tolerable good success: economic opportunities for women in New South Wales 1788-1830* (Sydney, 1983), p. 25.
[75] Chapter 6, p. 161
[76] CRO, Carlisle, D/BS/Scott.
[77] *Cumberland Pacquet* 18 April 1825, *Australian* 27 January 1825.
[78] Family information and *Municipality of Sorell Heritage Study: Thematic History,* (Sorell 1996) pp. 50-1. Sorell Heritage Survey re 'The Circle:site of Downward's windmill.'
[79] *Australian,* 21, 28 October, 13, 20, 27 November 1824, 7, 21 July, 1 September 1825, 19 January 1826.
[80] CRO, Carlisle, D/BS/Scott.
[81] CRO, Carlisle, D/BS/Scott.
[82] CRO, Carlisle, D/BS/Scott.
[83] CRO, Carlisle, DX/46/5.
[84] CRO, Carlisle, DX/46/5.
[85] Family information. Haines, *Life and death in the age of sail,* p. 168.
[86] CRO, Kendal, WDX 948/15.
[87] Haines, *Life and death in the age of sail,* p. 169.
[88] G. Handley (ed.) *Trollope the Traveller,* p. 138, M. Muir (ed.), *Anthony Trollope in Australia,* p. 67.
[89] Family information.
[90] CRO, Carlisle, D/mg/224/8.
[91] CRO, Carlisle, DX/67/37/1.
[92] CRO, Carlisle, DX 1755/1/1.
[93] CRO, Kendal, WDX 822.
[94] CRO, Carlisle, D/BS/Scott.
[95] CRO, Carlisle, DX/67/37/1.
[96] CRO, Carlisle, DX/67/37/1.
[97] CRO, Carlisle, D/Ken/3/28/2.
[98] Spark, *Outward Bound,* pp. 46, 48, 50-2.
[99] CRO, Kendal, WDX 822.
[100] Stuart, *The Emigrant's Guide,* p.159. Robertson, *History of Alston Moor,* pp. 42-3.
[101] Thompson, *Hudson, the early years.* B.H., R.L., Hodgson, E.C. Royle, E.G. Mullan, M.P. Clarke, J. Vipond, *Pioneer families,* Vol. 6 (Hudson Historical Society Records), p.16.
[102] S. Moodie, *Roughing it in the Bush* (1852, London 1986), p. 83.
[103] Thompson, *Hudson, the early years* and *Pioneer families,* Vol. 6, pp.16-17.
[104] www.trentvalleyarchives.com/gazette.htm. Accessed March 21 1009 quoting an article in the *Peterborough Examiner* July 17 1928.
[105] Strickland, *Twenty seven years in Canada West* Vol. 1, pp. 18-19, 31-2, 38, 45, 55, 64, 92, 112.

[106] CRO, Kendal ,WDX 822.
[107] One of several examples in *Sidney's Emigrant's Journal,* 1848-50.
[108] D. White (ed.), *News of the Plains and Rockies 1803-65,* Vols. 1-6 (Washington, 1999) Vol. 2, p. 366.
[109] *Ibid* Vol. 2, p. 219.
[110] Information from John Sharpe, Clifton.
[111] White (ed.), *News of the Plains and Rockies,* Vol. 2, p.16.
[112] *Ibid.* p. 139.
[113] Family information.
[114] Family information.
[115] Buckingham, A *journey through the Slave States,* pp. 181-2, 184-5.
[116] CRO, Kendal, WDX 169.
[117] *Sidney's Emigrant's Journal* 5 October 1848.
[118] Morris, *The Dalesmen of the Mississippi River.*
[119] Family information.
[120] Trollope, *North America,* pp. 160, 176.
[121] CRO, Carlisle, DX/67/37/1.
[122] CRO, Kendal, WDX 822.
[123] Family information.
[124] Family information.
[125] Dickens, *American Notes,* p. 166.
[126] J. Hamilton, *Places* (Calgary, 1971), pp. 47-50.
[127] M. Hiemstra, *Gully farm,* (London, 1955), p.55 onwards. Also, J. Sharpe and others, *Prairie Wool and Pussy Willows* (Committee collaboration), (North Battleford, c.1988).
[128] Family information.
[129] Family information.
[130] Family information quoting Harry Brunskill's unpublished memoir
[131] Family information quoting Harry Brunskill's unpublished memoir.
[132] Family information.
[133] Family information.
[134] Dr K. Hornsby, quoting from a family memoir.
[135] Family information.
[136] CRO, Carlisle, D/Ben/letters.
[137] CRO, Kendal, WDX 822.
[138] Family correspondence quoting Harry Brunskill's unpublished memoir.
[139] CRO, Carlisle, DX/46/5.
[140] Hughes, *Henry Mundy* pp. 78-81. The Mundys were from Buckinghamshire.
[141] E. Bennington, *The Robinsons of Moneymore* (New Zealand, 1983), p.12.
[142] Hart, *The Powley Connection,* pp.106-117.
Bennington, *The Robinsons of Moneymore,* p.11.
[143] Reed, The *Story of Canterbury,* pp. 130-140.
[144] Spedding, *Footsteps in retrospect,* p. 10.
[145] CRO, Carlisle, DX/806/3 and family information.
[146] Diary transcripts from T.W. Jones and L. Hewitson
[147] 'Journey to South Africa,' *CFHS Journal* 117, November 2005. J Nolan's memories.
[148] CRO, Carlisle, DX/301/91.
[149] CRO, Carlisle, DX/1070/1.
[150] Family information.
[151] Family information.
[152] CRO, Kendal, WDX 169. CRO, Whitehaven, D/BT/6/209/1.
[153] Family information. *Penrith Observer* 17 January 1865.
[154] Family information.
[155] Family information.
[156] Family information.

[157] *Letters from settlers and labouring emigrants*, 1843, Nelson section, p.64. Letter from Francis Jollie to William Blamire, December 1843.
[158] Family information quoting Harry Brunskill's unpublished memoir.
[159] Family information.
[160] Shepherd, *Hellgill*, p. 167.
[161] Family information.
[162] *C & W Herald* 24 April 1909.
[163] CRO, Carlisle, DX/806/3 and family information.
[164] CRO, Carlisle, DX/806/3 and family information.
[165] Family information.
[166] Family information and CRO, Carlisle, D/BS/Scott.
[167] Dr K. Hornsby quoting from the Calcott family memoir.
[168] A. H. Christian, *The search for Holmes, Robson, Hind, Steele and Graham* (Carlisle, 1984), p.2.
[169] Family information.
[170] Family information.
[171] Family information.
[172] *C & W Herald* 11 January 1913.
[173] *C & W Herald* 26 March 1910.
[174] *C & W Herald* 18 March 1911.
[175] Family information.
[176] Family information.
[177] *Whitehaven News* 14 July 2006. *C & W Herald* 28 October 2005.
[178] Family information.
[179] BPP 1873 LXI Emigration Report. p.37.
[180] *Daily Telegraph and Courier* 29 June 1855. N. Fogg, *Great Britain*, p. 127.
[181] Family information.
[182] CRO, Carlisle, D/67/37/1.
[183] Shepherd, *Hellgill,* pp. 296, 298.
[184] B. Palmer, 'Tom Penny: gentleman' *CFHS Newsletter*, 94, 2000.
[185] Family information.
[186] *Carlisle Journal* 26 February 1892.
[187] CRO, Carlisle, DX/67/37/1. Translated from very poor spelling.
[188] *Ibid.*
[189] *West Cumberland Times* and *Whitehaven News*. For example, 12 February, 7, 14, 28 May, 9 July, 13 August, 1, 8 October, 19 November, 3, 10 December 1903.
[190] Family information.
[191] Family information.
[192] Family information.
[193] Family information.
[194] Family information.
[195] *Maryport News* 9 September 1905.
[196] *Cumberland News* 6 March 1981- re 1881.
[197] *C & W Herald* 13 March 1909.
[198] *Cumberland Pacquet* 8 May 1913.
[199] *Maryport News* 23 December 1905.
[200] *Maryport News* 3 May 1905.
[201] CRO, Kendal, WDX 204. *Carlisle Journal* 25 September 1853.
[202] *West Cumberland Times* 27 March 1901.
[203] *Whitehaven News* 27 June 1895. *Cumberland Pacquet* 19 June 1913.
[204] *West Cumberland Times* 14 September 1918.
[205] *Cumberland Pacquet* 13 March 1913.
[206] Belshaw, *Colonisation and community*, pp. 202-3.
[207] Belshaw, *Colonisation and community*, p. 52.

[208] Belshaw, *Colonisation and community*, pp. 202-3.
[209] *Penrith Observer* 23 February 1915.
[210] Royal Commission Report, quoted in B. Bowden and B. Penrose,' Dust, contractors, politics and silicosis,' *Australian Historical Studies,* 128 October 2006, pp. 89-107.
[211] CRO, Carlisle, D/67/37/1.
[212] *Cyclopaedia of NZ,* Vol. 4, Otago.
[213] Diary transcripts from T.W. Jones and L. Hewitson.
[214] *Cumberland Pacquet* 15 February 1905.
[215] *Cumberland Pacquet* 7, 21 January, 29 April 1909, and family information.
[216] *Cumberland Pacquet* 11 March 1909.
[217] *Cumberland Pacquet* 27 May 1909.
[218] CRO, Kendal, WDX 822.
[219] T.H. Watkins, *Gold and silver in the west: the illustrated history of an American dream* (Palo Alto, 1971), pp. 135-6.
[220] *Cumberland Pacquet* 24 April 1913.
[221] Watkins, *Gold and silver in the West*, p. 93. *Cumberland Pacquet* 23 September 1909.
[222] CRO, Whitehaven, D/Mg/224/2.
[223] CRO, Carlisle, DX/301/87.
[224] Family information.
[225] CRO, Carlisle, DX/451.
[226] CRO, Kendal, WDX 822.
[227] CRO, Kendal, WDX 1005.
[228] CRO, Carlisle, DX/1755/1/4.
[229] CRO, Kendal, WDX 822.
[230] Family information.
[231] Family information.
[232] Family information.
[233] CRO, Carlisle, D/BS/Scott.
[234] Family information.
[235] Family information.
[236] CRO, Kendal, WDX 822.
[237] CRO, Carlisle, D/67/37/1.
[238] CRO, Kendal, WDX 822.
[239] D. Whitelock, *Adelaide 1836-1976* (Queensland 1977), pp. 216-8.
[240] Reed, A.H. *The story of Hawke's Bay*. (Wellington, 1958), p. 119.
[241] Reed, *The story of Hawke's Bay*, p. 292.
[242] *Cyclopaedia of New Zealand*, Volume 4, Otago.
[243] E. Olssen, *A History of Otago*, (Dunedin, 1984), pp. 68,
[244] *Lyttelton Times* 15 December 1880.
[245] P. R.May, *The west coast gold rushes*, (Christchurch, 1967), pp. 177-8.
[246] May, *West coast gold rushes,* p. 323.
[247] May, *West coast gold rushes*, pp. 330-6, 341.
[248] Dart. *The Powley connection*, pp. 231-3., 236.
[249] Spedding, *Footsteps in retrospect*, pp. 13-16.
[250] *C & W Herald* 13 July, 10 August 1907.
[252] D. Whitelock, *Adelaide 1836-1976* (Queensland, 1977), pp. 224-42, p. 226.
[252] CRO, Kendal, WDX 1005.
[253] D. Snowman, 'New World Overtures' in *History Today*, January 2010, pp. 35-41.
[254] CRO, Kendal, WDX 822.
[255] *C & W Herald* 19 September 2004, 2 October 2004.
[256] *C & W Herald* 13 July, 10 August 1907.
[257] Family information.
[258] *C & W Herald* 19 September 2009. *Maryport News* 28 January 1905.
[259] CRO, Carlisle, DX/301/87.

[260] CRO, Carlisle, DX/1070/1.
[261] CRO, Kendal, WD/AG/Box 3.
[262] CRO, Kendal, WPR 9/257.
[263] CRO, Carlisle, D/BS/Scott.
[264] CRO, Kendal, WDX 822.
[265] CRO, Carlisle, D/BS/Scott.
[266] CRO, Kendal, WDY 33/1.
[267] CRO, Carlisle, D/Mg/224/2.
[268] CRO, Kendal, WDX 211/3.
[269] CRO, Carlisle, DX/301/74.
[270] *Homesick*, A poem by Christopher Gelder. Family information.
[271] CRO, Kendal, WDX 822. Cat posies –could these be catkins?
[272] CRO, Carlisle, DX/249/14.
[273] Spark, *Outward Bound*, pp. 46, 48, 50-2.
[274] CRO, Kendal, WDX 822.
[275] CRO, Carlisle, DX/67/37/1.
[276] Spedding, *Footsteps in retrospect*, p. 35.

Chapter Six: Returned emigrants and sojourners.

[1] BPP 1873 LXI, Emigration report. pp. 340-3. Baines, *Migration in a mature economy*, pp. 29, 21-2, 279.
[2] BPP 1903 LXXXII, Emigration and immigration Tables. p.762.
[3] *C & W Herald* 12 May 1906.
[4] W.S. Shepperson, *Emigration and disenchantment: portraits of Englishmen repatriated from the United States* (Oklahoma, 1965), p. 5. BPP 1910 LXVI Emigration Report. pp. 73-90, p. 79.
[5] BPP 1912-13 LX EIO Report, pp. 615-32. BPP 1917-18 XXXV, Census Report. p. 512. A new system meant that numbers 'could be flawed' but the accuracy was 'now greatly improved.'
[6] Baines, *Migration in a mature economy*, pp. 128-40, p. 130.
[7] BPP 1917-18 XXXV, Census Report 1911, p. 766.
[8] BPP 1850 XXXVII, Emigration Report, pp. 838-9.
[9] BPP 1850 XXXVII, Emigration Report, pp. 838-9. 1852 XVIII, Emigration Report, 1873 XVIII, Emigration Report, p. 344.
[10] BPP 1917-18 XXXV, Census Report 1911. p.766.
[11] Registrar General's Report, 1874.
[12] BPP 1862 XXII, Emigration Report, pp. 1-220, p. 25,
[13] Dickens, *American Notes*, p. 204.
[14] P.F. Haslam, 'The story of John and Rebecca Fearon,' *CFHS Newsletter* 96 (August, 2000).
[15] E. Richards, 'Running home from Australia: intercontinental mobility and migrant expectations in the nineteenth century' in Harper (ed.) *Emigrant Homecomings: the return movements of emigrants, 1600-2000* (Manchester, 2008), pp. 77, 80-3.
[16] E.T. Parson *Land I can own* (Ottawa, 1981), p. 25.
[17] Dickens, *American Notes*, p. 204.
[18] Family information.
[19] Family information.
[20] Family information.
[21] *C & W Herald* 14 November 1908.
[22] Census enumerations.
[23] Family information and 1901 census.
[24] Spedding, *Footsteps in retrospect*, pp. 19-20, 28-36, 38-39.
[25] These examples are cited in Shepherd, *Hellgill*, pp. 297-8.
[26] Richards, 'Running home from Australia' in Harper (ed.) *Emigrant Homecomings*, pp. 88-9, quoting South Australia Archives 7/54/2/5/1912.

[27] Family information.
[28] Erickson, *Emigration from Europe*, pp. 149-50.
[29] CRO, Carlisle, D/HW/1.
[30] *Keswick Reminder* 16 January 2009.
[31] See Chapter 5, Mining section, pp.131-2
[32] *Cumberland Pacquet* 21 October 1909.
[33] S. Richardson, 'William Willan: a Westmorland gold mining prospector in South Africa,' *CFHS Newsletter* 115, (May, 2005).
[34] *Cumberland Pacquet* 22 April 1909.
[35] S. Rickard, (ed.), *George Barrington's Voyage to Botany Bay,* (Leicester, 2001), p. 20.
[36] BPP 1835 XI, Report on gaols, p. 345.
[37] A. Brooke and D. Brandon, *Bound for Botany Bay: British convict voyages to Australia* (London, 2005), p. 114.
[38] S. Nicholas and P.R. Shergold, 'Convicts as workers,' in S. Nicholas (ed.), *Convict Workers: re-interpreting Australia's past* (Cambridge, 1988), pp. 62-84, 76-7.
[39] Brooke and Brandon, *Bound for Botany Bay*, p. 60.
[40] R. Hughes, *The Fatal shore: a history of the transportation of convicts to Australia 1787-1868* (London,1987), quoting L.L. Robson, pp. 159-61. Nicholas and Shergold, 'Convicts as workers,' p. 7.
[41] Nicholas and Shergold, 'Convicts as workers,' p. 95.
[42] *Ibid.*, p. 46.
[43] Family information. I. Terry, *Municipality of Sorell Heritage Study: Stage 1, Thematic history* (Sorell, 1996).
[44] A.G.L. Shaw, *Convicts and the colonies: a study of penal transportation from Great Britain and Ireland to Australia and other parts of the British Empire* (London, 1966), p. 149.
[45] *Australian Convict Index 1788-1868.* Accessed via Ancestry.co.uk, 22/09/07.
[46] F. Jackson, 'They travelled abroad,' *CFHS Newsletter* 120, 2006.
[47] Information from Dr J. Barnes.
[48] I. Ashbridge, *Cumbrian crime from a social perspective* (Cramlington, 1999), p. 12.
[49] Local newspapers. Edwin Fox Museum, Picton, NZ via Liz Hawkins.
[50] CRO Carlisle D/BS/Scott
[51] *New South Wales Census*,1828. M.R. Sainty and K.A. Johnson (eds.) (Sydney, 1980)
[52] CRO Carlisle D/BS/Scott. *The Australian*, 23 December 1824, 3 February 1825. Hughes, *The Fatal Shore*, pp. 203-243.
[53] Glenridding is at the head of Ullswater.
[54] T.A. Heathcote, *The Indian army: the garrison of British Imperial India 1822-1922* (Newton Abbott, 1974). N. Robins, The *Corporation that changed the world: how the East India Company shaped the modern multi-national (London, 2006).*
[55] Heathcote, *The Indian Army*, pp. 130-2.
[56] CRO, Carlisle, DX 249/14.
[57] *Ibid.*
[58] *Cumberland Pacquet* 20 December 1842. Penrith and Warcop church and cemetery records.
[59] BPP 1847 XLI, Return of sickness and mortality 1825-44, p. 67. BPP 1875 XLIII Return of sickness and mortality 1841-73, p. 485.
[60] *Cumberland Pacquet* 22 March, 26 April, 12 July, 20 December 1842, 18 February 1909.
[61] CRO, Carlisle, DRC/1/8.
[62] Census 1881, 1891.
[63] CRO, Kendal, WDX 652. *C & W Herald* 24 April 1909.
[64] *Carlisle Journal* 14 November 1871.
[65] Family correspondence.
[66] CRO, Carlisle, D/Pen/Malay/6/28.
[67] CRO, Carlisle, DX 451.

[68] *West Cumberland Times* 12 January 1901.
[69] *Maryport News* 25 February 1903, *C & W Herald* 19 May 1906.
[70] CRO, Carlisle, DX 301/ 87-92.
[71] E.F. Knight, *Railways in Rhodesia* (London, 1904), pp. 42, 49.
[72] CRO, Carlisle, DX 301/87-92.
[73] CRO, Carlisle, DX/301/75.
[74] CRO, Carlisle, DX 451.
[75] *Kirkby Stephen and Appleby Messenger* 1891, CRO, Kendal, WDX 190.
[76] G.T. Hutchinson, *From the Cape to the Zambesi* (London, 1905), pp. 126-8.
[77] CRO Carlisle, DX/301/83-7.

Chapter Seven: Conclusion
[1] Baines, *Migration in a mature economy*, p. 282.
[2] Bailyn, *Voyagers to the west*, p. 5.
[3] CRO, Kendal, WDY 566.
[4] CRO, Kendal WDX 822.
[5] Family information.
[6] *Cumberland Pacquet* 28 September 1905, *C & W Herald* 22 March 1913.
[7] Shepperson, *British emigrants to North America*, p.245.
[8] R. W. Warwick, 'A New Zealand Memorial,' *CFHS Newsletter* 97 (November, 2000), p.24. T Cockerill, 'The English Cemetery, Pourta de la Cruz, Tenerife, Canary Isles,' *CFHS Newsletter*, 102, February 2002, p. 35. Vere Langford Oliver, 'Cumbrian references in Tombstones in Barbados' in *CFHS Newsletter* 94, February 2004, p. 15.
[9] Family information.
[10] Family information.
[11] *C & W Herald* March 30 1912.
[12] Information from John Sharpe.
[13] *C & W Herald* November 15 2008 and John Sharpe.
[14] *C & W Herald* July 25, September 5 1908.
[15] Family information.
[16] *C & W Herald* March 24 1902.
[17] *C & W Herald* September 11 1909.
[18] Family information.
[19] *C & W Herald* 11 March 1911.
[20] J.Cowan, *Settlers and pioneers*, p.30.
[21] *C & W Herald* May 25 1907.
[22] *C & W Advertiser* January 25 1859.
[23] *Southland People: a dictionary of Otago, Southland biography* (Dunedin 1998) p.59.
[24] *Maryport News* November 18 1905.
[25] *Cyclopaedia of NZ*, Vols. 1-6.
[26] Westmorland Gazette 19 March 1904.
[27] *C & W Herald* March 20 1909.
[28] I. Terry, *Sorell*, p. 50, Heritage survey notes.
[29] Family information.
[30] Family information.
[31] Family information.
[32] CRO Kendal, WDX 822. K. Thompson, 'Maryport emigrants in Australia,'quoting *Maryport Advertiser* 19 February 1886. *CFHS Newsletter* 114 (2005).
[33] *Penrith Observer* 17 June 1865. Family information.

Bibliography.

Official Publications
Census of England and Wales 1841-1911

Published Tables and Reports
BPP   British Parliamentary Papers.
BPP 1843 XXIII
BPP 1852-3 LXXXV
BPP 1863 LIII
BPP 1873 LXXI
BPP 1883 LXVIII
BPP 1893-4 CIV
BPP 1902 CXVIII
BPP 1903 LXXXVI
BPP 1917-18 XXXV
Census Enumerations
1841-1901 Accessed via Ancestry.com
Government Papers
NB. From 1839 to 1873, Emigration Reports are the Annual General Reports of the
Colonial, Land and Emigration Commission. From 1887 to 1916, Emigration Reports
are the Annual Reports of the Emigrant's Information Office.
RC = Royal Commission
SC = Select Committee
BPP 1821 XVII, Report on emigration.
BPP 1821 LX, SC Report on agricultural distress.
BPP 1822 V, SC Report on agricultural distress.
BPP 1822 XX, Report on the State of New South Wales.
BPP 1824 XIX, Report on transportation.
BPP 1826 XXVI, SC Report on emigration.
BPP 1826-7 V, SC Report on emigration.
BPP 1830 XXIX, Emigration to the Colonies.
BPP 1830 XXIV, Report on emigration.
BPP 1833 V, SC Report on the state of agriculture.
BPP 1833 XXVI, Emigration report.
BPP 1833 V, SC Report on agriculture. Mr Blamire's evidence.
BPP 1834 XXVII, Report from H.M. Commissioners on the Poor Law.
BPP 1835 XI, Report on gaols.
BPP 1836 XL, Report on emigration.
BPP 1837 XLII, Report from agent for emigration to Canada.
BPP 1837-8 XL, XVII, XLVII, Emigration Reports.
BPP 1837-8 XXII, Report on transportation.
BPP 1837-8 XL, Emigration Report.
BPP 1840 XXIV, Report on the condition of handloom weavers.
BPP 1841 XXXI, III, Emigration Reports.
BPP 1841 IV, Report on South Australia.
BPP 1842 XV, XVII, Report on the employment of children and young persons in mines.
BPP 1842 XXXI, Return of emigrants and passengers to Quebec.
BPP 1843 XXXIV, Emigration Report.
BPP 1844 XXXI, Emigration Report.
BPP 1847 XLI, Return of Sickness and Mortality in India 1825-44.
BPP 1847 XXVI, XXXIX, XXXIII, Emigration Reports.
BPP 1847-8 XL, Report of Poor Law Commissioners.
BPP 1847-8 XLVII, Emigration Report and Passenger Returns.

BPP 1849 XXXVII, XXII, Emigration Reports.
BPP 1850 XXXV, Report on the Australian Colonies.
BPP 1850 XXXVII, Emigration Report.
BPP 1851 XXII, Report on emigration and Colonial land.
BPP 1851 XL, XXI, XXL, Emigration Reports.
BPP 1851 XL, Registrar General's Report.
BPP 1851 XXII, Emigration Report.
BPP1851 XXI, Steam communication with India.
BPP 1852 XVIII, XXXIV, Emigration Reports.
BPP 1852-3 XL, Emigration Report.
BPP 1852-3 LXVIII, Emigration Report.
BPP 1854 XLVI, Emigration Report.
BPP 1857-8 XLI, Emigration Report.
BPP 1860 LX, Report on shipping.
BPP 1861 L, Report on wages and earnings of agricultural labourers.
BPP 1861 XL, Emigration Report.
BPP 1862 XXII, Emigration Report..
BPP 1868-9 XIII, Reports of Commissioners on the employment of children, young
    persons and women in agriculture.
BPP 1873 XVIII, LXI, Emigration Reports.
BPP 1873 LIII, Report on wages and earnings of agricultural labourers.
BPP 1874 XXIII, Part II, Report on Friendly and Building Societies.
BPP 1875 XLIII, Return of sickness and mortality in India 1861-73.
BPP 1881 XVI, XVII, RC on the depressed condition of the agricultural interest.
BPP 1883 LIV, Election report.
BPP 1887 LVII, Emigration Report.
BPP 1888 LXXIII, Emigration Report.
BPP 1889 LV, Emigration Report.
BPP 1890 XLIX, Emigration Report.
BPP 1890-1 LVI, Emigration Report.
BPP 1890-1 XL, SC on Colonisation Report.
BPP 1893 LVI, Emigration Report..
BPP 1893-4 LX, Emigration Report.
BPP 1895 XVII, RC on Agricultural Depression.
BPP 1895 LXX, Emigration Report, Report on Canada.
BPP 1896 LVIII, Emigration Report.
BPP 1897 LXI, Emigration Report..
BPP 1898 LIX, Emigration Report.
BPP 1899 LVIII, Emigration Report.
BPP 1900 CII, Emigration Report.
BPP 1901 XLVI, LXXXVIII, Emigration Reports.
BPP 1902 CXVI, Emigration Report.
BPP 1902 LXVI, Report after Colonial Conference.
BPP 1903 LXXXII, Report on passenger movements.
BPP 1903 XLIV, Emigration Report.
BPP 1904 LIX, 106, Emigration Reports.
BPP 1905 LXII, Emigration Report.
BPP 1905 LIII, Report on work of the Salvation Army in the Colonies.
BPP 1906 XCVI, Report on General Election, Illiteracy.
BPP 1906 LXXVII, Emigration Report.
BPP 1906 XCVI, Election Report.
BPP 1906 CXXXIV, Return of passenger movements.
BPP 1907 LVI, XCVII, LXVII, Emigration Reports.
BPP 1908 LXX, 112, Emigration Reports.

BPP 1909 LIX, CIII, Emigration Reports.
BPP 1910 CIX, LXVI, Emigration Reports.
BPP 1911 LX, XLV, Emigration Reports.
BPP 1912-13 LX, Emigration and Census Reports.
BPP1912-13 111, Census Report.
BPP 1912-13 XVI, RC Report on the Dominions.
BPP 1913 XLV, RC Report on the Dominions.
BPP 1913 LV, XLV, Emigration and Census Reports.
BPP 1914 LX, LXIX, Emigration Reports.
BPP 1914-16, Emigration Report.
BPP 1917-18, XXXV Census Report 1911.
And, selected Registrar General's Annual Reports.

Miscellaneous Records

CRO, Kendal
WDX 147/6,WDX 147/7 Bateman family papers. Letters from Australia.
WDX 169   Atkinson letter.
WDX 190   *Kirkby Stephen and Appleby Monthly Messenger* March 1891.
WDX 204   Letters to the Taylor family at Crosby Ravensworth from America.
WDX 652   Photograph of A.R. Tucker, Bishop of Uganda 1899-1911.
WDX 822   Letters from abroad, including 14 letters from the Hodgson family in
    Pittsburgh, and Charteris Creek to the Salkeld family of Fell Dykes, Hilton, Appleby,
    1833-1867 and from the Anderson relatives, 1895.
WDX 848/7-15   Papers concerning Brunskill and related families.
WDX 1005   Letters from William and George Crook in New York 1832, 1836.
WPR 9/257   T. R. Holmes' Log Book on H.M.S. President visiting Callao,
    Valparaiso and other ports in South America, 1855-57.
WDY 159   Typescript of Robert S. Hall's Diary, 1853-54.
WD/AG/Box 3   Rathnell letters.
WDY 33/1   Letter from James Walker.
WDX 190   *Kirkby Stephen and Appleby Monthly Messenger.*
WRX 259   Robert Hall's Journal
WDX 948   Letters from George and Sarah Brunskill.
WDX 211/3   Letters from William Milner.
WDY 566   Letters from Joseph Dover.
WDFC/M   Wesleyan and Primitive Methodist records.
WDX 148   Gibson family letters.
WDX 152   Thompson family letters.
WDX 358   Staveley letters.

CRO, Carlisle
D/BS/Scott   Letters from New South Wales.
DX 249/14   Pattinson letters.
DX/46/5-7   J. Gibson letters.
DX 301/75-92   E. Metcalfe letters.
DX 451   Letters to Longtown.
DX 249/23   Ferguson letters.
DX/67/37   S. Madgen letters.
DX/806/3   Tinning letters.
DX/1070/1   W. Shaw letter.
DX 1755/1/1   T. Raine, letter from Wisconsin.
DX 1755/1/4   R.Harrison, letter from Buffalo, NY.
DX/301/75   J. Rodgers' visit to Paris.

D/BT/6/209/1	R. Gibson letters.
D/Ken.3/2 8/2	G. Molloy letter.
DRC/1/8	Dr Gardiner in Danzig.
D/Pen/Malay/6/28	Report on the Gedong Estate.
PR/57/67/1	P. Carrick letter.
D/Ben/letters.	Letter to R. Benson.
DX/46/5	Gibson letters.
DX/249/14-23	Ferguson letters.

CRO, Whitehaven
YDX 481 Account of Joseph Graves' journey from Cockermouth to Manchester, 1837.
D/Mg/224/2   Letter from J. Hudson.
D/BT/6/209/1   Letter from W. Atkinson.

Library of the Grand United Lodge of England & Wales
Records of the foundation of Overseas Lodges.

Newspapers: Sample years only.
  Penrith Observer
  Carlisle Journal
  Cumberland Pacquet
  Carlisle Patriot
  Cumberland & Westmorland Advertiser
  Cumberland & Westmorland Herald
  Cumberland News
  Daily Telegraph and Courier
  Daily Telegraph
  Keswick Reminder
  Lyttelton Times
  Maryport News
  Nelson Examiner
  Otago News
  The Australian
  The Press
  West Cumberland Times
  Whitehaven News

Unpublished Material
Dickson, G.C. and Johnston, J.W. *Diary transcripts.*
Hudson, Paul. S. *English emigrants to New Zealand 1839-1850: an analysis of the work of the New Zealand Company.* (Ph.D. thesis, Lancaster, 1996).
Spedding. N.S. *Footsteps in retrospect.*
Extracts of Iredale and Calcott family memoirs supplied by Dr K. Hornsby.
Extracts and quotations from family histories sent by relatives.
Internet sources
www.trentvalleyarchives.com/gazette.htm.
Australian Convict index accessed via Ancestry .co.uk

Primary Sources
Adams, C W. *A spring in the Canterbury Settlement* (London, 1853/ Christchurch, 1971).
Australian Handbook and Almanac (Sydney, 1877).
Bradshaw's Railway Guides, selected years from 1842 (London).
Bright, J. *Handbook for emigrants and others* (London, 1841).
Buckingham, J.S. *A journey through the slave states of North America* (1842, London, 2006).

Bulmer, T. *History, Topography and Directory of Cumberland* (Preston, 1901).
Bulmer, T. *History & Directory of West Cumberland* (Penrith, 1901, Whitehaven, 1994).
Bulmer, T. *History, Topography & Directory of Westmorland* (Preston, 1885).
Bulmer, T. *History, Topography and Directory of East Cumberland* (Preston, 1884).
Caird, J. On the agricultural statistics of the United Kingdom, *Journal of the Statistical Society of London,* 31 (1868).
Canada and the Western States Handbook, (London, 1859).
Cassell's Emigrant maps and guides. Canada East, North America, New South Wales, Cape Colony, California, United States, Western Australia, South Australia (London, 1870).
Collins, S.H.*The Emigrants' Guide to the USA* (London, 1840, 1971)
Creighton, M. *Carlisle* (London, 1906).
Cyclopaedia of New Zealand: industrial, descriptive, historical, biographical: facts, figures, illustrations. Volumes 1-6,
Vol. 1. Wellington Provincial District — v. 2. Auckland Provincial District — v. 3. Canterbury Provincial District — v. 4. Otago and Southland Provincial Districts — v. 5. Nelson, Marlborough, and Westland Provincial Districts — v. 6. Taranaki, Hawkes's Bay, and Wellington Provincial Districts. (Wellington, 1897-1908).
Dickens, C.*American Notes* (London, 1842, 1892).
Fowler, J. *Journal of a tour through the State of New York in 1830* (London, 1831, New York, 1970).
General Directory of South Africa (London, 1889, 1890, 1905, 1908).
Granville, A.B. *Spas of England & other principal bathing places* (London, 1841).
Gray, C. *Sisters in the wilderness: the lives of Susanna Moodie and Catherine Traill* (London, 2001).
Hammond, J.L. and B. *The Village Labourer 1760-1832: a study in the government of England before the Reform Bill* (London, 1911, Gloucester, 1987).
Hastings, L.W. *The emigrants' guide to Oregon & California* (Princeton, 1845, 1932).
Hayward, J. *Gazeteer of the United States of America* (Philadelphia, 1854).
Hopkins, J.C.*Morang's Annual register of Canadian Affairs* (Toronto, 1901).
Hursthouse, C. *An account of the settlement of New Plymouth in New Zealand* (London, 1849).
Hutchinson, G.T. *From the Cape to the Zambesi* (London, 1905).
Jollie's Cumberland Guide and Directory (Carlisle, 1811, Whitehaven, 1995).
Kelly's Directory Cumberland & Westmorland (London, 1905, 1906).
Kelly's Directory General Directory of South Africa (Cape Town, 1905).
Knight, E.F. *Railways in Rhodesia* (London, 1904).
Letters from settlers and labouring emigrants in the New Zealand Company's settlements of Wellington, Nelson & New Plymouth (London, 1843).
MacDougall, R. *The emigrant's guide to North America,* E. Thompson (ed.) (1841, Reprint Ottawa, 1998).
Mannex & Co. *History, Topography and Directory of Westmorland with Lonsdale and Amounderness in Lancashire* (Preston, 1851, Whitehaven, 1978).
Mannex & Whellan *History, Gazetteer and Directory of Cumberland* (Beverley, 1847, Whitehaven, 1974).
Marshall, W.*The Review and Abstract of the county reports to the Board of Agriculture: Northern department,* Vol. 1. (York, 1818, New York, 1968).
Moodie, S. *Roughing it in the bush* (1852, London 1986).
Morris, Harrison & Co. *Commercial Directory & Gazetteer of the County of Cumberland* (Nottingham, 1861).
Morang's Annual Register of Canadian Affairs (Toronto, 1902)
Newhall, J. *A glimpse of Iowa in 1846: the emigrant's guide and State directory* (Iowa, 1846/1957).
New South Wales Census, 1828 (see under Sainty (ed.) 1980).

New Zealand and Australia Guide (London, 1843).
New Zealand Post Office Directory 1885-86 (London, 1885).
Nugent, F.W. *New Zealand: a field for emigration* (London, 1886).
Parson and White, *History, Directory and Gazetteer of Cumberland and Westmorland* (Leeds, 1829, Beckermet, 1976).
Paton, W. B. *Handbooks on British Colonies*, Canada, Australia, New Zealand (London, 1910).
Pennefeather, F.W. *New Zealand: a field for emigration* (London, 1886).
Pigot's Directory of Cumberland, Lancashire and Westmoreland (Manchester, 1828-9, Norwich, 1995).
Population of the United States 1860 (Eighth census report).
Post Office Directory of Westmorland and Cumberland (London 1858, Kendal 2009).
Post Office Directory of Cumberland and Westmorland (London, 1894).
Post Office Directory of Lancashire, (London, 1858).
Quarterly Review 'South Africa and Rhodesia' (January, April 1901).
Shaw, A.G.L. (ed.) *The history of Tasmania* by J West (1853, Sydney, 1971).
Sidney's Emigrant's Journal 1848-52 (London).
Stanford's Emigrant's Guide (London, 1854)
Strickland, S. *Twenty seven years in Canada west or the experience of an early settler.* Vol. 1 (London 1853, Bibliolife 2009), Vol. 2 (London 1853, Michigan, MLibrary, 2009)
Stuart, C. *The Emigrant's Guide to Upper Canada* (London, 1820).
Thompson, E. (ed.) *The Emigrant's Guide to North America* (Ontario, 1841, 1998).
Trollope, A. *North America* (London, 1862, 1968).
Trollope, A. *Australia and New Zealand* London 1873/1968).
USA govt. papers *The USA in 1860 compiled from original returns of the 8th census* (Washington, 1864).
Ware, J.E.*The Emigrant's Guide to California* (St Louis, 1849).
West, J. *The history of Tasmania* (1853, Shaw ed. Sydney 1971).
Whitaker, J.*An Almanack for the year of our Lord 1869* (London, 1869).
Whitaker's Almanacks – selected years (London).
Wilson, J. (ed.) *The Victoria History of the county of Cumberland* (London, 1905/1968).

Secondary Sources
TCWAAS Transactions of the Cumberland and Westmorland Antiquarian and Archaeological Society.
CFHS Cumbria Family History Society.
VCH Victoria County History.
Addison, V. *Black Sheep and Diamonds* (Carlisle, 2003).
Alcott, B.S., Gerber, D.A., Sinke, S.A. (eds.) *Letters across borders: the epistolary practices of international emigrants.* (New York, 2006)
Allan, R.M. *Nelson: a history of early settlement* (Wellington, 1965).
Arnold, R.*The Farthest Promised Land: English villagers, NZ immigrants of the 1870s* (Wellington, 1981).
Artibise, A.F.J. *Winnipeg: A social history of urban growth* (Montreal, 1975).
Ashbridge, I.*Cumbrian crime from a social perspective* (Cramlington, 1999).
Ashcroft, L.*Vital Statistics: The Westmorland 'census' of 1787* (Kendal, 1992).
Bailyn, B.*The peopling of British North America: an introduction.* (New York, 1986).
Bailyn, B. *Voyagers to the west: a passage in the peopling of America on the eve of the Revolution* (New York, 1987).
Baines, D. *Migration in a mature economy: Emigration: emigration and internal migration in England and Wales 1861-1900* (Cambridge, 1985).
Barnes, F. *Barrow and District* (Barrow-in-Furness, 1968).
Beckett, J.V. *Coal and tobacco: The Lowthers and the economic development of west Cumberland 1660-1760* (Cambridge, 1981).

Belich, J. *Making People: History of New Zealanders* (New Zealand, 1996).
Belshaw, J.D. *Colonisation and community: The Vancouver Island coalfield and the making of the British Columbian working class* (Montreal, 2002).
Benington, E. *The Robinsons of Moneymore* (New Zealand, 1983).
Best, G. *Mid-Victorian Britain 1851-75* (London, 1971).
Bloomfield, G T. *New Zealand: a handbook of historical statistics* (Boston, 1983).
Borrie, W.D. *Immigration to New Zealand 1854-1938* (Canberra, 1991).
Bowden, B. & Penrose, B. 'Dust, contractors, politics and silicosis' *Australian Historical Studies* 128 (October, 2006).
Broeze, F. British inter-continental shipping and Australia 1813-1850, *Journal of Transport History*, NS 4 (1978).
Broeze, F.'Distance tamed: steam navigation to Australia & New Zealand from its beginning to the outbreak of the Great War', *Journal of Transport History*, 3rd ser. 10 (1989).
Brogan, H. *The Penguin History of the United States* (London, 1985).
Brooke, A & Brandon, D. *Bound for Botany Bay: British convict voyages to Australia* (London, 2005).
Bueltmann, T. 'Where the measureless ocean between us will roar: Scottish emigration to New Zealand, personal correspondence and epistolary practices, c.1850-1920,' *Immigrants and Minorities* 25 (2005).
Carrier, J.N.H. & Jefferies, J.R. *External migration, Study No. 6. Statistics 1815-1950* (London, 1953).
Carrothers, W.A. *Emigration from the British Isles: with special reference to the development of overseas dominions* (London, 1929/1965).
Charlwood, D. *The long farewell* (London, 1981).
Checkland, S.G. The *rise of industrial society in England 1815-1885* (London, 1964).
Christian, A.H. *The search for Holmes, Robson, Hind, Steele and Graham* (Carlisle, 1984).
Clark, M. *A short history of Australia* (Melbourne, 1961).
Clarke, D. *This other Eden* (Milburn, 1985).
Clarke, M.P. 'The John Hodgson family of Cote St Charles,' *Pioneer Families*, Vol. 6, Hudson Historical Society Records.
Clifton, S. Letter from home, *CFHS Newsletter* 102 (2002).
Cocker, M. *Rivers of blood, rivers of gold* (London, 1998)
Cockerill, T. The English Cemetery, Pourta de la Cruz, Tenerife, Canary Isles,' *CFHS Newsletter 102* (2002).
Coleman, T. *Passage to America: a history of emigrants from Great Britain to America in the mid-nineteenth century* (London, 1972).
Coleman, T. *The Liners: a history of the north Atlantic crossing* (London, 1976).
Cowan, J. *New Zealand Centennial Survey, Vol. IV, Settlers and pioneers* (Wellington, 1940).
Crouzet, F. *The Victorian economy* (London, 1982).
Current, R.N. *Wisconsin: a bicentennial history* (New York 1977).
Dodgshon, R.A. and Butlin, R.A. (eds.), *An historical geography of England & Wales* (1st and 2nd editions. (London, 1978, 1990).
Donaldson, M. and Parsons, M. *The Parsons family* (M Peyton, ed.) Hudson Historical Society Records.
Elton. J. 'Journey to South Africa', *CFHS Newsletter* 117 (2005).
Erickson, C.J. 'The encouragement of emigration by British Trade Unions, 1859-1900,' *Population Studies* 3 (1949-50).
Erickson, C.J. 'Who were the English and Scots emigrants to the United States in the late nineteenth century?' in *Population and Social Change*, D.V. Glass and R. Revelle (eds.) (London, 1972).
Erickson, C.J. *Invisible immigrants: the adaptation of English & Scottish Immigrants in nineteenth century America* (Cornell, 1972).

Erickson, C.J. *Emigration from Europe 1815-1914: select documents* (London, 1976).
Erickson, C.J. 'Emigration from the British Isles to the USA in 1831,' *Population Studies* 35 (1981).
Erickson, C.J. 'Emigration from the British Isles to the USA in 1841,' Part I, *Population Studies* 43 (1989).
Erickson, C.J. *Leaving England: Essays on British emigration in the nineteenth century* (Cornell, 1994).
Faragher, J.M. *Women and men on the overland trail* (Yale, 1979).
Ferguson, J.A. A journey with Captain Wood and his mysterious tablet: Part 2, *CFHS Newsletter* 117 (2005).
Fischer D.H. *Albion's seed: four British folkways to America* (Oxford, 1989).
Fischer, D.H, and Kelly, J.C. *Bound Away: Virginia and the westward movement* (Charlottesville, 2000).
Fitzpatrick, D. *Oceans of consolation: personal accounts of Irish migration to Australia* (Cork, 1994).
Fogg, N. *The voyages of the Great Britain: life at sea in the world's first liner* (2002, London 2004).
Freeman, M. *Social investigations and rural England 1870 -1914* (London, 2003).
Galloway, L.E. & Vedder, R.K. 'Emigration from the United Kingdom to the United States, 1850-1913' *Journal of Economic History* 31 (1971).
Gerber, D.A. *Authors of their lives: The personal correspondence of British immigrants to North America in the nineteenth century* (New York, 2006).
Glass, D.V. & Revelle, R. (eds.) *Population and Social Change* (London, 1972).
Grant, J. and Serle, G. *The Melbourne Scene 1803-1956* (Melbourne, 1957).
Gray, C. *Sisters in the Wilderness: the lives of Susanna Moodie and Catherine Traill* (London, 2001).
Greenwood, E.C. *Pioneer settlements in Upper Canada* (Toronto, 1933, reprint 1969).
Greenwood, G. *Australia: a social & political history* (Sydney, 1955).
(London, 1993).
Haines, R 'Indigent misfits or shrewd operators: government assisted emigrants from the United Kingdom to Australia 1831-60.' *Population Studies* 48 (1994).
Haines, R. The idle and the drunken won't do there: poverty, the new Poor Law and nineteenth century government assisted emigration to Australia from the United Kingdom, in *Australian Historical Studies* 28, 108 (1997).
Haines, R. *Life and death in the age of sail: the passage to Australia* (London, 2006).
Hallas, C. 'The Northern Region,' in Thirsk (ed.) *Agrarian History* Vol. 7 (Cambridge, 2000).
Hamilton, J. *Places* (Calgary, 1971).
Hammerton, J.A. *Emigrant gentlewomen: Genteel poverty & female emigration 1830-1914*, (London, 1979).
Handley, G. (ed.) *Trollope the traveller: selection from Anthony Trollope's travel writings*
Harper, M. *Adventurers and Exiles* (London, 2003).
Harper, M. (ed.) *Emigrant homecomings: the return and movement of emigrants 1600-2000* (Manchester, 2005).
Harriman, B. *The British in Peru* (Peru, 1984).
Harrington Local History Society *Harrington through the years* Vols. 1-5 (c.2000).
Harris, A. *Sailing to Australia: shipboard diaries by nineteenth century British emigrants* (Manchester, 1994).
Hart, J. *The Powley Connection: Northern England to southern New Zealand* (Auckland, 1997).
Haslam, P.F. 'The story of John and Rebecca Fearon,' *CFHS Newsletter* 96 (August, 2000).
Hawkings, D.T. *Bound for Australia* (Chichester, 1987).
Hay, D. *Whitehaven: a short history* (Whitehaven, 1966).

Heathcote, T.A. *The Indian army: the garrison of British Imperial India 1822-1922* (Newton Abbott, 1974).
Herd, A. 'More New Zealand notes,' *CFHS Newsletter* 97 (November, 2000).
Herd, M.A. *American immigration* (Chicago, 1960).
Heussler, R.C. *Yesterday's rulers: The making of the British Colonial Service* (Syracuse, 1963).
Hiemstra, M. *Gully Farm* (London, 1955).
Hill, M. *Gold: The California story* (Los Angeles, 1999).
Hinchcliffe, E. 'The Washingtons at Whitehaven and Appleby' *TCWAAS, NS* 71 (1971).
Hodgson, B.H. and R.L. 'The Grahams of Choisy,' *Pioneer Families Vol.* 6, Hudson Historical Society Records.
Hodgson, E.B. The Hodgsons of the Seigneury of Vaudreuil, *Pioneer Families* Vol.6, Hudson Historical Society Records.
Hodgson, R.L. The Hodgsons of Como, *Pioneer Families* Vol. 6, Hudson Historical Society Records.
Hodgson, B.H., R.I, Royle, E.C., Mullan, E.G., Clarke, M.P., Vipond, J. *Pioneer Families* Vol. 6. (Hudson Historical Records.)
Hollett, D. *From Cumberland to Cape Horn: the sailing fleet of Thomas & John Brocklebank of Whitehaven and Liverpool 1770-1900* (London, 1984).
Howells, G. 'Emigration and the new Poor Law: Norfolk emigration fever of 1836' *Rural History* 11 (2000).
Howkins, A. 'Overview' in *Agrarian History* Vol. 7, Pt.2.
Horn, P. *Labouring life in the Victorian countryside* (London, 1984).
Hughes, E. *North Country life in the eighteenth century: Cumberland and Westmorland 1700 -1830*, Vol. 2 (Oxford 1965).
Hughes, L. *Henry Mundy: a young Australian pioneer* (Leighton Buzzard, 2003).
Hughes, R. *The Fatal shore: a history of the transportation of convicts to Australia 1787-1868* (London, 1987).
Hunter, J. *A dance called America* (Edinburgh, 1994).
Jackson, F. 'They travelled abroad and, or died abroad.' *CFHS Newsletter* 120 (2006).
Jones, M.A. 'The background to emigration from Great Britain in the nineteenth century.' *Perspectives in American History* 7 (1973).
Keesing (ed.), N. *Gold fever: The Australian goldfields 1851 to the 1890s* (Sydney, 1967).
Lancaster, J.Y. 'The wreck of the Geltwood' in *Harrington through the years* Vol. 2. *(c.*2000)
Lancaster J.Y and D. Wattleworth. *The iron and steel industry of West Cumberland* (Workington, 1977).
Lancaster, S. (ed.) Thompson, J. *Hudson: the early years up to 1867* (Hudson, 2004).
Langton, J. and Morris, R.J. *Atlas of Industrialising Britain 1780-1914* (London 1986).
Lawton, R. 'Population and Society' in Dodgshon and Butlin (eds.) *An historical geography of England & Wales,* 2nd edition. (London, 1990).
Lawton, R. and Pooley, C.G. *Britain 1740-1950: an historical geography* (London, 1992).
McCarthy, A. 'Personal letters, oral testimony and Scottish migration to New Zealand in the 1950s: the case of Lorna Carter' in Immigrants *and Minorities* 23 (2005).
McCourt, E. *Saskatchewan* (Toronto, 1968).
MacDonald, J. and Richards, E. 'The Great Emigration of 1841: Recruitment for New South Wales in British emigration fields,' *Population Studies* 51 (1997)
MacGregor, J.G. *A history of Alberta* (Edmonton, 1972).
MacRaild, D.M. *Labour in British society 1830-1914* (London, 2000).
Mandell, R.C.*Wisconsin: a history* (Wisconsin, 1973).
Mandell, S. 'Winners at a Cumberland goose-carding in New Zealand,' *CFHS Newsletter* 97 (2000).
Marais, J.S. *The colonisation of New Zealand.* (London, 1968).
Marshall, J.D. 'Kendal in the late seventeenth and eighteenth centuries,' *TCWAAS*, NS 75

(1975).

Marshall, J.D. and Walton, J.K. *The Lake Counties from 1830 to the mid-twentieth century* (Manchester, 1981).

May, P.R. *The west coast gold rushes* (Christchurch, 1962/7).

Milne, M. *No telephone to Heaven* (Stockbridge, 1999).

Mingay G.E. *The transformation of Britain 1830-1939* (London, 1986).

Mingay, G.E. *Rural life in Victorian Britain* (London, 1976).

Morgan, M. *One man's gold rush: the Klondike* (Seattle, 1967).

Morris, D. *The Dalesmen of the Mississippi River* (York, 1989).

Morris, H.'Cumbrian references on tombstones in Barbados,' *CFHS Newsletter* 94 (2000).

Muir, M. (ed.) *Anthony Trollope in Australia* (Adelaide, 1949).

Mullan, E.G. *A bit of local history: the Lancaster family,* Hudson Historical Society Records.

Murdoch. A. *British emigration 1603-1914* (Basingstoke, 2004).

Murray, J. *Proclaim the Good News: a short history of the Church Missionary Society* (London, 1985).

Nicholas, S. (ed.), *Convict workers: reinterpreting Australia's past* (London, 1988).

Nicholas, S. and Shergold, P.R. 'Convicts as workers,' in Nicholas, S. (ed.), *Convict workers: reinterpreting Australia's past* (London, 1988).

Nugent, W. *Crossings: the great trans-Atlantic migrations 1870-1914* (Bloomington, 1992).

Oliver, V.L. 'Cumbrian references in Tombstones in Barbados' in *CFHS Newsletter* 94, (2004).

Olssen, E. A history of Otago (Dunedin, 1984)

Ormsby, M.A. (ed.) *A pioneer gentlewoman in British Columbia* (Vancouver, 1976).

Palmer, B. 'Tom Penny – gentleman,' *CFHS Newsletter* 94 (2000).

Parnaby, B. *The Jeffersons of Whitehaven* (Cumbria, 2005).

Parson, E.T. *Land I can own* (Ottawa, 1981).

Pawson, E. 'The framework of industrial change 1730-1900' in Dodgshon and Butlin (eds.) *An historical geography of England & Wales* (1st edition), (London, 1978).

Perrott, M. *A tolerable good success: Economic opportunities for women in New South Wales 1788-1830* (Sydney, 1983).

Petrowski, C. *A bride's passage: Susan Hathorn's year under sail* (Boston, 1997).

Phillips, C.H. *The East India Company 1784-1834* (Manchester, 1961).

Pike, A. 'Our sole Tasmanian member,' *CFHS Newsletter* 114 (2005).

Pooley, C.G. and Whyte, I.D. *Migrants, emigrants and immigrants: a social history of migration* (London, 1991).

Prince, H. C. 'The changing rural landscape' in Thirsk, (ed.) *Agrarian History 1750-1850,* Vol. 6 (Cambridge, 1989)

Raby, G. *The making of rural Australia: an economic history 1788-1860* (Oxford, 1996).

Reed, A.H. *The story of Canterbury: the last Wakefield settlement* (Wellington, 1949).

Reed, A.H. *The story of early Dunedin* (Wellington, 1956).

Reed, A.H. *The story of Hawke's Bay* (Wellington, 1958).

Richards, E. How did poor people emigrate from the British Isles in the nineteenth century?' *Journal of British Studies* 32 (1993).

Richards, E. *Britannia's children; emigration from England, Scotland, Wales and Ireland from 1600* (London, 2004).

Richards, E. 'The limits of the Australian emigrant letter,' Chapter 2 in Elcott et al (ed.) *Letters across borders: the epistolary practices of international emigrants* (New York, 2006).

Richards, E. 'Running home from Australia: intercontinental mobility and migrant expectations in the nineteenth century' in Harper (ed.) *Emigrant homecomings: the return movements of emigrants, 1600-2000* (Manchester, 2008).

Richardson, S. 'William Willan: a Westmorland gold mining prospector in South Africa'

CFHS Newsletter 115 (2005).
Rickard, S. (ed.) *George Barrington's voyage to Botany Bay* (Leicester, 2001).
Rigg, A.N. *Cumbria, slavery and the textile industrial revolution* (Kirkby Stephen, 1994).
Roberts, E.H. (ed.) *Sugden's history of Arlecdon and Frizington* (Cockermouth, 1897, 1997).
Robertson, A. *A history of Alston Moor* (Alston, 2002).
Robertson, E.J. *Early New Zealand* (Melbourne, 1958).
Robins, N. *The Corporation that changed the world: how the East India Company shaped the modern multi-national* (London, 2006).
Rose, J. 'Willingly to school: the working class response to elementary education in Britain, 1875-1918,' *Journal of British Studies* 32 (1993).
Rowe, G. 'Extracts from William Shortridge's Diary, 1891', *CFHS Newsletter* 96, (2000).
Rowe, K. Maryport emigrants in Australia, *CFHS Newsletter* 114 (2005).
Royle, E.C. *Pioneer Settlers in Hudson: the Blenkinships.* Hudson Historical Society Records.
Russell, M.M. *The Family Forest* (Manchester 2000).
Sainty, M.R. and Johnson, K.A. (eds.) *Census of New South Wales 1828* (Sydney, 1980).
Savill, D. *Sail to New Zealand: the story of Shaw, Savill and Company, 1858-82* (London, 1986).
Schlissel, L. *Women's diaries of the westward journey* (New York, 1982).
Schurer, K. 'The role of the family in the process of migration.' In Pooley and White (eds.) (London, 1991).
Scott, D. *Cumberland and Westmorland* (London, 1920).
Serle, G. *The rush to be rich: a history of the colony of Victoria* (Melbourne, 1971).
Sharpe, J. and others. *Prairie Wool and Pussy Willows*, (Committee collaboration), (North Battleford, SK. c.1988).
Shaw, A.G.L. *Convicts and the colonies: a study of penal transportation from Great Britain and Ireland to Australia and other parts of the British Empire* (London, 1966).
Shepherd, M.E. *From Hellgill to Bridge End: aspects of economics and social change in the Upper Eden Valley, 1840-95* (Hatfield, 2003).
Shepperson, W.S. *British emigration to North America: projects and opinions in the early Victorian period* (Oxford, 1957).
Shepperson, W.S. *Emigration and disenchantment: portraits of Englishmen repatriated from the United States* (Oklahoma, 1965).
Short, B. 'Rural Demography' in Thirsk, (ed.) *The Agrarian History of England and Wales,* Vol. 7, Pt. 2 (Cambridge, 2000).
Southland People: a dictionary of Otago, Southland biography (Dunedin 1998).
Smith, C. *Carlisle to Canada: a family chronicle* (Carlisle, 2006).
Snowman, D. 'New World Overtures' in *History Today,* January 2010.
Spark, E. *Outward Bound: my diary* (Alston, 2002).
Summerson, H. *An ancient squire's family: the history of the Aglionbys c.1130-2002* (Carlisle, 2007).
Tapp, W.E. *Britain to America: mid-nineteenth century immigrants to the United States* (Illinois, 1999).
Terry, I. *Municipality of Sorell Heritage Study: Stage 1, Thematic history* (Sorell, 1996).
Thirsk, J. (ed.), The *Agrarian History of England and Wales,* Vols. 6 and 7 (Cambridge 1989, 2000).
Thompson, J. (ed. Lancaster) *Hudson: the early years up to 1867* (Hudson, 2004).
Thompson, K. 'Maryport emigrants in Australia,' *CFHS Newsletter* 114 (2005).
Thompson, R.N. 'The working of the Poor Law Amendment Act in Cumbria 1836-71,' *Northern History* 15 (1979).
Trohear, M. *Round trip to America* (Cornell, 1993).
Trohear, M. 'Snippets from the *Whitehaven News*,' *CFHS Newsletter* 113 (2004).
Turnbull, J.W. 'The Turnbulls of Castle Gardens, Workington' *CFHS Newsletter* 115

(2005).

Twomey, C. 'Without natural protectors: responses to wife desertion in Gold Rush Victoria.' *Australian Historical Studies,* 28 (1997), pp 22-36.

Van Vugt, W.E. *Britain to America: mid-nineteenth century immigrants to the United States* (Illinois, 1999).

Vipond, J. *The Viponds of Hudson,* Hudson Historical Society Records.

Warwick, R.W. 'A New Zealand Memorial,' *CFHS Newsletter* 97 (2000).

Watkins, T.H. *Gold and silver in the west: the illustrated history of an American dream* (Palo Alto 1971).

White, D.A. (ed.), *News of the plains and Rockies 1803-65,* Vols. 1-6 (Washington, 1999).

White, P.W. and Woods, R. *The geographical impact of migration* (London, 1980).

Whitelock, D. *Adelaide 1836-76* (Queensland 1977).

Wilkie, W.E. *Dubuque on the Mississippi 1788-1988* (Wisconsin, 1987).

Wood P.J. *Women of the Waimakariri* (New Zealand, 1993).

Wyman, M. *Round Trip to America 1830-1930* (Cornell, 1993).

Index of People

Some family names are very common in the area which is further complicated by duplicated personal names. Although in most cases references to a name below will be to the same person this cannot be taken as a certainty and may refer to a different generation or even to a different family.

212

213

General Index.

215

217

219

220